1-11-61

YOUTH PROGRAMS
FOR CHRISTIAN GROWTH

Youth Programs
for
Christian Growth

RUTH SCHROEDER

ABINGDON PRESS

NEW YORK   NASHVILLE

1149281

To the Pioneers

a fellowship of Christian youth who
are blazing new trails for Christ

Contents

Basic Christian Beliefs

Growth in Christian Discipleship

Basic Christian Beliefs

1. The Bible Through the Ages

PRELUDE: "Break Thou the Bread of Life"

CALL TO WORSHIP:

> Father of mercies, in Thy Word
> What endless glory shines!
> Forever be Thy name adored
> For these celestial lines.
>
> Here the Redeemer's welcome voice
> Spreads Heavenly peace around;
> And life and everlasting joys
> Attend the blissful sound.
>
> O may these heavenly pages be
> My ever dear delight!
> And still new beauties may I see,
> And still increasing light!
>
> Divine Instructor, gracious Lord,
> Be Thou forever near;
> Teach me to love Thy sacred Word,
> And view my Saviour there.
> —ANNE STEELE

RESPONSE (to be sung by the entire group):

> Break Thou the bread of life,
> Dear Lord, to me,

As Thou didst break the loaves
Beside the sea;
Beyond the sacred page
I seek Thee, Lord;
My spirit pants for Thee,
O living Word!
—MARY A. LATHBURY

PRAYER:

We thank thee, O Lord, for thy Word, which is the bread of life for men's souls. Give us an eagerness to know thee through the pages of thy Word and to follow thy teachings in our daily lives. Help us to appreciate the power of the Bible across the ages and to discover its message for the day in which we live. AMEN.

HYMN: "How Firm a Foundation" or "Tell Me the Old, Old Story"

THE OLD TESTAMENT SPEAKS ABOUT THE WORD OF GOD:

The law of the Lord is perfect, reviving the soul; the testimony of the Lord is sure, making wise the simple; the precepts of the Lord are right, rejoicing the heart; the commandment of the Lord is pure, enlightening the eyes; the fear of the Lord is clean, enduring for ever, the ordinances of the Lord are true, and righteous altogether.

How can a young man keep his way pure? By guarding it according to thy word. With my whole heart I seek thee; let me not wander from thy commandments! I have laid up thy word in my heart, that I might not sin against thee. Thy word is a lamp to my feet and a light to my path.[1]

THE NEW TESTAMENT SPEAKS ABOUT THE WORD OF GOD:

For whatever was written in former days was written for our instruction, that by steadfastness and by the encouragement of the scriptures we might have hope. All scripture is inspired by God and profitable for teaching, for reproof, for correction, and for training in righteousness, that the man of God may be complete, equipped for every good work. All flesh is like grass and all its glory like the flower of grass. The grass withers, and the flower falls, but the word of the Lord abides for ever.[2]

POEM:

> I paused last eve beside the blacksmith's door,
> And heard the anvil ring, the vesper's chime,
> And looking in I saw upon the floor
> Old hammers, worn with beating years of time.
> "How many anvils have you had?" said I,
> "To wear and batter all these hammers so?"
> "Just one," he answered. Then with twinkling eye:
> "The anvil wears the hammers out, you know."
> And so, I thought, the anvil of God's Word
> For ages skeptics' blows have beat upon,
> But though the noise of falling blows was heard
> The anvil is unchanged; the hammers gone.[3]
> —JOHN CLIFFORD

LEADER:

The Bible is not the book of the month or the book of the year. It is the book of the centuries. The actual writing of the Bible took place over a period of at least fifteen hundred years. The Bible is a collection of sixty-six separate books, and many different people had a part in recording God's message for mankind. As various individuals experienced the presence of God in their lives, they wrote down the ideas God revealed to them. For example, before he wrote the immortal Shepherd Psalm, the psalmist knew God as his Shepherd.

Through the ages the Bible has been recorded in many different forms. The early passages of the Old Testament were written many centuries before Christ, on the skins of animals, on wax tablets, and even on bricks and pieces of earthenware. Later the Old Testament books were recorded on long sheets of papyrus (a writing material formed by pressing together thin strips of the papyrus plant). These long pieces of papyrus were rolled into large, bulky scrolls. The books of the Old Testament were first written in Hebrew, the language of the people whom God used in a special way to make known his will to mankind.

The New Testament was written in Greek, the language of the civilized world of Jesus' day. It was recorded, not only on rolled scrolls, but also on sheets of papyrus which were stacked in large piles.

11

The story of how the Bible has blazed its way through the centuries into more than one thousand different languages is one of the most thrilling chapters in the history of mankind. We will hear the dramatic stories of four men who, at great cost to themselves, have given the Bible to men and women in their native tongues.

I. THE STORY OF WYCLIFFE

John Wycliffe lived from 1320-84, a period when the wealth of England belonged to a small group, while the rest of the people lived almost like slaves. The church was dominated by the pope in Rome and was interested only in obtaining money from the people of England in order to enhance Rome's glory. Because Wycliffe desired to improve the lot of the common man, he was hated by church leaders and by wealthy aristocrats.

Wycliffe was a scholar who knew the power of God's Word. He decided that the people of England should read the Bible for themselves —an unheard-of practice in that day! With the help of a few friends he translated the entire Bible into English—the first translation of God's Word into the English language.

The church authorities were furious. They had no intention of allowing the common people to read the Bible for themselves! They burned Wycliffe's translations of the Bible whenever they could get hold of them. Nevertheless, copies of Wycliffe's Bible continued to spread through the land—all of them patiently copied *by hand* by Wycliffe and his co-workers. There are still 170 handwritten copies of the Wycliffe Bible in existence today.

Having the Bible in their own language started the English people on the long road to political and religious freedom. Economic and social reforms were begun which were resisted by church authorities and political leaders. They rightly blamed Wycliffe's translation of the Bible for many of these changes. Forty-four years after Wycliffe's death, his enemies dug up his body, burned it, and cast his ashes into the river in order to disgrace his memory. History, however, has accorded Wycliffe a place of great honor. He is often called "the Morning Star of the Reformation."

II. THE STORY OF TYNDALE

Almost two hundred years after the time of Wycliffe another English scholar and reformer was born. His name was William Tyndale, and, like Wycliffe, he had a great concern for the common man. The English language had changed and developed since Wycliffe first translated the Bible into English, and a new translation was needed. Furthermore, the printing press had been invented, and Tyndale was determined to produce copies of the Bible—not by the hundreds, but by the thousands.

The church officials of England refused permission for Tyndale to translate the Bible into English, so in 1524 Tyndale went to Germany, not realizing that he would never see his native land again. Enemies of Tyndale followed him to Germany and hampered his work, but before long many copies of Tyndale's English New Testament were finding their way into England—well hidden in bales of cloth and barrels of flax and wheat! The more the church officials denounced and burned the New Testaments, the more eagerly did the people buy and read the books.

Before Tyndale finished translating the Old Testament, persecution of Protestant leaders was surging throughout Europe. Tyndale was imprisoned and in 1536, during a public demonstration of hatred, was strangled to death and his body burned. He willingly gave his life in order that men might discover for themselves the comfort, power, and inspiration of God's Word.

III. THE STORY OF CAREY

William Carey, an English shoe cobbler who studied maps of the world while he repaired shoes, answered God's call to take the Gospel to India. In 1793 Carey, his wife, and four small children left England by sailboat to make the long, dangerous voyage to India. The family endured unbelievable hardships. Their first home in India was a bamboo house near a dense jungle inhabited by tigers and deadly cobras. They had very little food to eat. All of them became sick with tropical fevers, and one of the children died.

The first years in India were spent in language-study and in translating the Bible into Bengali, the language of many of the people of

India. William Carey discovered that, although lower- and middle-class Indians showed great interest in his Bengali translation of the Bible, the high-caste people felt that a sacred book should be written in Sanskrit, the literary language of India. Whereupon, Carey began the long and difficult task of learning Sanskrit and translating the entire Bible in the language of the scholars.

Carey established the first Christian hospital in India, the first Christian schools, and the first orphan's home. He organized dozens of churches in various parts of India. People from the highest castes were won to Christ and had fellowship with low-caste Christians—an unheard-of practice in the India of that day. In the midst of these important activities William Carey continued his work of translating the Bible, until he and his associates had translated and printed the Bible, or portions of the Bible, into forty-four of the languages and dialects of India.

William Carey was a man of faith and vision. He demonstrated in his own life the motto which he suggested to his fellow Christians in England: "Attempt great things for God. Expect great things from God."

IV. THE STORY OF JUDSON

Adoniram Judson and his young wife, Ann, were the first American missionaries to carry the message of Christ to a distant land. They arrived in Burma in 1813, a time when Burma was ruled by a cruel tyrant who looked with disfavor upon all foreigners.

Judson's first concern was to master Burmese, one of the most difficult languages in the world. After many months of study he translated the book of Matthew into the Burmese language. He also began in their own tongue to tell the people of Burma about the message of Jesus. It was six long years before Judson won his first Burmese convert to Christ—six years of sickness, privation, and persecution by government officials.

As other Burmese declared their acceptance of Christianity, government persecution increased, and Judson intensified his efforts to complete the translation of the New Testament into Burmese. At last, in 1825, ten years after his arrival in Burma, Judson finished his translation of the New Testament.

Very soon afterward war was declared between Burma and England. Along with many other foreigners, Judson was arrested and placed in the death prison at Ava, a windowless dungeon where the heat and filth were almost unbearable. Ann went every day to government officials, seeking relief for her husband, and finally gained permission to take food and water to him. While Adoniram Judson was chained to iron fetters in the death prison, a daughter, Maria, was born to his wife. As soon as she was able, Ann, carrying the tiny baby to the prison with her, again brought food to her husband.

The Judsons were concerned about the safety of the priceless translation of the New Testament. Since their home had been raided several times by Burmese soldiers, Ann sewed the manuscript into an old, soiled pillow, which she gave to her husband in the prison. One day Judson and the other prisoners were dragged from the dungeon, chained together, and forced to march under a blazing sun to another prison ten miles away. Although he begged wildly for the dirty pillow, Judson was forced to leave it behind. After seven long months in the second prison Judson was suddenly released to act as an interpreter for the government.

The war was over at last and the Judsons were allowed to return to their work at Rangoon, where the Burmese Christians welcomed them eagerly. Imagine the joy of Ann and Adoniram Judson on discovering that these faithful friends had rescued the soiled pillow from the prison and kept it carefully as a remembrance of the Judsons! Little did these humble Christians realize that they had preserved the one precious copy of the New Testament in ther own language!

Adoniram's joy was soon dimmed. Ann Judson died while he was on a journey to Ava, and soon afterward the little daughter, Maria, also died. In his sorrow and loneliness Judson turned once more to translating the Word of God into the language of the land that had brought him such great suffering and loss. By 1835 the entire Bible had been translated into Burmese, but Judson immediately began a revision of his translation, which was not completed until 1840. The Judson Burmese Bible—a masterpiece of forceful style and unsurpassed beauty—is still used today by the Christians of Burma. It has been the means of bringing to thousands of Burmese people the light and love of the gospel of Jesus Christ.

LEADER:

Marching as it has across the centuries into the lives of people of more than a thousand different languages, the Bible has had a glorious history. And the end is not yet in sight! In recent years, with missionaries on every continent working at the task of Bible-translating, the Bible has made its appearance in an average of twelve new languages each year. God's Word continues to march onward in the many, varied languages of mankind, bringing to men of all races and tribes the life-transforming message of the risen, living Lord.

HYMN (may be sung by the entire group or by a soloist): "O Zion, Haste" or "We've a Story to Tell to the Nations"

CLOSING PRAYER:

We thank thee, O God, for the triumphant advance of thy Word into the numerous languages of mankind. Help us to appreciate and cherish thy Word and to be more grateful for the price that was paid to make the Bible available in our own language. May we be more loyal to Christ, who gives the Bible its great message and meaning. In his name we pray. AMEN.

2. How the Bible Helps Us Today

PRELUDE: "Open My Eyes, That I May See"

CALL TO WORSHIP:

> Lamp of our feet, whereby we trace
> Our path, when wont to stray;
> Stream from the fount of heavenly grace,
> Brook by the traveler's way.
>
> Bread of our souls, whereon we feed,
> True manna from on high;
> Our guide and chart, wherein we read
> Of realms beyond the sky.
>
> Word of the ever living God,
> Will of His glorious Son;
> Without thee how could earth be trod,
> Or heaven itself be won?
>   —BERNARD D. BARTON

PRAYER:

We are grateful, our Father, for the beauty and splendor of thy Word. Guide us as we think together about the Bible and as we discover ways in which the Bible helps us in our everyday experiences. Enable us to know and to love the Saviour who is depicted in the pages of thy Word. May we have a greater understanding of his will and way for our lives. In the Master's name we pray. AMEN.

HYMN: "I Love to Tell the Story" or "Thy Word Is Like a Garden, Lord"

LEADER:

I will meditate on thy precepts, and fix my eyes on thy ways. I will delight in thy statutes; I will not forget thy word. Open my eyes, that I may behold wondrous things out of thy law.[1]

RESPONSE (may be sung by the entire group or as a solo):

> Open my eyes, that I may see
> Glimpses of truth Thou hast for me;
> Place in my hands the wonderful key
> That shall unclasp, and set me free.
> Silently now I wait for Thee,
> Ready, my God, Thy will to see;
> Open my eyes, illumine me,
> Spirit divine!

LEADER:

Not every one who says to me, "Lord, Lord," shall enter the kingdom of heaven, but he who does the will of my Father who is in heaven. Every one then who hears these words of mine and does them will be like a wise man who built his house upon the rock.[2]

RESPONSE:

> Open my ears, that I may hear
> Voices of truth Thou sendest clear;
> And while the wave-notes fall on my ear,
> Everything false will disappear.
> Silently now I wait for Thee,
> Ready, my God, Thy will to see;
> Open my ears, illumine me,
> Spirit divine!

LEADER:

Teach me, O Lord, the way of thy statutes; and I will keep it to the end. Give me understanding, that I may keep thy law and observe it with my whole heart.[3]

RESPONSE:

> Open my mouth, and let me bear
> Gladly the warm truth everywhere;
> Open my heart, and let me prepare
> Love with Thy children thus to share.
> Silently now I wait for Thee,
> Ready, my God, Thy will to see;
> Open my heart, illumine me,
> Spirit divine! [4]
>
> —CLARA H. SCOTT

LEADER:

The purpose of the Bible is to help us understand what God is like. God gradually made himself known to many different people through many centuries. These ideas about God are recorded for us in the Bible. We find the final and complete message about God in the life and teachings of Jesus. The Old Testament, with its gradual revelation of God, is a preparation for Jesus' coming. The New Testament tells about Jesus and the way in which he can empower and transform human life.

The Bible, with its message of Jesus and the life he lived upon the earth, is a book of practical and personal help for every young person and adult. John summarized his Gospel by saying that these words "are written that you may believe that Jesus is the Christ, the Son of God, and that believing you may have life in his name."

An informal dramatization will be presented, showing some of the ways in which the Bible can provide help, guidance, and inspiration for young people today.

INFORMAL DRAMATIZATION:

BIBLE READING WITH A PURPOSE

(DICK *is reading his Bible in the living room of his home.* JACK *and* SALLY *enter and are welcomed cordially by* DICK.)

JACK: We thought we'd drop by and see what you were doing, Dick.

DICK: That's swell. Sit down and stay awhile.

SALLY: What were you reading, Dick? I noticed you had a book in your hand when we came to the door.

DICK: Why, yes, I did. I was reading the Bible.

JACK: The Bible! I didn't know you ever read the Bible!

DICK: What's wrong with the Bible? Isn't it worth reading?

JACK: Why, I suppose so. A person expects to hear ministers read the Bible at church, but I didn't think people read it at home—for pleasure.

DICK: The more one reads the Bible, the more fun it becomes. I read the Bible a long time before it had much meaning for me.

SALLY: What do you mean, Dick.

DICK: For a long time I read the Bible because of a sense of duty. I didn't understand much of what I was reading. I didn't have a definite plan of Bible-study and didn't get much help from my reading. Now it's different!

JACK: What's different—the Bible?

DICK: The Bible is the same, Jack. I guess my attitude is different.

JACK: I don't follow you! Either you read the Bible, or you don't!

DICK: There's more to it than that! A person's attitude toward the Bible is important. I read it now to see what message it has for me— how it can help me with my daily problems.

JACK: I still don't follow you! The Bible was written hundreds of years ago. It can't help us with the problems of a scientific age.

SALLY: Not so fast, Jack! There may be more to this matter of Bible-reading than you or I realize. Tell us, Dick, how the Bible has helped you with your problems.

DICK: First of all, the Bible tells about Jesus and the type of life he lived. It tells about experiences Jesus had with the people of his day.

JACK: How does that have anything to do with the twentieth century?

DICK: Human nature hasn't changed much through the centuries, Jack. No one is ever really satisfied with his life. All of us need forgiveness for our sins.

JACK: So the Bible reminds us of our sins, and that is supposed to make us happy?

DICK: The Bible does much more than that. It tells us of Jesus, who not only forgives our sins, but gives us strength to live better and

20

to keep from repeating the same mistakes in the future. Jesus wants to be our Saviour, but he also wants to be our Leader and Guide.

SALLY (*wistfully*): I often have questions about what is right and what is wrong. I often wish I had some sort of guide to better living.

JACK: But Jesus lived almost two thousand years ago. How can he guide us today?

DICK: The Bible tells us that Jesus is a living Leader—one who understands all our problems and wants to help us with them. The Bible also gives many of Jesus' teachings. They are not rules and regulations that applied just to the day in which Jesus lived. His teachings are basic principles which apply to our age and to every age. Bible-reading is much more helpful when you are looking for important principles and are trying to apply them to your own life.

SALLY: You spoke about having a plan of Bible-study, Dick. What did you mean by that?

DICK: The minister at our church gave us an outline of the New Testament to guide us in our Bible-reading. He suggested that we first read the book of Mark, then the other three Gospels, the book of Acts, the letters of Paul, and the rest of the New Testament. Many of the young people in our church are reading the New Testament in this way. Our pastor helps us with any passages that are difficult for us to understand. We're almost through with the New Testament; then we'll tackle the Old Testament. We've already found many principles which help us with our daily problems and experiences.

JACK: I'll have to admit that this sounds like a practical type of Bible-reading. What are some of these principles you've discovered?

DICK: I've marked some of them in my Bible. (DICK *opens his Bible and reads Matt. 16:24-25; 20:25-27; John 13:34-35; 3:16-17.*)

SALLY: Those teachings do have a message for us today, Dick. I know I could use them in my own life.

DICK: These are only a very few of the great teachings of the Bible. The more we read the Bible, the more these teachings help us to live an abundant, worth-while life. Jesus said, "I came that you might have life, and have it abundantly." The teachings of the Bible add joy and purpose to our lives.

JACK (*thoughtfully*): Come to think of it, Dick, you are a happy sort of fellow! You don't seem to get down in the dumps like the rest of us do. Maybe there's something to this Bible-reading business after all!

SALLY: I'm sure you get a lot of help from the Bible, Dick. Could Jack and I get in on this Bible-reading plan you were telling us about?

JACK: I'll say you can! I'll give you an outline of the New Testament to use as a guide, and you'll discover for yourselves the value of Bible-reading with a purpose!

HOW THE BIBLE HELPS US TODAY (may be read by a young person, or copies may be prepared so that it may be read in unison by the entire group):

1. The Bible helps us know God as he is revealed in Jesus Christ. It describes the abundant, eternal life which only Christ can provide.

2. The Bible helps us discern right from wrong and find forgiveness for our sins. It gives us strength to overcome temptation.

3. The Bible helps us walk in daily fellowship with Christ as our Saviour and Friend. It gives us guidance in our day-by-day decisions and experiences.

4. The Bible gives us inspiration for living a radiant, worth-while life. It helps us develop Christlike attitudes, motives, and desires.

5. The Bible challenges us to use our strength in constructive activities and purposeful endeavors.

6. The Bible inspires us to dedicate our time, talents, and possessions to Christ in order that they may be used for the advancement of his kingdom upon the earth.

SOLO OR DUET: "Sing Them Over Again to Me" or "O Word of God Incarnate"

CLOSING PRAYER AND BENEDICTION:

Our Father, we thank thee for the words of truth and wisdom which we find in thy Word. We are especially grateful for the message of Jesus Christ and his redeeming love. Help us to read the Bible with greater earnestness and find in it words of forgiveness and guidance for our daily lives. Send us forth with a desire not only to study thy Word more diligently, but also to share its message with others. In the name of Christ, our Redeemer. AMEN.

3. What God Is Like

Prelude: "This Is My Father's World"

Call to Worship:

> O God, whose smile is in the sky,
> Whose path is in the sea,
> Once more from earth's tumultuous strife,
> We gladly turn to Thee.
>
> Now all the myriad sounds of earth
> In solemn stillness die;
> While wind and wave unite to chant
> Their anthems to the sky.
>
> We come as those with toil far spent
> Who crave Thy rest and peace,
> And from the care and fret of life
> Would find in Thee release.
>
> O Father, soothe all troubled thought,
> Dispel all idle fear,
> Purge Thou each heart of secret sin,
> And banish every care.
>
> Until, as shine upon the sea
> The silent stars above,
> There shines upon our trusting souls
> The light of Thine own love.[1]
>
> —John Haynes Holmes

23

THE LORD'S PRAYER (in unison)

HYMN: "There's a Wideness in God's Mercy" or "How Gentle God's Commands"

LEADER:

No man can achieve a complete understanding of God. The words of a poet cannot adequately describe God. Great hymns of praise cannot depict his full majesty. A human mind cannot comprehend the complete grandeur and greatness of God.

We can, however, by turning to God's Word, receive help and guidance in our search for God. If we study the Bible in a spirit of earnest seeking after God, we will obtain an increasingly clear understanding of what God is like.

READER I:

Yet, O Lord, thou art our Father; we are the clay, and thou art our potter; we are all the work of thy hand.

Pray then like this:

> Our Father who art in heaven,
> Hallowed be thy name,
> Thy kingdom come,
> Thy will be done
> on earth as it is in heaven.

If you then, who are evil, know how to give good gifts to your children, how much more will your Father who is in heaven give good things to those who ask him?

For although there may be so-called gods in heaven or on earth—as indeed there are many "gods" and many "lords"—yet for us there is one God, the Father, from whom are all things and for whom we exist, and one Lord, Jesus Christ, through whom are all things and through whom we exist.[2]

READER II:

God is our heavenly Father. He is interested in each one of us, his children. He loves us and wants us to respond to his love and to have fellowship and companionship with him. He is eager to give us strength and guidance and to help us discover life at its glorious best. Even when we make mistakes and disobey him, God continues to love us. He is anxious for us to realize our sinfulness and to seek his forgiveness.

Jesus gave us a wonderful picture of God in the parable of the Prodigal Son. The young son was thoughtless and headstrong. He went to a distant country and lived a sinful life, causing his father grief and sorrow. The son finally realized his wrongdoing and started on the long journey toward home. While he was still a great distance from home, he saw someone hurrying toward him. It was his father, who had often watched for his absent son. The father ran to the boy, threw his arms about him, and kissed him. "Bring quickly the best robe, and put it on him," he said to the servants. "Prepare a great feast and let us eat and make merry; for this my son was dead, and is alive again; he was lost, and is found."

God, our heavenly Father, is like the father of the Prodigal Son.

HYMN: "Dear Lord and Father of Mankind" or "Father Almighty, Bless Us with Thy Blessing"

READER I:

Lord, thou hast been our dwelling place in all generations. Before the mountains were brought forth, or ever thou hadst formed the earth and the world, from everlasting to everlasting thou art God.

But the hour is coming, and now is, when the true worshipers will worship the Father in spirit and truth, for such the Father seeks to worship him. God is spirit, and those who worship him must worship in spirit and truth.[3]

READER II:

God is spirit. A physical body does not limit him to one geographical area or to one small segment of time. He can be with his children in all parts of the world through all centuries of time. God is a person, with all the characteristics of personality raised to perfection. This wondrous personality of God is clothed, not in bone and flesh, but in a spiritual body, the glory of which we cannot describe or imagine.

Human personality—the real person or soul which dwells within the physical body—is made in the image and likeness of God. We cannot see—with our physical eyes—the real self or soul of a friend.

25

We see only the body which houses the soul. Neither can we see God with our physical eyes, for he is spirit. He is unhampered by the limitations and weaknesses of a physical body. He therefore is eternal and unchanging. He is from everlasting to everlasting. He is our God—our Strength and our Redeemer—forever and ever.

HYMN: "O God, Our Help in Ages Past" or "Guide Me, O Thou Great Jehovah"

READER I:

Holy, holy, holy is the Lord of hosts; the whole earth is full of his glory. For thus says the high and lofty One who inhabits eternity, whose name is Holy: I dwell in the high and holy place, and also with him who is of a contrite and humble spirit.

As obedient children, do not be conformed to the passions of your former ignorance, but as he who called you is holy, be holy yourselves in all your conduct; since it is written, "You shall be holy, for I am holy." [4]

READER II:

God is holy. He is worthy of worship and adoration. As we study the Bible and obtain a better understanding of God, we become increasingly aware of his holiness and majesty. We worship him with a deep sense of awe and reverence, realizing our own unworthiness.

God's holiness is a concept almost beyond our human comprehension. It refers to the greatness, majesty, and glory of God. This term also includes the righteousness of God. It is well for us to realize that God is a loving, heavenly Father. It is also important that we understand that God is the ultimate standard of righteousness, justice, and truth. Because God is holy and righteous, he has woven into the fabric of the universe, laws that are moral and right. We cannot break the moral and physical laws of the universe and escape the consequences of our actions.

A realization of God's holiness stirs within us a spirit of humility and repentance. We are then in a position to receive the forgiveness and salvation which God has provided for us in Jesus Christ.

SOLO: "Lord of All Being, Throned Afar"

READER I:

I have not hid thy saving help within my heart, I have spoken of thy faithfulness and thy salvation; I have not concealed thy steadfast love and thy faithfulness from the great congregation. It is good to give thanks to the Lord, to sing praises to thy name, O Most High; to declare thy steadfast love in the morning, and thy faithfulness by night. The steadfast love of the Lord never ceases, his mercies never come to an end; they are new every morning; great is thy faithfulness.

God is faithful, by whom you were called into the fellowship of his Son, Jesus Christ our Lord. God is faithful, and he will not let you be tempted beyond your strength, but with the temptation will also provide the way of escape, that you may be able to endure it.[5]

READER II:

God is faithful. The more we understand God and come into fellowship with him, the more certain we are that he is faithful and dependable. The more we know of God, the more we know that he is worthy of trust in this life and throughout eternity. We can experience his faithfulness in forgiving our sins and in helping us with everyday problems and temptations.

The faithfulness of God gives us confidence as we face the problems of the present, and hope and assurance as we face the unknowable future. Because God is faithful, we have the certainty that, in spite of the prevalence of evil in the world, right will eventually triumph. God will ultimately work out his own all-wise plan and purpose for the world.

SOLO: "Great Is Thy Faithfulness" (This hymn may be read effectively as a poem while the pianist plays the hymn's music as an accompaniment.)

READER I:

But God shows his love for us in that while we were yet sinners Christ died for us. For I am sure that neither death, nor life, nor angels, nor principalities, nor things present, nor things to come, nor powers, nor height, nor depth, nor anything else in all creation, will be able to separate us from the love of God in Christ Jesus our Lord.

So we know and believe the love God has for us. God is love, and he who abides in love abides in God, and God abides in him. For God so loved the world that he gave his only Son, that whoever believes in him should not perish but have eternal life.[6]

READER II:

God is love. This is the simplest and most adequate definition that we have of God. All the other qualities of God are bound together and given expression in this one supreme attribute. God's love is purposeful, its purpose being the salvation of each individual human soul. In order to make certain of man's salvation from sin, God took on the limitations of human flesh and came to earth in the person of Jesus Christ. His life upon the earth was a life of perfect love. When we say, "God is love," we are saying that "God is like Christ." There is no better description of God's love.

SOLO: "Love Divine, All Loves Excelling"

LEADER:

God is our heavenly Father. He is interested in each one of us, his children.

God is spirit. He is therefore eternal and unchanging.

God is holy. He is worthy of our worship and adoration.

God is faithful, giving to us confidence and assurance.

God is love. He is like the love which Christ demonstrated in his life and in his death.

Because we have caught a clearer glimpse of what God is like, let us give to him in greater measure our love, our loyalty, our lives—our all.

CLOSING PRAYER AND BENEDICTION:

We are thankful, O God, that you love us and are concerned with our problems and temptations. We are grateful that you revealed yourself to us in Jesus Christ and that Jesus demonstrated to us what your love is like. Help us respond to your love by trusting you more completely and serving you more wholeheartedly.

"To the King of ages, immortal, invisible, the only God, be honor and glory, for ever and ever." AMEN.[7]

4. How God Makes Himself Known to Us

PRELUDE: "Joyful, Joyful, We Adore Thee"

CALL TO WORSHIP:
The heavens are telling the glory of God; and the firmament proclaims his handiwork. O Lord, how manifold are thy works! In wisdom hast thou made them all; the earth is full of thy creatures. O come, let us sing to the Lord; let us make a joyful noise to the rock of our salvation! Let us come into his presence with thanksgiving; let us make a joyful noise to him with songs of praise! [1]

RESPONSE (to be sung by the entire group):
> Holy, holy, holy, Lord God of hosts!
> Heaven and earth are full of Thee;
> Heaven and earth are praising Thee,
> O Lord most high! [2]
> —MARY A. LATHBURY

PRAYER:
We praise thee, O God, for the beauty and wonders of thy universe. We praise thee, too, for thy Son, Jesus Christ, and for the loveliness of the life which he lived upon the earth. Help us draw upon thy strength and resources so that our lives may be radiant and worth while. AMEN.

HYMN: "Joyful, Joyful, We Adore Thee" or "Praise the Lord! Ye Heavens, Adore Him"

POEM:

> God of the earth, the sky, the sea,
> Maker of all above, below,
> Creation lives and moves in Thee;
> Thy present life through all doth flow.
>
> Thy love is in the sun-shine's glow,
> Thy life is in the quickening air;
> When lightnings flash and storm winds blow,
> There is Thy power, Thy law is there.
>
> We feel Thy calm at evening's hour,
> Thy grandeur in the march of night,
> And when the morning breaks in power,
> We hear Thy word, "Let there be light."
>
> But higher far, and far more clear,
> Thee in man's spirit we behold,
> Thine image and Thyself are there,—
> The in-dwelling God, proclaimed of old.
>   —SAMUEL LONGFELLOW

LEADER:

God is the Creator and Ruler of the universe. He is also the loving, compassionate Father who yearns for the well-being of his children. He is a God who, desiring the companionship of his children, seeks to make himself known to each one of us. An informal dramatization, "God Speaks in Many Ways," will suggest to us some of the ways in which God makes himself known to mankind.

INFORMAL DRAMATIZATION:

GOD SPEAKS IN MANY WAYS

(*Three young people are discussing a sermon which they have heard on God's presence in men's daily affairs.*)

Don: I couldn't follow Reverend Denton in that sermon of his this morning.

Marge: Neither could I! He spoke as if God were as near to us as the next-door neighbor. Somehow I can't think of God as a Person who is interested in the little affairs of my daily life.

Don: Neither can I, Marge. It is easier for me to think of God as the Creator of the universe—the supreme Being who keeps the stars in their courses, and that sort of thing.

Marge: What's the matter with you, Steve? This must be a record of some kind—your sitting still five minutes without saying anything!

Steve: I've been thinking, and that's a real effort!

Don: Thinking? That's some type of record too!

Steve: I'm serious for once, and I guess that's also breaking a record or something! God seems vague and faraway to me too. But after hearing Reverend Denton's sermon, I have the feeling that we could know God better—that God could be real to us like he is to Reverend Denton.

Don: We've been created with intelligence—or so we like to believe. I think we're supposed to manage our own affairs. Why should God bother with us? Let him run the universe, and I'll run my own life!

Marge: That makes God too impersonal, Don. There are times when I wish I had some of God's wisdom to help me make the right decisions.

Don: But you just said you didn't think God was interested in the little affairs of your life.

Marge: I don't know God very well, Don, but I need him in my life and I'd like to know him better.

Steve: That's exactly the way I feel. By the way, I jotted down a few scripture passages which Reverend Denton mentioned this morning. Maybe they could help us learn more about God.

Marge: Let's see what they say. Here's a Bible.

Steve: The first one is Ps. 19:1. You look up that one, Don.

Don (*reads Ps. 19:1*): Why, that's the very thing I was talking about. God is the Creator of the universe. We can look at the stars and see his glory.

Steve: You're right, Don. The universe reminds us of God's power

31

and majesty. But Reverend Denton said this morning that there are many ways in which God makes himself known to us. He suggested that we read I Kings 19:11-13.

MARGE: I'll look up these verses. (*Turns to I Kings 19:11-13 and reads.*) That was a strange experience that Elijah had.

STEVE: Maybe it wasn't so strange. Maybe God does speak to us in time of need.

DON: What do you mean? We can't hear God speak with our physical ears!

STEVE: That's right! I think the voice of God is an inner voice—a voice that we hear within our minds and souls if we're in tune with God. I'll read the next verse on this list. (*Turns to Ps. 46:10 and reads this verse.*)

MARGE: I guess you've got something, Steve! "Be still, and know that I am God." Maybe that verse means that if we think quietly about God, we'll be able to know him and hear his voice.

DON: Maybe there is something to this business of listening for God's voice. What's the next Scripture on your list?

STEVE: The next one is in the ninth chapter of Acts. I think it tells about Saul's conversion. After his conversion he was known as Paul.

DON: I'll look it up. (*Reads Acts 9:3-17.*)

MARGE (*thoughtfully*): Paul's life was completely changed after this experience. God must have spoken to him in some way.

STEVE: I think God spoke to Paul directly and that he also spoke to him through Ananias. Ananias knew that Paul had persecuted the Christians, but he was willing to go to Paul and help him in his time of great need. I wonder if God doesn't speak to us today through the lives of earnest, Christian people.

DON: I guess you're right, Steve. Maybe God was speaking to us this morning through Reverend Denton.

MARGE: God probably tries to speak to us in the church services every Sunday, but we usually aren't listening very attentively.

STEVE: I think God also speaks to us through the Bible. This next verse tells us about the Bible. (*Reads Ps. 119:105.*)

DON: Marge said something about needing guidance in making decisions.

MARGE: That's right. If I read the Bible more, I'd probably get some help in making decisions and knowing what's right and wrong.

STEVE: Reverend Denton said this last scripture passage is the most important one of all. I've forgotten what it's about.

MARGE: So have I, but I'll soon tell you all about it! Here it is. (*Reads John 14:6-9.*) How could we forget this passage, Steve? It really is the most important one of all.

STEVE: You're right, Marge. That's the reason Jesus came to earth—to show us what God is like and to help us know him.

DON: I guess Jesus is our best picture of God. The stars and other wonders of nature remind us of God, but they don't tell us very much about him.

MARGE: Jesus said, "He who has seen me has seen the Father." We don't have to worry any more about what God is like. He's like Jesus. I guess Reverend Denton was right after all. If God is like Jesus, he is interested in our everyday problems and experiences. He is as near—or nearer—than our next-door neighbor!

STATEMENT OF FAITH IN GOD:

(May be read by a young person, or enough copies may be provided so the entire group may read it in unison.)

I believe in God, the Creator and Sustainer of the universe. I believe that he is all powerful and that he is guiding the destiny of the universe and of mankind. The wonders and glories of nature reveal his majesty and power.

I believe in God, the eternal Father. I believe that he loves every one of his children and that he tries to reveal himself to each one of us. God makes himself known to us through the Bible, through the lives of earnest Christians, and by means of the "inner voice" which we hear within our minds and souls.

I believe in God as he is revealed in Jesus Christ. I believe that Jesus is the final and complete revelation of God. Because God has revealed himself to me in the life, death, and resurrection of Christ, I desire to trust him more fully and to follow his guidance more perfectly in my daily life.

HYMN (may be sung softly by the entire group as a hymn of dedication): "Have Thine Own Way, Lord" or "I Need Thee Every Hour"

CLOSING PRAYER:

O God of love and mercy, we praise thee for the way in which thou hast revealed thyself in Jesus Christ. We are grateful that we can know thee as a daily Companion who shares our problems and burdens. May we have a greater awareness of thy presence with us in the everyday experiences of life. Through Jesus Christ our Lord. AMEN.

5. The Reality of Jesus
1149281

PRELUDE: "What a Friend We Have in Jesus"

CALL TO WORSHIP:

> Lord Jesus, make Thyself to me
> A living, bright reality;
> More present to faith's vision keen
> Than any outward object seen;
> More dear, more intimately nigh
> Than even the sweetest earthly tie.
> —ANONYMOUS

RESPONSE (by the entire group): First stanza of "My Faith Looks Up to Thee"

PRAYER:
We thank thee, O Lord, for thy presence with us at this very moment. Guide our thoughts and our words during this hour of meditation and worship. Help us to be more certain of thy reality and more aware of thy nearness in our daily experiences. May we open our minds and souls to thy guidance. May we know thee with certainty as our Saviour and Friend. AMEN.

HYMN: "What a Friend We Have in Jesus" or "Blessed Assurance, Jesus Is Mine"

LEADER:
As young people, we are interested in what is real and genuine. We have little patience with a product which does not fulfill its claims or with a person who "puts on airs," pretending to be more important

than he really is. "Is this the real thing?" is a common question on the lips of youth.

Most young people desire to discover true values in friendship, marriage, religion—in life itself. When young people are confronted with the basic truths of Christianity, in language which they can understand, they respond to the challenge of the Christian message. Youth are attracted to Jesus Christ and his way of life, and when the Christian way is presented simply and directly, they answer wholeheartedly: "This is genuine. This is the real thing!"

Since Jesus Christ is at the center of our Christian faith and of life's true realities, he will be presented as a living reality, not only in the first century, but just as truly in this twentieth century in which we live.

TALK I:

THE REALITY OF JESUS IN THE FIRST CENTURY

During his public ministry, Jesus became a dynamic reality to the men, women, and youth about him. He said to Peter, Andrew, James, and John, "Follow me," and they left their families, friends, and fishing business and became his closest companions. Jesus was exceedingly real to these men. He walked along the dusty roads of Galilee with them, talking with them, laughing with them, sharing his great hopes and yearnings with them.

The reality of Jesus became the central experience in the lives of his disciples. They saw the miracles of healing which he performed. They heard his incomparable teachings. They had not yet experienced his reality in its highest realm, but Peter, in a moment of divine revelation, exclaimed, "Thou art the Christ, the son of the living God."

The Cross was the crucial point in the faith of the disciples. The Master was intensely real to them as a Person in human form. Then they saw Jesus the man nailed upon a cross and placed securely within a tomb. Small wonder their hopes were crushed and the fires of faith burned low! If they were to experience the true reality of Jesus, they must know him, not just as Jesus the man, but as the risen Christ. Did they experience his presence after the Resurrection, when he no longer daily walked the dusty roads with them? Was Jesus real to them then? That was the crucial test of their faith.

The most significant fact of history is that Jesus was able to prove his resurrection to his followers. The success of his mission upon the earth and the survival of his message hinged upon that pivotal point. This remarkable lesson which Jesus taught his disciples was a twofold process: he proved his resurrection to his followers *through their physical senses;* he proved his continued presence with them *without the use of their physical senses.* He led them from the realm of physical sight to the realm of faith—the most significant step an individual ever takes.

Three incidents illustrate this vital lesson which the early followers of the Master learned.

1. Mary Magdalene, on the first Easter morning, was weeping at the tomb. She had not yet comprehended the fact of the Resurrection and thought that someone had moved Jesus' body to another place. Jesus himself appeared, but her faith could not yet grasp the fact of his presence. Then Jesus spoke her name only the one word "Mary," but it was enough. By the tone of his voice as he uttered that familiar word, she recognized him—through the physical sense of hearing. Jesus then made a strange request, "Touch me not; for I am not yet ascended to my Father." Why this unusual request? Jesus was helping her take that crucial step from sight to faith. He was leading her beyond the need of physical senses in order to recognize his presence. And Mary learned her lesson. She hurried immediately to the disciples to share with them her new-found faith in the risen Lord.

2. Cleopas and another disciple were walking sorrowfully from Jerusalem to their home in Emmaus. Jesus joined them, but they were not aware of his presence. To them the Resurrection was not yet a reality. When they reached Emmaus, the two disciples invited Jesus to stop at their home for a simple evening meal. Jesus took bread and broke it and gave thanks. In that familiar act they recognized him— through the physical sense of sight. Then he vanished immediately from their midst. Why? He did not want them to depend further on their physical senses. He desired that they know him, not through the physical eyes, but through the eyes of faith.

3. Thomas refused to accept the report of the other disciples that they had seen the Lord. He had to have proof—tangible proof. "Unless I put my finger into the print of the nails," he said, "and put my hand into his side, I will not believe." Tangible evidence was not as necessary as Thomas had thought. One week later, when Thomas was present, Jesus appeared to the disciples. Thomas did not wait to examine the nail prints and the sword wound. He immediately exclaimed in awe and wonder, "My Lord and my God." One glimpse of the radiant Presence was proof enough.

The early disciples learned well the tremendous lesson of experiencing the presence of Christ by faith rather than by sight. Jesus was more real to them after the ascension than he had ever been in the days of his physical presence. They manifested far more courage, insight, and fearlessness than they had exhibited when Jesus had been with them in the flesh. It was their awareness of the empowering presence of their Lord that enabled them to overthrow empires and to start a mighty conflagration of transforming power that has not ceased to illumine the hearts and minds of men down to this present day.

SOLO: (If a soloist is not available, the words may be read as a poem.)
"Are ye able," said the Master,
   "To be crucified with me?"
"Yea," the sturdy dreamers answered,
   "To the death we follow Thee."

"Lord, we are able."
   Our spirits are Thine.
Remold them, make us,
   Like Thee, divine.
Thy guiding radiance
   Above us shall be
A beacon to God,
   To love and loyalty.

—EARL MARLATT

Talk II:

THE REALITY OF JESUS IN THE TWENTIETH CENTURY

The center of our Christian faith is still a Person—the person of Jesus Christ. How can young people in this present century know this Person in a vital, intimate way? How can they know with certainty that he is their Saviour, Leader, and Friend?

1. Young people who desire to know the reality of Jesus must give Jesus a place in their thinking. We should think, first of all, of Jesus as our Saviour. All of us have sin and selfishness in our lives. We are guilty of shallowness and littleness, living narrow, ordinary lives when Christ calls us to a life of wide horizons and high purposes. All of us need a Saviour to save us from our littleness and our sin. Jesus is God's answer to the problem of sin. He came to bridge the gap which sin causes between God and man. We need to think about his life, his teachings, his death and resurrection, his influence upon the history of mankind. We will never understand fully the magnitude of his message and mission. But as we think about him and seek his forgiveness and power, we will experience inner peace and joy such as we have never known, and in a unique and wonderful way he will become real to us as our Saviour.

Young people should also think of Jesus as their Leader and Guide. Most young people have perplexities and uncertainties. They feel the need of a divine Leader who can give them strength and direction for their lives. When they think seriously of Jesus and the way he has challenged and guided men through the centuries, they gladly turn their lives over to him. When they earnestly trust his wisdom and leadership, he becomes real to them as their Leader and Guide.

Young people should think of Jesus as a Friend and Companion. Here is the realm in which they may indeed know the reality of Jesus. Once a young person meets the exacting demands of Christian discipleship, he then experiences the most satisfying fellowship that life can bring. Because they have not completely dedicated their lives to him, too many are missing the thrill of knowing the true reality of Jesus. When young people follow the Master and do his will, he becomes real to them as their Comrade and Friend.

2. When a person's thoughts are centered on Jesus Christ, it logically follows that his actions will give evidence that he is a follower of the Master. Someone has said that every Christian is a "sermon in shoes." Far more people hear the "sermons in shoes" that are preached by humble Christians than hear the verbal sermons of the world's great preachers. There are thousands of young people who can be reached for Christ and the Church, not by ministers, but by Christian young people, who, at school, at work and play, are consistent followers of the Master. A Christian young person will be considerate and kind, not only to close friends, but also to young people who have few friends, to little children, to the aged, the afflicted, and to members of other races.

3. If a young person is giving Jesus a vital place in his thoughts and actions, he will desire to take time for prayer and meditation. In fact, when a person thinks seriously about Jesus as Saviour, Guide, and Friend, that is meditation. And when one earnestly yearns to be like Jesus, that is one form of prayer. A poet has given us a helpful definition of prayer: "Prayer is the soul's sincere desire, unuttered or expressed." The same poem closes with this earnest request:

> O Thou by whom we come to God—
> The Life, the Truth, the Way!
> The path of prayer Thyself hast trod;
> Lord, teach us how to pray! [1]
> —James Montgomery

4. An earnest Christian young person will appreciate the privilege, not only of fellowship with Christ, but also of fellowship with other Christians. When Christian people have a deep awareness of Jesus' reality, they come together eagerly and frequently for fellowship and prayer; they carry on the work of Christ in a spirit of oneness and accord. Fellowship with Jesus Christ and with fellow Christians and service for the Master become the most significant aspects of life.

5. Young people will become more aware of the reality of Jesus if they allow everyday experiences to remind them of the presence of the Master. A piece of bread and a cup of grape juice are familiar objects, and yet they have a rich and sacred meaning when they are

used in the observance of the Lord's Supper. The Communion service should never become a ritualistic form. It should be so full of meaning and significance that all who participate are aware of the divine Companion in their midst.

There is no better reminder of the radiant Presence of our Lord than the symbol of light. Surely a lighted candle will cause every Christian youth to think of the Light of the world and of the glory and beauty of his life. The stars dotting the heavens on a clear night should remind the Christian of the majestic radiance of God as he is revealed in Jesus Christ.

If a young person desires to increase his awareness of the Master's presence, he will think of his Lord as he looks about him. When he sees a stream of clear running water, he will be reminded of the Water of life, of the One who promised: "Whosoever drinks of the water that I shall give him shall never thirst." When a Christian sees sheep grazing peacefully in a meadow, he will be inspired by thinking of the Good Shepherd who looked with compassion upon the multitudes because they were like sheep having no shepherd. Upon entering a doorway, a follower of the Master may think of the One who said: "I am the door; by me if any man enter in he shall be saved." Jesus also said: "Behold, I stand at the door and knock: if any man hear my voice and open the door, I will come into him, and will sup with him, and he with me."

Having prayed humbly and sought the Lord eagerly, the earnest Christian youth will discover the radiant, reassuring presence of the living Christ. He will know then, without a shadow of doubt, that he has found the basic reality from which all other realities of life gain their significance and essential meaning.

SOLO:

> "Are ye able?" Still the Master
> Whispers down eternity,
> And heroic spirits answer
> Now, as then, in Galilee.

> "Lord, we are able."
> Our spirits are Thine.

Remold them, make us,
Like Thee, divine.
Thy guiding radiance
Above us shall be
A beacon to God,
To love and loyalty.
—EARL MARLATT

CLOSING PRAYER:

We thank thee, O Christ, for those through the centuries who have experienced thy presence and power. We are grateful that they have kept the torch of the gospel burning brightly and have passed on the light from generation to generation to our present day. Help each one of us to know thee in a vital, personal way and to eagerly share our knowledge of thee with those about us. AMEN.

6. What Jesus Means to Us

PRELUDE: "Saviour, Like a Shepherd Lead Us"

CALL TO WORSHIP:

> O Christ, the Way, the Truth, the Life,
> Show me the living way,
> That in the tumult and the strife,
> I may not go astray.
>
> Teach me Thy Truth, O Christ, my Light,
> The Truth that makes me free,
> That in the darkness and the night
> My trust shall be in Thee.
>
> The Life that Thou alone canst give,
> Impart in love to me,
> That I may in Thy presence live,
> And ever be like Thee.[1]
>
> —GEORGE L. SQUIER

PRAYER:

Help us to find in thee, O Christ, the way, the truth, and the life. May we walk in thy way, understand thy truth, and experience the abundant life which thou alone canst give. Help us to open our minds and hearts to thee so that we may be filled with the light of thy love. Lead us each day along the right pathway, for we need thy guidance in all the experiences of life. In thy name we pray. AMEN.

HYMN: "Saviour, Like a Shepherd Lead Us" or "The King of Love My Shepherd Is"

SCRIPTURE: John 14:1-6

TALK I:

CHRIST IS THE WAY

Jesus described in exalted terms his ministry and mission. Coming from the lips of one who lived as he did, these amazing claims seem reasonable and appropriate. Of all the descriptions which Jesus gave of himself, one of the most meaningful is expressed in the simple phrase, "I am the way."

Jesus is the way to God. "No one comes to the Father," he said, "but by me." It is through Christ that we know what God is like. Christ is the only way to an adequate understanding of God. He is the only way to intimate fellowship with God. Christ is God revealing himself to mankind. He is God taking on the limitations of human flesh so that we might know God and have fellowship with him.

The pathway to God, which Christ provided for us, has a cross at the very center of it. The cross is an essential part of Christ's ministry on the earth. Since God is holy and righteous, he cannot ignore our sins. The Cross is God's plan for dealing with sin in the lives of his children. The Cross proves that God loves us in spite of our sins.

A certain boy refused to tell the truth about a wrong he had committed. The boy's father, not daring to overlook his son's wrong-doing, sent him to the attic to sleep. The father kept thinking of the boy—alone in the dark attic. Finally he carried a blanket to the attic and slept on the floor beside his son during the night. The father did not ignore the boy's sin, but he shared the sin and the consequences of that sin.

Christ shared the guilt and shame of our sins. He identified himself with sinful man, taking upon himself the sins of all mankind. On the cross he paid in full the penalty for our sins. By his death on the cross Christ made it possible for us to come before God with clean hands and pure hearts. Christ is the way to forgiveness, the way to

44

fellowship with God. He is the pathway to eternal life. "I am the way," Jesus said. "No one comes to the Father, but by me."

LEADER:

Thou art the Way: to Thee alone
From sin and death we flee;
And he who would the Father seek
Must seek Him, Lord, by Thee.

SOLO: First stanza of "O Jesus, I Have Promised"

TALK II:

CHRIST IS THE TRUTH

Through the ages men have had a deep, inner longing to know the truth about life and death, about right and wrong, about God and man. The amazing scientific discoveries of recent years have stirred within us a greater desire to discover the truth, not only about natural laws, but about life itself. The theories of men do not satisfy us, for other men may be as mistaken as we about the true meaning of life. In Christ, however, we discover one who is more than man—one who can say with authority, "I am the truth."

Christ is truth. He is the truth about man. In him we find the answer to the riddle of man and why he has been placed upon this planet. In Christ we find the answers to the problems and perplexities of our own individual lives. Christ is the truth about what each one of us should be. We do not know how evil we are until we meet Christ face to face. Only Christ can show us what we ought to be and give us power to become the person of our highest dreams. Only Christ, by the giving of his love, can illumine our darkened lives with light.

When we catch a real glimpse of Christ, we discover the truth about sin. We realize the seriousness of sin, and, for that reason, we have a deep sense of guilt. We may scarcely recognize this feeling of guilt because it is pushed into our subconscious minds, but it is there. It expresses itself in many ways. The more critical we are of

45

others, the more guilt we feel within ourselves. Only when we completely acknowledge our sin and accept the Father's forgiveness as it has been offered to us in Christ, can we find relief from our sense of guilt.

Christ is the truth about God. He demonstrated by his life and death what God is like. By his life, death, and resurrection, he proved that he was God in human form. The purpose of his life upon the earth was to give us the truth about God. To feel the warmth and radiance of Christ's love is to know God and to trust him to guide and sustain us through all the uncertainties of life's tomorrows.

Christ is the truth about life. When, by knowing Christ and his forgiveness, we have established a right relationship with God, life becomes meaningful and satisfying. We must live each day in right relationship with God as he has been made known to us through Christ. When we open our minds and souls to the love of Christ and earnestly seek his guidance and strength, only then will we discover the true meaning and purpose of life. Jesus said, "If you continue in my word, you are truly my disciples, and you will know the truth, and the truth will make you free."

LEADER:

> Thou art the Truth: Thy Word alone
> True wisdom can impart;
> Thou only canst inform the mind,
> And purify the heart.

SOLO: Second stanza of "O Jesus, I Have Promised"

TALK III:

CHRIST IS THE LIFE

One cannot think of Christ without thinking of life—life so vibrant and full of meaning that it has an eternal quality about it. The forces of evil were arrayed against Jesus, but were unable to overcome the power of his life. Even death itself was no match for the enduring quality of his life. He arose from the grave, proving that life—eternal life—is victorious over both sin and death.

46

The Gospel of John declares: "In Christ is life and that life is the light of men." Through the centuries the light of Christ has glowed like a torch in the darkness, and all the forces of evil have not been able to put out the light of his life.

To share the eternal life of Christ is to find the true meaning and purpose of life. Only when we experience the power of the eternal Christ in our lives, will our questions about life and death be satisfactorily answered. Only in Christ can we know the kind of life that is worthy of eternity. Through Christ we can experience that kind of life now. It is a life which sees the spark of eternal value in every human soul and tries daily to bring forth the good and noble in every man. It is a life of love that rejoices in fellowship with God and with one's fellow men.

Jesus said, "I came that they may have life, and have it abundantly." It is through Christ that we can understand, appreciate, and experience life that is abundant and eternal.

LEADER:

> Thou art the Life: the rending tomb
> Proclaims Thy conquering arm;
> And those who put their trust in Thee
> Nor death nor hell shall harm.
>
> Thou art the Way, the Truth, the Life:
> Grant us that way to know,
> That truth to keep, that life to win,
> Whose joys eternal flow.[2]
> —GEORGE WASHINGTON DOANE

SOLO: Fourth stanza of "O Jesus, I Have Promised"

CLOSING PRAYER:

We are thankful, O Christ, for all you have meant to us in the past. Help us discover the greater meanings and values which you can give to our lives in the days ahead. We are grateful that you are the Way, the Truth, and the Life. May we experience in fuller measure the abundant life which you have made available for us, and may we share this glorious life with others.

"Now to him who by the power at work within us is able to do far more abundantly than all that we ask or think, to him be glory in the church and in Christ Jesus to all generations, for ever and ever. AMEN." [3]

7. Understanding the Holy Spirit

PRELUDE: "Holy Spirit, Truth Divine"

CALL TO WORSHIP:

> Oh, Haunting Spirit of the Ever True,
> Keep thou the pressure of thy way upon us.
> We see a world too big to grasp;
> We glimpse a city too far off to reach;
> We trudge a way too long to walk;
> We feel a truth too pure to understand,
> We have a purpose that we cannot prove;
> A life to live beyond the power of living;
> A vision, time nor energy cannot contain;
> But faith that all our effort will not be in vain.
> Oh, Haunting Spirit of the Ever True,
> Keep thou the pressure of thy way upon us.[1]
> —ALLAN KNIGHT CHALMERS

RESPONSE (to be sung in unison):

> Spirit of the living God,
> Fall afresh on me;
> Spirit of the living God,
> Fall afresh on me.
> Melt me, mold me, fill me, use me;
> Spirit of the living God,
> Fall afresh on me.
> —ANONYMOUS

PRAYER:

Our Father, may we have a greater understanding of the Holy Spirit and of his presence and power in the world today. May we follow the leadership of thy Spirit and allow him to direct our thoughts and actions. AMEN.

HYMN: "Holy Spirit, Truth Divine" or "Spirit of Life in This New Dawn"

LEADER:

The Holy Spirit is presented to us in the Bible, not as a vague influence, but as a Person. According to God's Word, the Holy Spirit has the characteristics of a person. He possesses knowledge, feeling, and the power to lead and guide. He encourages, instructs, and reproves. The Holy Spirit can be grieved; he also rejoices when we respond to his guidance.

The Holy Spirit not only has personality; he also possesses diety. This means that he is a divine person. He has attributes and powers which belong only to God. He is God at work in the world today. He is God at our side to guide and help us. The Holy Spirit is equal in majesty and power to God the Father and God the Son.

We will be able to understand more about the Holy Spirit as we turn to God's Word and consider a number of scripture passages which refer to the Holy Spirit.

READER I:

In the beginning God created the heavens and the earth. The earth was without form and void, and darkness was upon the face of the deep; and the Spirit of God was moving over the face of the waters.[2]

READER II:

These are the two opening verses of God's Word. The Holy Spirit is mentioned—in the opening sentences of the Bible—as having a part in the creation of the universe. The Holy Spirit—like the Father and the Son—is from everlasting to everlasting. He is without beginning and without end. The Holy Spirit had a part in the creation of the universe, and he has a part in carrying out God's eternal plan for the universe and for mankind.

READER I:

The Old Testament writers refer on many occasions to the Holy Spirit. They give us many helpful ideas regarding the work and witness of the Holy Spirit.

The psalmist prayed: "Create in me a clean heart, O God, and put a new and right spirit within me. Cast me not away from thy presence, and take not thy holy Spirit from me."

Isaiah wrote: "The Spirit of the Lord God is upon me, because the Lord has anointed me to bring good tidings to the afflicted; he has sent me to bind up the brokenhearted, to proclaim liberty to the captives, and the opening of the prison to those who are bound."

Joel gave God's promise of a greater outpouring of the Holy Spirit in the future: "And it shall come to pass afterward, that I will pour out my spirit on all flesh; your sons and your daughters shall prophesy, your old men shall dream dreams, and your young men shall see visions."

Micah declared: "But as for me, I am filled with power, with the Spirit of the Lord, and with justice and might, to declare to Jacob his transgressions and to Israel his sin."

Zechariah wrote: "Not by might, nor by power, but by my Spirit, says the Lord of hosts." [3]

READER II:

The Old Testament writers had an ever-growing understanding of the work of the Holy Spirit. They were able to experience, in a limited measure, the power and helpfulness of God's Spirit. God revealed to the prophet Joel that at a future date the Holy Spirit would be present upon the earth in greater power. God made known to Zechariah that his work upon the earth would be accomplished, not by human might or power, but by the power of the Holy Spirit.

READER I:

And when Jesus was baptized, he went up immediately from the water, and behold, the heavens were opened and he saw the Spirit of God descending like a dove, and alighting on him; and lo, a voice from heaven, saying, "This is my beloved Son, with whom I am well pleased."

And Jesus came and said to them, "All authority in heaven and on earth has been given to me. Go therefore and make disciples of all nations, baptizing them in the name of the Father and of the Son and of the Holy Spirit." [4]

READER II:

At the time of Jesus' baptism, and again when Jesus gave his final commission to his disciples, the Holy Spirit is mentioned in connection with the Father and the Son. The Holy Spirit is a part of the Trinity— equal in power and glory to the Father and the Son.

READER I:

And I will pray the Father, and he will give you another Counselor, to be with you for ever, even the Spirit of truth, whom the world cannot receive, because it neither sees him nor knows him; you know him, for he dwells with you, and will be in you. But when the Counselor comes, whom I shall send to you from the Father, even the Spirit of truth, who proceeds from the Father, he will bear witness to me. Nevertheless I tell you the truth: it is to your advantage that I go away, for if I do not go away, the Counselor will not come to you; but if I go, I will send him to you. And behold, I send the promise of my Father upon you; but stay in the city, until you are clothed with power from on high. [5]

READER II:

On various occasions Jesus repeated the promise which had first been given by Joel, that the Holy Spirit would come into the world in greater power. Jesus told his disciples that when he returned to the Father, the Holy Spirit would come into their lives and be their Helper and Guide. The Holy Spirit would enable the disciples to carry on the work that Jesus had instructed them to do. Jesus told his disciples to remain in Jerusalem until they had been empowered by the Holy Spirit.

READER I:

When the day of Pentecost had come, they were all together in one place. And suddenly a sound came from heaven like the rush of a mighty wind, and it filled all the house where they were sitting. And there appeared to them tongues as of fire, distributed and resting on each one of them. And they were all filled with the Holy Spirit and began to speak in other tongues, as the Spirit gave them utterance.[6]

READER II:

The disciples remained in Jerusalem, as Jesus had told them to do, and on the day of Pentecost, which was fifty days after Jesus' resurrection, the Holy Spirit came to earth in increased power and glory. The disciples were filled with the Holy Spirit, receiving new courage, strength, and power. They were now ready to obey the great commission of Christ and carry the message of salvation to all nations of the earth.

READER I:

Jesus answered, "Truly, truly, I say to you, unless one is born of water and the Spirit, he cannot enter the kingdom of God. That which is born of the flesh is flesh, and that which is born of the Spirit is spirit.[7]

READER II:

The Holy Spirit has been at work in the lives of men, women, and youth through the centuries. The Holy Spirit's power is of great importance to each one of us today. The Holy Spirit makes it possible for us to experience the salvation which Christ has provided. The Spirit of God enables us to see the sin in our lives and to realize our need of a Saviour. The Holy Spirit reveals to us that Jesus Christ is the only answer to our deepest needs. The power of the Holy Spirit makes it possible for us to know Christ as Saviour and Lord, thus becoming a part of Christ's kingdom.

READER I:

But the Counselor, the Holy Spirit, whom the Father will send in my name, he will teach you all things, and bring to your remembrance all that I have said to you. For the kingdom of God does not mean food and drink but righteousness and peace and joy in the Holy Spirit. May the God of hope fill you with all joy and peace in believing, so that by the power of the Holy Spirit you may abound in hope. But the fruit of the Spirit is love, joy, peace, patience, kindness, goodness, faithfulness, gentleness, self-control; against such there is no law.[8]

READER II:

Once we have become a part of Christ's kingdom, the Holy Spirit continues to be our teacher, guide, and helper. It is the power of the Holy Spirit which enables us to grow and develop in the Christian life. The Holy Spirit gives us strength to overcome sinful habits and to discover more fully God's will for our daily lives. The Holy Spirit encourages us in our prayer life and guides us in an understanding of the Bible.

When we follow the leadership of the Holy Spirit, we will develop Christlike attitudes and motives. We will demonstrate in our daily lives the fruits of the Spirit: love, joy, peace, patience, kindness, goodness, faithfulness, gentleness, and self-control.

HYMN: "Breathe on Me, Breath of God" or "Holy Spirit, Hear Us"

POEM:

> Gracious Spirit, dwell with me!
> I myself would gracious be;
> And, with words that help and heal,
> Would Thy life in mine reveal;
> And, with actions bold and meek,
> Would for Christ, my Saviour, speak.
>
> Truthful Spirit, dwell with me!
> I myself would truthful be;
> And, with wisdom kind and clear,
> Let Thy life in mine appear;
> And, with actions brotherly,
> Speak my Lord's sincerity.
>
> . . . .
>
> Holy Spirit, dwell with me!
> I myself would holy be;
> Separate from sin, I would
> Choose and cherish all things good,
> And whatever I can be
> Give to Him who gave me Thee.[9]
>   —THOMAS TOKE LYNCH

CLOSING PRAYER:

O Spirit of God, fill our minds and our lives anew with thy presence and power. We realize how weak and sinful we are when we rely on our own strength. We need thy guidance and leadership in our daily experiences. Turn our hatred into love, our criticism into compassion, our complaining into gratitude and praise. Reveal to us in greater measure the greatness and glory of the Lord Jesus. In his name we pray. AMEN.

8. How the Holy Spirit Helps Us Today

PRELUDE: "Spirit of God, Descend upon My Heart"

CALL TO WORSHIP:

> O Spirit of the Living God,
> Thou Light and Fire Divine:
> Descend upon Thy church once more
> And make it truly Thine!
> Fill it with love and joy and power,
> With righteousness and peace,
> Till Christ shall dwell in human hearts,
> And sin and sorrow cease.[1]
> —HENRY HALLAM TWEEDY

PRAYER:

Our Father, we thank thee for sending thy Spirit into the world to be our Helper and Guide. As we think together about the work of the Holy Spirit in the world today, may the Spirit dwell in greater measure in our own lives and minds. Guide us in our study of the Holy Spirit, and may we be responsive to the leading of thy Spirit in every area of our lives. AMEN.

HYMN: "Gracious Spirit, Dwell with Me" or "Come, Thou Almighty King"

LEADER:

The Bible suggests many ways in which the Holy Spirit is a source of helpfulness to mankind. The vast power and resources of the Holy

56

Spirit are available to us. All we need to do is open our minds and lives to the influence and leadership of God's Spirit. Perhaps a summary of the ways in which the Holy Spirit desires to be of help will enable us to understand more fully the power and presence of the Holy Spirit in the world today.

READER I:

Jesus answered, "Truly, truly, I say to you, unless one is born of water and the Spirit, he cannot enter the kingdom of God." [2]

READER II:

The power of the Holy Spirit makes it possible for us to know Christ as Saviour and Lord and to become a part of the kingdom of God.

READER I:

That which is born of the flesh is flesh, and that which is born of the Spirit is spirit.[3]

READER II:

There are two distinct areas of life—the physical and the spiritual. We enter the physical realm by means of physical birth. We enter the spiritual realm by means of a spiritual birth. It is the power of the Holy Spirit that enables us to experience this spiritual birth.

READER I:

And I will pray the Father, and he will give you another Counselor, to be with you for ever.[4]

READER II:

Jesus said that the Holy Spirit is the Comforter and Counselor of each one of his followers. The Holy Spirit will be with us forever.

READER I:

Even the Spirit of truth, whom the world cannot receive, because it neither sees him nor knows him; you know him, for he dwells with you, and will be in you.[5]

READER II:

Jesus also called the Holy Spirit the Spirit of truth. Those who close their minds to Christ cannot know or receive this Spirit of truth. Each one who is an earnest follower of the Master will know the Holy Spirit, for the Spirit dwells within the heart and mind of every Christian.

READER I:

But the Counselor, the Holy Spirit, whom the Father will send in my name, he will teach you all things, and bring to your remembrance all that I have said to you.[6]

READER II:

God sent the Holy Spirit to be our Teacher. The Holy Spirit will teach us the truths we should know about Christ and the Christian way of life.

READER I:

Nevertheless I tell you the truth: it is to your advantage that I go away, for if I do not go away, the Counselor will not come to you; but if I go, I will send him to you. And when he comes, he will convince the world of sin and of righteousness and of judgment.[7]

READER II:

The Holy Spirit helps us understand the seriousness of sin, the importance of righteousness, and the certainty of judgment.

READER I:

When the Spirit of truth comes, he will guide you into all the truth; for he will not speak on his own authority, but whatever he hears he will speak, and he will declare to you the things that are to come.[8]

READER II:

The Holy Spirit is also our Guide. He guides us in the understanding of truth and in the making of decisions which have to do with everyday living.

READER I:

You shall receive power when the Holy Spirit has come upon you; and you shall be my witnesses in Jerusalem and in all Judea and Samaria and to the end of the earth.[9]

READER II:

It is from the Holy Spirit that we receive spiritual power and

58

resources. The Holy Spirit gives us power to be witnesses for Christ in our local communities, throughout our nation, and to the uttermost parts of the earth.

READER I:

For the kingdom of God does not mean food and drink but righteousness and peace and joy in the Holy Spirit.[10]

READER II:

When the Holy Spirit dwells in us, our lives will be characterized by righteousness, peace, and joy. The Christian life is a joyous and worth-while way of living.

LEADER:

We have heard from God's Word a number of ways in which the Holy Spirit desires to help us in the everyday experiences of life. The ways in which the Holy Spirit inspires and challenges young people today will become more meaningful as we listen to a true story, "Pioneers for Christ."

STORY:

PIONEERS FOR CHRIST [11]

It was September, 1950. Five young people met one Sunday evening to talk about reaching other youth for Christ and the church. One of these young people had recently returned from military service in the Philippines. In addition, there were a young teacher beginning her first year of teaching, a girl who was employed in an insurance office, and a nurse who worked in a doctor's office. A young bank examiner completed the quintet.

"Why do many young people feel that they graduate from church when they graduate from high school?" one of them asked.

"Why don't young people have a more vital place in the life of our church?" asked another.

"Why aren't young people interested in using their talents and abilities in the work of the church?" still another inquired.

"I think we need a greater sense of fellowship," the ex-soldier said.

"We need closer fellowship with Christ and also a feeling of fellowship with each other."

"Fellowship" became the keyword of the new youth group from the very beginning. Each Sunday evening before the evening church service the group met for prayer and a discussion of topics vitally related to the daily experiences of youth. Growth took place slowly but consistently. By the end of the first year a dozen young people attended the Sunday evening meetings regularly.

Six years after its organization the fellowship of Pioneers, as the young people call themselves, has an active resident membership of more than seventy. During the six-year period more than two hundred young people have been active members of the group, serving not only in the youth group, but also in the wider ministry of the church.

Fellowship is still the keynote of the Pioneers. There is a spirit of genuine Christian fellowship in this group which takes in the stranger and makes him feel that he is an important part of the group. This spirit of fellowship is so vital that it binds together young people from various parts of the country and from different backgrounds and experiences. Airmen from a nearby air base, girls working in offices and shops, fellows working in offices and stores, students from several business schools and universities—all these young people are experiencing the meaning of the important truth that youth are one in Christ. Two Canadians, a young man from China, two Puerto Ricans, an Austrian, a Japanese-American, a girl from Denmark, and several Negro young people have been members of the group during its six-year history. As youth become aware of their common love and loyalty to Jesus Christ, national and racial barriers are surmounted.

Prayer was important to these young people when the Pioneer Fellowship was organized. It plays a vital part in the life of the group today. Each Wednesday evening a large number of Pioneers attend the Deeper Life Hour of the church. Following this service they meet for a youth-sharing session and prayer time, with all of the young people taking part in prayer. They pray earnestly for one another, for young people whom they are hoping to win to Christ, and for the work of Christ around the world. These young people also realize the importance of daily prayer and Bible-reading. They read the same book of the Bible in their daily devotions, and on Wednesday evenings they share verses and passages of Scripture which have been meaningful to them during daily devotional periods. The name they have given to this sharing experience each Wednesday evening is "Fellowship of Faith."

Fun is a natural outgrowth of the experiences of the Pioneers. Because these young people have a feeling of vital Christian fellowship, they have fun that is a joy to behold! What a variety of good times they enjoy: hayrides, miniature golf, roller skating, ice skating, basketball games, softball games, picnics, banquets, hymn-sings, and "Fellowship of Fun" each Sunday night after the evening church service.

Concern for other youth is another important characteristic of the Pioneers. Calling in the homes of young people has been one of the main emphases of the group during the six years of its existence. One night every two weeks is set aside as "calling night." The young people meet at the church for a brief time of instruction and prayer and to get the assignments for their calls. They call on prospects and on young people who have been absent from the group. This type of calling— month after month and year after year—pays big dividends in the long run. There are young people who have been called upon regularly for three or four years who are just beginning to attend Pioneer meetings. Many of the young people who are contacted become Christians and unite with the church. At a recent baptismal service eight of the eleven persons baptized were young people who had been contacted by the Pioneers.

Service to others has been an important goal of the Pioneer Fellowship through the years. The young people call periodically on all the shut-ins of the church, sometimes presenting brief devotional services in their homes. They also take regularly to the shut-ins, tape recordings of the church worship services. The young people sing Christmas carols and give gifts at Christmas time to each shut-in.

The Pioneers also conduct a Thursday evening service each month at the City Mission. Recently one of the men at the mission was impressed by the testimonies of the Pioneers. He talked to several of the young people after the service about the meaning of Christian discipleship. Two days later this man sent the following message to the young people by the superintendent of the mission: "Tell the young people they are responsible for my conversion. Tell them I'm going back to my home town and make a new start in life. Tell them to keep praying for me."

Back of all the other characteristics of the Pioneer Fellowship is this all-important one: *consecration to Christ.* From the very beginning there has been a nucleus of young people who placed loyalty to Christ and his Church above everything else. This spirit of dedication to Christ has been irresistible—it has constantly reached out and touched the lives of other youth.

On a recent Life Service Sunday six young people from the Pioneer Fellowship publicly dedicated their lives to full-time Christian service. Eight others had previously made this important decision, making a total of fourteen from this one youth group who are making definite plans for full-time Christian work. A number of these young people have moved elsewhere to continue their preparation for their work for Christ. Still other members of the group have left for the armed services. All these young people who are away are remembered frequently in prayer by the young people back home. Once each month a youth paper, *Pioneer Trails,* makes its way to all the Pioneers who are scattered around the world.

One other aspect of the Pioneer Fellowship should be mentioned. The group has a splendid record as far as matrimony is concerned! In due time the ex-soldier, who served as the first president of the group, married the young nurse. The bank examiner married the schoolteacher. Since then ten other couples from this group have been united in marriage. Twelve Christian homes have been established as a direct result of this one youth group—an average of two each year. And the prospects are bright for the future! This is indeed *pioneering* of a high order.

The motto of the Pioneer Fellowship is taken from Heb. 12:2: "Looking to Jesus the pioneer and perfecter of our faith." Pioneers for Christ! Surely there is no greater challenge than that for youth. Christian youth do not follow the path of the pioneer in their own strength. It is the power of the Holy Spirit at work in the lives of these young people which makes it possible for them to be effective Pioneers for Jesus Christ.

SOLO: "Spirit of God, Descend upon My Heart"

CLOSING PRAYER:

O God, during these moments of quiet meditation may thy Spirit descend upon us and take possession of our minds and lives. May we look earnestly unto Jesus, the Pioneer and Perfecter of our faith. Help us to follow the leadership of the Holy Spirit as we endeavor to be courageous pioneers for Christ. AMEN.

9. The Meaning of Life

PRELUDE: "Take My Life, and Let It Be"

CALL TO WORSHIP:

> One ship drives east and another drives west
> With the selfsame winds that blow.
>> 'Tis the set of the sails
>> And not the gales
> Which tells us the way to go.
>
> Like the winds of the sea are the ways of fate,
> As we voyage along through life:
>> 'Tis the set of a soul
>> That decides its goal
> And not the calm or the strife.[1]
>> —ELLA WHEELER WILCOX

PRAYER:

Our Father, may our minds and souls be in tune with thee. By looking to thee for guidance, may we discover the true goals and purposes of life. May we dedicate our strength, our talents, and our love to thee. In the name of Christ we pray. AMEN.

HYMN: "Take My Life, and Let It Be" or "Thou My Everlasting Portion"

LEADER:

Life has meaning and purpose. Man, with his ability to think and to love, is not a victim of chance. To be a man, with all of man's yearnings for a better life, must be an experience of tremendous worth.

To be human, with human weaknesses and yet with the amazing potentialities of humanity, must have eternal value and purpose.

Man is a strange and complex creature. We fail to understand the hopes and feelings of our closest friends. We often do not understand ourselves. It is helpful to turn to God's Word for guidance in our quest for knowledge regarding man and the meaning of life.

The Bible describes two aspects of man's existence. Man is depicted as a physical being, whose life upon the earth is brief and uncertain. To place our faith in physical strength and material possessions is to be deceived and to miss the real meaning of life.

SCRIPTURE:

And he said to them, "Take heed, and beware of all covetousness; for a man's life does not consist in the abundance of his possessions." And he told them a parable, saying, "The land of a rich man brought forth plentifully; and he thought to himself, 'What shall I do, for I have nowhere to store my crops?' And he said, 'I will do this: I will pull down my barns, and build larger ones; and there I will store all my grain and my goods. And I will say to my soul, Soul, you have ample goods laid up for many years; take your ease, eat, drink, be merry.' But God said to him, 'Fool! This night your soul is required of you; and the things you have prepared, whose will they be?' So is he who lays up treasure for himself, and is not rich toward God."

Come now, you who say, "Today or tomorrow we will go into such and such a town and spend a year there and trade and get gain"; whereas you do not know about tomorrow. What is your life? For you are a mist that appears for a little time and then vanishes. Instead you ought to say, "If the Lord wills, we shall live and we shall do this or that." As it is, you boast in your arrogance. All such boasting is evil.[2]

LEADER:

The Bible also emphasizes the spiritual aspect of man's life. The physical body of man houses an immortal spirit. To realize the importance of man's spiritual nature is the key to an understanding of the meaning of life.

SCRIPTURE:

So God created man in his own image, in the image of God he

created him. And the Lord God formed man of the dust of the ground, and breathed into his nostrils the breath of life; and man became a living soul.

And the tempter came and said to him, "If you are the Son of God, command these stones to become loaves of bread." But he answered, "It is written, 'Man shall not live by bread alone, but by every word that proceeds from the mouth of God.'"

Jesus answered, "Truly, truly, I say to you, unless one is born of water and the Spirit, he cannot enter the kingdom of God. That which is born of the flesh is flesh, and that which is born of the Spirit is spirit. Do not marvel that I said to you, 'You must be born anew.'"

For it is the God who said, "Let light shine out of darkness," who has shone in our hearts to give the light of the knowledge of the glory of God in the face of Christ. But we have this treasure in earthen vessels, to show that the transcendent power belongs to God and not to us. So we do not lose heart. Though our outer nature is wasting away, our inner nature is being renewed every day.[3]

LEADER:

"Treasures for Earth and Heaven" is an informal skit which illustrates the twofold nature of man's existence—the physical or material aspect of life and the spiritual aspect of life. This skit is based on a familiar passage of Scripture: "Do not lay up for yourselves treasures on earth, where moth and rust consume and where thieves break in and steal, but lay up for yourselves treasures in heaven, where neither moth nor rust consumes and where thieves do not break in and steal. For where your treasure is, there will your heart be also."[4]

DRAMATIC PRESENTATION:

TREASURES FOR EARTH AND HEAVEN

(MARGIE *and* GLENDA *are spending Sunday afternoon together at Margie's home.*)

MARGIE: What did you think of our lively discussion in Sunday-school class this morning?

GLENDA: The discussion was tops! Did you notice that everyone in class had something to say? I think Mr. Peterson is a swell guy and a great teacher.

MARGIE: I agree, but there's one thing I don't get. Why does he keep talking about "treasures in heaven"? What's wrong with a few treasures on earth?

GLENDA: There's nothing wrong with enjoying things on earth, but material values are not as important as spiritual values.

MARGIE: You're as bad as Mr. Peterson—always talking about "spiritual values." For myself, I'm interested in things I can see and feel— like a new car, for example.

GLENDA: I like new cars too—especially red ones! But things you see and feel aren't enough. Even a new car wouldn't be much fun if you had no one to enjoy it with you!

MARGIE: Different people have different ideas about life. Why can't each person live his own life without someone else always reminding him of his religious duties?

(DENNIS, MARGIE's *older brother, enters the room, interrupting the girls' conversation.*)

DENNIS: What in the world are you gals arguing about?

MARGIE: Why don't big brothers mind their own business? We're not arguing about anything. Glenda and I are discussing today's Sunday-school lesson.

DENNIS: This is a surprise! I didn't know you two ever had a serious thought!

GLENDA: Why don't you join us, Dennis? Do you ever have any serious thoughts? What did you think of Mr. Peterson's lesson this morning?

DENNIS: I think "Old Pete" had some very good ideas—especially when he said there's a lot more to life than machines and gadgets.

MARGIE: You ought to talk! You have a car and money for clothes and all kinds of gadgets. We're still in school and can't work, and you try to tell us that clothes and cars aren't important!

DENNIS: They're important, Margie, but they're not all of life. They are not even the most important part of life.

MARGIE: This sounds strange coming from you, Dennis! It seems to me that your car is plenty important to you.

DENNIS: All of us think too much about material possessions. I know

I do. That's why we need discussions like we had this morning to remind us that man is a lot more than the clothes he wears or the car he drives.

GLENDA: You're right, Dennis. We take for granted our most important possessions.

MARGIE: What do you mean by that?

GLENDA: Oh, lots of things! We can hear, see, speak, think, and remember. We can also make friends and have fellowship with one another and with God.

MARGIE: You said something awhile ago, Glenda, about a car not being much fun unless someone enjoyed it with you. I guess you're right. If I ever have a car, I want someone I like real well to share it with me.

DENNIS (*jokingly*): This sounds like a great confession! I believe Margie's about to reveal the great secret of her life!

MARGIE: I'm serious, Dennis! Love and friendship *are* important— maybe even more important than the car!

GLENDA: Good for you, Margie! I knew you'd come through with the right idea! Man is more than a physical being. He has spiritual qualities that are more important than his physical body or his material possessions.

DENNIS: Our physical life is important, but it's temporary and uncertain. The moral and spiritual qualities are eternal.

MARGIE (*excitedly*): Then, that's why Mr. Peterson talks about "treasures in heaven"! Love, friendship, and service are for this life and for eternity too. We might call them treasures for *both* earth and heaven.

GLENDA: Treasures for earth and heaven! That's a wonderful thought, Margie! Mr. Peterson will go for that idea! Let's tell him about it right away!

LEADER:

The meaning of life becomes clearer to us as we think of the characteristics which distinguish man from lower forms of life. Man has intelligence, which means he has the power to reason, remember, analyze, and to plan his activities. Man also has a moral nature. He has the power to choose between right and wrong. Man is a social

68

being, capable of having love and concern for others. He is at his best in association with others. In addition, man has a spiritual nature. He is capable of fellowship with God. He was created for fellowship with God and is never able to put God entirely out of his life.

Unfortunately, the capabilities of man are marred by sin. Man is unable to live up to the best that he knows. Sin harms the inner spiritual nature of man just as diseases harm the physical body. Man needs a power beyond himself to help him overcome the forces of evil which are at work in his mind and soul. This power can be found only in God as he has revealed himself in Christ. Christ alone provides adequate motivation for victorious living. He alone gives real meaning and true significance to human life.

POEM:

> O Thou great Friend to all the sons of men,
>> Who once appeared in humblest guise below,
> Sin to rebuke, to break the captive's chain,
>> And call thy brethren forth from want and woe,—

> We look to thee! thy truth is still the Light
>> Which guides the nations, groping on their way,
> Stumbling and falling in disastrous night,
>> Yet hoping ever for the perfect day.

> Yes; thou art still the Life, thou art the Way
>> The holiest know; Light, Life, the Way of heaven!
> And they who dearest hope and deepest pray,
>> Toil by the Light, Life, Way, which thou hast given.[5]
>>> —THEODORE PARKER

HYMN: "O Jesus, I Have Promised" or "Jesus—Thou Joy of Loving Hearts"

CLOSING PRAYER:

We are thankful, O Christ, that we can find in thee a true understanding of the meaning of life. May we have the wisdom to realize that spiritual values are of greater importance than physical or material ones. Help us earnestly to seek thy forgiveness and guidance and to draw upon thy resources as we meet the problems and make the decisions of everyday living. In thy name we pray. AMEN.

10. Finding the Answer to Sin

PRELUDE: "Dear Lord and Father of Mankind"

CALL TO WORSHIP:

> Great Master, touch us with Thy skillful hand;
> Let not the music that is in us die
> Great Sculptor, hew and polish us; nor let,
> Hidden and lost, Thy form within us lie!
>
> Spare not the stroke! do with us what thou wilt!
> Let there be naught unfinished, broken, marred;
> Complete Thy purpose, that we may become
> Thy perfect image, Thou our God and Lord! [1]
>
> HORATIUS BONAR

PRAYER:

Touch our lives, O Christ, so that we may become more like thee in our thoughts, words, and deeds. May we look to thee for forgiveness and for strength to turn away from our selfishness and sin. In thy name we pray. AMEN.

HYMN: "Lord, for Tomorrow and Its Needs" or "Jesus, Saviour, Pilot Me"

LEADER:

Sin is the universal problem of mankind. Basically, sin is a wrong attitude toward God. It is an attitude of self-sufficiency, the feeling that one can get along without God's help. The problem of sin cannot be solved until an individual recognizes his need of God and experiences a right relationship with God.

Every person who is honest with himself knows that there are frequent occasions when his thoughts and actions do not measure up to his highest ideals and aspirations. There are times when we have serious questions about what is right and wrong, but most of us fail every day to live up to what we already know is right and good. We need new insight into the meaning of life; but, even more than this, we need forgiveness for our failure to translate our present understanding of life into daily living. We need strength and power to live according to the knowledge we already possess.

Christ is God's answer to the problem of sin. He came to seek and to save those who are lost and those who, because of their sin, cannot find their way to God. On the cross Christ gave his life as a sacrifice for our sins. By faith in him we can receive forgiveness for our sins, and, having had the barrier of sin removed, we can live in daily fellowship with God.

We will hear two stories of individuals who found in Christ the answer to the problem of sin. The first story is the historical account of Zacchaeus, a man who came in contact with Jesus Christ during the days of Christ's ministry on the earth. The second story is an experience that might happen in the life of any youth in our day. It is the story of a young man who discovered Christ through contacts with his own church and youth group. He, too, found in Christ the answer to the problem of sin.

SCRIPTURE: Luke 19:1-10

STORY:

ZACCHAEUS FINDS THE WAY

As Jesus made his final journey to Jerusalem, he was not thinking of himself or of the cross that stood at the end of the journey, but of the people who needed his help along the way. At Jericho, fifteen miles from Jerusalem, great crowds thronged about Jesus as he made his way through the narrow streets of the city. In this great city of more than a hundred thousand people lived a lonely and unhappy man by the name of Zacchaeus.

Zacchaeus was a man of wealth. He was the chief tax collector of

Jericho, and because of this, he was hated by his fellow countrymen, the Jews, who looked upon him as a traitor and a collaborator with Rome. Moreover, Zacchaeus was a part of a corrupt system which allowed tax collectors to take all the taxes they could get from the people, keeping for themselves the money above the amount that had to be sent to Rome. Zacchaeus' conscience troubled him because of the way in which he had secured his wealth.

Zacchaeus had heard interesting tales about Jesus of Nazareth. He knew that Matthew, a former tax collector, was now one of the Master's disciples. Evidently, Jesus was a friend even of tax collectors for Rome! When Zacchaeus learned that Jesus was passing through Jericho, he determined to see this man who was interested in all people—including tax collectors.

Hurrying from his spacious home, Zacchaeus was dismayed to discover that the street was already crowded with people. Being a very short man, it would be impossible for him to see Jesus in such a crowd. As he pondered what to do, Zacchaeus noticed a big sycamore tree. Forgetting his dignity as chief tax collector, he quickly climbed that tree. Zacchaeus did not know, as he watched eagerly for Jesus, that Jesus was interested in him and looking for him.

When Jesus came to the sycamore tree, he stopped and peered into the tree. He saw the bright-eyed little man. "Zacchaeus," Jesus called, "make haste and come down; for I must stay at your house today."

Zacchaeus could scarcely believe his own ears. Was it true that the famous Teacher was calling him, a despised taxgatherer, by name? After one look at the Master's smiling face, Zacchaeus scrambled down the trunk of the sycamore tree like a young school boy. He eagerly led Jesus to the largest house on the street and received him joyfully into his home.

The curious spectators were not prepared for this turn of events. They thought the Master was playing a joke on the unpopular little tax collector. They didn't think for a minute that Jesus really intended to stay at the home of a publican. When they saw Jesus disappear inside Zacchaeus' house, their tongues began to wag. "Did you ever hear of such a thing? He has gone to be the guest of a man who is a sinner!"

Zacchaeus had his servants prepare a delicious dinner for the Master.

During the meal there was time for pleasant conversation and also time for our Lord to tell Zacchaeus about the way of eternal life. Zacchaeus realized that, more than anything else in the world, he wanted the abundant life which Jesus offered. His words proved the earnestness with which he accepted Jesus' offer of salvation.

"Behold, Lord," he said, "half of my possessions I will give to the poor, and if I have defrauded anyone of anything, I will restore it fourfold."

Jesus knew that the man spoke with sincerity. "Today salvation has come to this house," he said to Zacchaeus. And then he added these unforgettable words; "For the Son of man came to seek and to save the lost."

Zacchaeus had found the answer to the problem of selfishness and sin. In Jesus Christ he had found the way to life that is abundant, satisfying and worth while.

SCRIPTURE: Matt. 7:7-8; 11:28-29

STORY:

TOM HARRISON MAKES A DISCOVERY

Life was at sixes and sevens for Tom Harrison. Because he had been late to work three mornings in a row, he was in trouble with his boss. Furthermore, he couldn't keep his mind on the columns of figures he was supposed to tabulate, and his boss had hinted that if his work didn't improve, he might as well look for another job.

Tom was also at cross purposes with his parents. His father had reminded him repeatedly to mow the lawn and for three successive Saturdays his mother had asked him to clean the basement. He had promised to perform these tasks, but had succeeded in doing neither. In addition to this, he had been untruthful to his parents on various occasions. His father and mother objected to his taking his girl friend, Sally, to Tuckermans, a questionable gathering place for a rather fast crowd of young people. Tom had told his parents a number of times that he was going to Sally's house or to a show, when in reality he and Sally had gone to Tuckermans.

It was surprising, as Tom thought about it, how quickly he and

Sally had entered into the activities at Tuckermans. The atmosphere of the place was very different from anything they had known before. It troubled Tom that he and Sally had started drinking with the crowd at Tuckermans. He knew that his parents and his friends at church were opposed to drinking and to some of the other activities that went on at Tuckermans. Tom realized that going to such a questionable place gave him a grown-up feeling of independence and daring, but he kept wondering if by so doing, he was adopting a wrong set of standards for his life. Was he also causing Sally to develop wrong habits and ideals?

With all these confusing thoughts clamoring for the attention of his mind, it was no wonder that Tom's work at the office was slipping and that he couldn't even keep his mind on such routine jobs as mowing the lawn and cleaning the basement.

Tom finally decided, as he drove home from work one afternoon, that it was wrong for him and Sally to go to Tuckermans. It was doubly wrong to tell his parents they were going to some other place. Tom also realized that it would be rather difficult to stop going to Tuckermans. They had promised the crowd they would be there that very night. If they didn't appear, they would be ridiculed by various members of the group. He could hear the fellows say, "I guess Tom and Sally have chickened out. I suppose they've gone back to the Sunday-school gang."

As Tom thought of the Sunday-school gang, his conscience gave him real trouble. He and Sally had skipped church for three Sundays. They had scarcely seen their church friends for more than a month. They had even missed the last youth fellowship party—an event they usually would not think of missing. Why, it had been at a youth fellowship party a year ago that he had met Sally. They used to talk about the good times they had with the young people at the church and how much the group meant to their lives.

Tom had very little to say during dinner that evening. As soon as dinner was over, he drove to Sally's house, helped Sally into the car, and without a word, set out in the direction of Tuckermans.

All of a sudden Tom stopped the car and exclaimed, "Sally, do you really want to go to Tuckermans tonight?"

"Oh, Tom," she replied, "I don't want to go at all! I used to think it was exciting to go there, but it isn't a bit of fun anymore. I would have told you sooner, but I thought you liked it there so much."

"You should have told me how you felt," Tom said. "I'm sorry I've taken you there so many times."

"Tom," Sally asked, "do you ever miss the gang at church? I heard they're having another party at the church tonight."

Tom swung his car around so fast that gravel flew in all directions, and in a very few minutes he and Sally were greeting their friends at the church. Tom returned to his own home later that night after a wonderful evening of Christian fun and fellowship. When he reached his own room, he prayed more earnestly than he had ever prayed before:

"Thank you, God, for showing me the way back to fellowship with you and with Christian friends. Forgive me for the mistakes I've made, for the sinful things I've done, and for the poor example I have been to others. Help me to rededicate my life to Christ and to the work of his kingdom. May I love Christ more devotedly and serve him more faithfully in the future. AMEN."

Tom went to bed that night with a peace of mind and heart that he had not known for many weeks. He had found the answer to the problem of sin by experiencing the forgiveness, peace, and power of God.

SCRIPTURE: I John 1:5-9

LEADER:

Let us have a period of silent prayer as we humbly confess our sins to God, remembering that if we confess our sins, God will forgive our sins and cleanse us of all unrighteousness.

PERIOD OF SILENT PRAYER (as the pianist plays softly "Dear Lord and Father of Mankind")

SOLO: "Dear Lord and Father of Mankind"

CLOSING PRAYER AND BENEDICTION
    If I have wounded any soul today,

If I have caused one foot to go astray,
If I have walked in my own willful way,
Dear Lord, forgive![2]
—C. M. BATTERSBY

"Now to him who is able to keep you from falling and to present you without blemish before the presence of his glory with rejoicing, to the only God, our Savior through Jesus Christ our Lord, be glory, majesty, dominion, and authority, before all time and now and for ever." AMEN.[3]

11. Discovering the Way of Salvation

PRELUDE: "My Faith Looks Up to Thee"

CALL TO WORSHIP:

Thy will, O God, is best,
By Thee the victory's won,
In Thy strong will we find our rest,
Thy will, O God, be done.

Thy will, O God, is strong,
Resist Thy power can none,
Thy throne is raised above all wrong,
Thy will, O God, be done.

Thy will, O God, is law,
Thy word through worlds hath run,
Teach us to say with holy awe,
Thy will, O God, be done.

Thy will, O God, is love,
Thou art our shield and sun,
In earth below, in heaven above,
Thy will, O God, be done.

Thy will, O God, is life,
Thy life and ours is one,
Be Thou our master in the strife,
Until Thy will is done.[1]

—HUGH THOMSON KERR

PRAYER:

"O God, grant that I may never seek to bend the straight to the crooked, that is, thy will to mine; but may I ever bend the crooked to the straight, that is, my will to thine." AMEN.[2]

HYMN: "Stand Up, Stand Up for Jesus" or "Lead On, O King Eternal"

LEADER:

Jesus said, "I am the way, and the truth, and the life; no one comes to the Father, but by me." Christ is the way to God. He is the way to the abundant, eternal life. He is the way of salvation which God has provided for mankind. How do we discover this way of salvation? What attitudes of mind and heart are necessary if we are to experience God's plan for our lives?

SCRIPTURE: Mark 1:14-15; Matt. 16:24-25; John 8:12

TALK I:

THE MEANING OF REPENTANCE

If young people are to discover the way of salvation, they must understand and experience the meaning of repentance. This word has a far deeper significance than most young people realize.

First of all, true repentance involves a feeling of our need of God's help. This is the point at which we must start if we are to experience God's salvation. We must realize that we have deep spiritual needs which we cannot meet by our own efforts. In other words, we must have a true sense of humility. Most of us think too highly of ourselves, but there are some who do not recognize their true value and worth as human personalities. Humility is looking at ourselves in true perspective. It is seeing ourselves as human beings in need of God's salvation. True humility is a recognition of our God-given potentialities and a realization that we cannot experience the fulfillment of these potentialities without God's help.

Repentance is not only a feeling of our need of God, but it is also an earnest seeking after God's help. It is a realization that God's help comes to us through Jesus Christ. Repentance means that we realize our need of a Saviour.

True repentance, therefore, is far more than regret for one's sins. There must be a change of mind—a changed attitude toward sin, toward self, and toward God. A person who is repentant realizes the seriousness of sin; he knows that he cannot solve the problem of sin by his own strength. He therefore seeks the help and forgiveness of God. Repentance is the act of giving up false pride and self-sufficiency. It is turning from a self-centered life to a Christ-centered life.

The Prodigal Son had regret for his mistakes and wrongdoing. But he went far beyond regret in his thinking and his actions. Mere regret would not have taken him beyond self-pity. It would not have challenged him to leave the field in which he was feeding pigs. The Prodigal Son felt a deep need for his father's companionship and love. He realized that his own sin had separated him from his father and that he was no longer worthy to be his father's son. He was willing to work as a hired servant for his father. He was willing to make the long, difficult journey back to his father's home. He did more than stay among the pigs, feeling sorry for himself. He *turned from* the place of sin and despair and *returned to* his father.

True repentance is *turning from* selfishness and sin. It is *turning to* Christ for forgiveness and strength.

HYMN: "I Need Thee Every Hour" or "Come to the Saviour Now"

TALK II:

THE MEANING OF FAITH

After realizing our need of salvation and turning to Christ for help, we are challenged to place our faith or trust in Christ as our Saviour. We recognize in Christ the answer to our deep sense of need and our yearning for a life of meaning and purpose.

This act of faith makes possible a new person in Christ—a person with new attitudes, new purposes, new hopes and aspirations. This is the beginning of the adventure of Christian discipleship. It is an act of faith because we do not know all the answers about God or about life at the beginning. We take the first step by faith, believing that we will find further answers as we continue our journey. We are like an engineer on a train which makes a night run from Kansas City to Chicago. The engineer does not wait until he has a light on his engine that will shine from Kansas City to Chicago. He leaves the station at Kansas City, confident that as his train moves forward during the night, the light on the engine will continue to throw its rays several hundred feet ahead of the train. The tracks will be illuminated—a few hundred feet at a time—all the way from Kansas City to Chicago.

Faith means that we confidently begin the adventure of Christian discipleship, even though our light of knowledge is very small. We are certain that additional light will illumine our pathway as we continue to seek help from Christ. We know that millions of Christians through the centuries have taken this journey of faith, and we can profit from their experiences. We know that we can receive help from the Bible and from prayer. We have seen the lives of people in our own day transformed by faith in the Christian message. We believe this message will do as much for us. So we eagerly begin the journey of the Christian life.

The act of faith that makes possible our salvation is faith in a Person—Jesus Christ. It is faith in God as he has revealed himself in Christ. True Christian faith is knowing God because we have met Jesus Christ. It is responding with gratitude to the love of God because we have seen God's love demonstrated in the life and death of Christ. Faith is trusting our lives to God's leadership because we have seen God's concern for mankind at work in Jesus Christ. Faith goes beyond repenting for our sins. It is accepting Christ's death on the cross as a sacrifice that pays the penalty for our sins. Faith is depending on Christ to remove the blight of sin from our lives and to enable us to experience the abundant, eternal life.

Christian faith is a way of life. It is daily fellowship with God through Jesus Christ. Faith is yielding our lives to the will and purposes of God. "Not my will, but thine be done" is the essence of true faith.

SOLO: First and second stanzas of "My Faith Looks Up to Thee"

Talk III:

THE MEANING OF OBEDIENCE

Salvation is a continuing experience. It begins with a repentant spirit and an act of faith in Christ. It continues as an ever-increasing and ever-unfolding adventure of fellowship with Jesus. Obedience to Christ is necessary if we are to experience this continuing challenge of Christian discipleship.

Salvation involves the acceptance of Jesus as our Saviour from sin. It also includes the acceptance of Jesus as our Master and Lord. Salvation requires repentance and faith; it also demands obedience. Christian discipleship is a compelling and exacting way of life. It is a challenge, an adventure that calls for complete dedication of life to him. "No one can serve two masters," Jesus said. "Whoever does not bear his own cross and come after me, cannot be my disciple."

Intimate companionship with Christ is dependent on a spirit of obedience to Christ's will for our lives. "You are my friends," Jesus said, "if you do what I command you." Notice the condition! If we are obedient to Christ, we will experience the joy of intimate fellowship with him.

On another occasion Jesus said, "If you love me, you will keep my commandments." In order to know the commands of Christ, we must study the teachings of Jesus as they are recorded in the Gospels. We should read and reread these teachings until our minds are saturated with them, until the words of Jesus become a vital part of our thoughts, our attitudes, and our actions.

The motto of our daily lives should be to do the will of Christ in every word and deed. Obedience requires that we let Christ direct every area of our lives. He should be the Master and Guide of our home life, our school life, of our vocation or job, and of our social activities. Christian discipleship demands that we say to Christ: "Here, Lord, is my life—every nook and corner of it. I am not qualified to direct my own life. I turn it over to you. Use me according to your purposes, and guide me in every experience of life."

Our lives should conform to the will and purposes of God. It is the height of arrogance to think that God should change his plans to conform to our petty schemes and ideas. A boat may be tossed and battered by the storm, but the captain knows that he must bring his craft to the harbor. It would be folly for the captain to wish that the shore line would change and reach out to the boat. It is the position of the boat that must be changed. The boat must make its way to the shore line and find a safe harbor there. When we think of obedience to God, we realize that our lives must be changed and brought into conformity to the will of God. It is foolishness to think of trying to bend the will of God to conform to our wishes and desires. We must redirect our lives so that they will make their way to the shore line of God's will. There they will find strength and stability and a safe harbor.

Solo: "Have Thine Own Way, Lord!"

Closing Prayer:

We are thankful, our Father, for the way of salvation which you have provided for us through Jesus Christ. Help us to feel our need of thy salvation and to seek thee in a spirit of humility, faith, and obedience. May each one of us be aware of Christ's presence in our midst during these moments of prayer and dedication. Help us to dedicate our lives more completely to Christ and to know him in a vital, personal way as our Saviour, Lord, and Friend. Amen.

12. Let Christ Come In

SUGGESTIONS TO THE LEADER:
To add to the effectiveness of the service, a large picture of "The Light of the World" by William Holman Hunt or "Christ at Heart's Door" by Warner Sallman should be displayed as a part of the worship center. Make arrangements for the room lights to be turned off and a spotlight shown on the picture at the appropriate time. The pastor and the youth sponsor should remain after the meeting to talk with those who desire to make decisions for Christ.

PRELUDE: "Living for Jesus a Life That Is True"

CALL TO WORSHIP:

> Every Youth has a quest to make,
>   For life is the King's Highway,
> And a joyous heart is the script we take
>   On the road of Everyday.
>
> Every Youth has his gifts to guard,
>   As he fares to a far-off goal;
> A body pure, and a mind unmarred,
>   And the light of a lovely soul.
>
> Every Youth has a task of his own,
>   For the Father has willed it so.
> Youth seeks the way, and He alone,
>   Can show him the path to go.
>
> Every Youth has a lovely Guide,
>   From the vale to the mountain crest;

83

For the Unseen Friend who walks beside,
Is the Way and the End of the Quest.[1]
—MARY S. EDGAR

HYMN: "Now in the Days of Youth" or "Living for Jesus a Life That Is True"

SCRIPTURE:

Jesus said to them, I am the bread of life; he who comes to me shall not hunger, and he who believes in me shall never thirst. I am the living bread which came down from heaven; if any one eats of this bread, he will live for ever; and the bread which I shall give for the life of the world is my flesh.

For God so loved the world that he gave his only Son, that whoever believes in him should not perish but have eternal life. For God sent the Son into the world, not to condemn the world, but that the world might be saved through him. He who believes in him is not condemned; he who does not believe is condemned already, because he has not believed in the name of the only Son of God.

Behold, I stand at the door and knock; if any one hears my voice and opens the door, I will come in to him and eat with him, and he with me.[2]

LEADER:

More than nineteen hundred years ago a Man was born contrary to the laws of life. He was reared in obscurity, yet his name is spoken in the far corners of the earth, and his praises sung by countless millions.

He never wrote a book, yet more books have been written about him than any other man in the world's history. He never attended college, but thousands of colleges have been erected by the inspiration of his life. His wisdom is beyond correction and his knowledge of life unsurpassed.

He was not an architect, but he has inspired the erection of the most magnificent cathedrals on the face of the earth. He was not an artist, but he has touched the hidden genius within the hearts of men and caused more paintings to be hung in famous galleries than any man who ever lived.

He never wrote a hymn, but the inspiration of his love has caused many thousands of hymns to be written. He was not a musician, yet he has inspired men to write the greatest of oratorios.

Love was his only weapon, yet he has overthrown empires and changed the course of nations.

He was sinless. No man could convict him of sin. At his trial the judge said, "I find no fault in him." At the foot of the cross upon which he died the soldier who nailed him there cried, "truly this man was the Son of God."

He arose from the grave because he was the Son of God. Death could not destroy him; the grave could not hold him. He lives today! He is the Good Shepherd seeking for lost sheep. He is the Light of the world for the darkened hearts of men. He is the Truth for those who seek to know the right. He is the Bread of life for those who hunger and thirst after righteousness. He is the Saviour of mankind. He is the one and only hope of the world!

PRAYER:

Our Father in heaven, we thank thee for the untold blessings which Christ has brought into the world. We thank thee for his matchless beauty, love, and power. Help us to respond to his majesty and grace and to welcome him eagerly into our hearts and lives. May our lives be flooded with the radiance of his spirit. AMEN.

RESPONSE: (as a solo or by the entire group)

> Into my heart, into my heart,
> Come into my heart, Lord Jesus;
> Come in today, come in to stay,
> Come into my heart, Lord Jesus.[3]
>   —HARRY D. CLARKE

STORY:

THE INN OF LIFE [4]

The Inn of Life is a favorite stopping place on life's main highway. The innkeeper's name is old Hugh Manity. He has a number of guests in his inn. Listed in the guest register are Work, Play, Love, and Worship. On another page of the register are the names of other guests: Impurity, Unbelief, Jealousy, and Selfishness.

A young man entered the inn one night and registered at the desk. He was shown to his room, and being weary, soon fell asleep. A few hours later he was awakened by the large hall clock, sounding the strokes of midnight. Then he heard another sound. Someone was knocking at the door of the inn. The knocking continued, but no one went to the door. The young man turned on the light and went out in the hall. He saw other guests. They, too, were wondering who was knocking. He hurried downstairs and discovered old Hugh Manity, the innkeeper, with a number of his guests about him. The young man recognized Work, Play, Love, and Worship. They were standing on one side of the innkeeper, and on the other side were Impurity, Unbelief, Jealousy, and Selfishness.

The person at the door continued knocking. Then he spoke in a clear, distinct voice, "Behold, I stand at the door and knock; if any one hears my voice and opens the door, I will come in to him and eat with him, and he with me."

Old Hugh Manity did not go to the door; he merely stood there and listened to the knocking. Finally Worship came up to the innkeeper and said, "Let him in. He is a wonderful person. He has brought joy to my heart ever since I first knew him. You would like him as a guest in your inn. Why don't you open the door and let him in? He would bring great joy to your life too." Hugh Manity paid little attention to Worship and did not open the door.

Then, Work approached the old innkeeper and spoke earnestly: "Open the door and let this carpenter in. He is one who knows how to work. He is interested in working people, for he is a worker himself. I have known him for many years. He befriends everyone. Why don't you let him come in?" But old Hugh Manity made no move to open the door.

Next Play turned to Hugh and said: "Won't you open the door and let him in? I can play and enjoy life and still be a friend of this man, for he once said, 'I came that they may have life, and have it abundantly.' He will make your life joyous and worth while if you let him come into the inn. Please open the door." But old Hugh was firm. His heart seemed to be set, and he did not open the door.

Love then spoke to the innkeeper: "There would be more love in your heart if you would let him into your life. He would be a great blessing to you and to the guests in your inn. By his presence he radiates a spirit of love and good will. Why don't you let him in?"

The knocking continued, but Hugh Manity did not go to the door. His other guests took advantage of his indecision. Selfishness approached the innkeeeper and said: "Don't let him come in. He will give you no rest. He will want you to visit the sick; he will want you to give money; he will want you to be doing things for other people all the time. I can't remain a guest at your inn if you let him in."

Jealousy spoke to old Hugh Manity next: "You and I made a compact a number of years ago. We promised to stick together come what may. You cannot keep your bargain if you let him in. If he comes in, I go out, never to return. I cannot stay in the same inn with him." Old Hugh was troubled. He heard the knock again. The Christ was knocking at the door!

Unbelief stepped up quickly to old Hugh Manity and said: "Leave him outside. You have an objective mind and a good personality. Everything is going well with you. Leave this intruder outside. If he comes in, you will no longer be comfortable. He is not your type. He will make you believe a lot of foolish ideas. He will tell you that you will be completely changed by just following him. He will even make a promise that when you die, you will live again. He will tell you about his miraculous birth, about his sacrificial death. He even claims that on the third day he arose from the dead! I cannot be a friend of yours if you let him come in. I will leave and never return!"

Then Impurity spoke to the old innkeeper: "You like my company, and I like your inn, but if you let this person come in, I can no longer be a guest of yours. I do not feel one bit comfortable in his presence. If he comes, I go!"

Old Hugh listened to the knock again. He was exceedingly perplexed, not knowing which of the voices to heed. And then suddenly something happened. Love rushed over to Hugh Manity and fell on her knees in front of him, pleading earnestly: "Please let him in. All of us need him. The whole world needs him. He is the answer to man's doubts and fears. He is the only answer to the world's great need!"

That did it! Old Hugh Manity walked over to the door and flung it open, and the Lord Christ entered in! And down on their knees went Love, Work, Play, and Worship. And out into the night went

Impurity, Unbelief, Jealousy, and Selfishness. There was a bright radiance within the inn that had never been there before. Old Hugh Manity's face was aglow with light, and he said joyously: "I never knew the Son of God before. Welcome! Welcome to the Inn of Life!" (At this point the room lights are turned off, and a bright spotlight is thrown on the picture of Christ knocking at the door.)

The parable is simple. To every young person's heart there come certain undesirable guests, such as Selfishness, Jealousy, Unbelief, and Impurity. Christ, the great Light of the world, knocks at your heart's door and wants to come in. If he comes into your life, these unwelcome guests must leave. Only the worthy guests can remain: Worship, Work, Play, and Love. Many times he has knocked at the door of your heart. Why not let him come in? "Behold, I stand at the door and knock," Christ says. "If any one hears my voice and opens the door, I will come in!"

LEADER:

Christ will not force his way into your life or mine. We have been given the power of choice, and we must make the decision as to what our relationship with Christ shall be. We must open the door of our heart and invite him to lead and direct our lives. When we do so, he will gladly enter in and become our Redeemer, Friend, and Guide. Let each of us welcome the Saviour of the world into our hearts and lives.

PERIOD OF SILENT PRAYER (as the pianist plays softly "O Jesus, Thou Art Standing")

SOLO: "O Jesus, Thou Art Standing"

PRAYER:

We thank thee, O Christ, that thou art willing to become our Saviour and Guide. We are often perplexed and in need of thy help and thy power. We eagerly open the door of our lives to thee. Enter, we pray, and take possession of all that we are and have. In thy name we pray. AMEN.

LEADER:

Those who desire to make their decision for Christ and to dedicate their lives to him are invited to remain at the front of the room to talk briefly with our sponsor and our pastor. Additional guidance will be given regarding the meaning of Christian discipleship. After the benediction, will those who are remaining come quietly to the front of the room, while the others refrain from talking and leave the room in a spirit of prayer and meditation.

BENEDICTION:

May our thoughts, our motives, and our decisions be acceptable unto thee, O God, and may the radiant presence of the living Christ abide with each one of us now and through all of life's tomorrows. AMEN.

13. How Christ Changes Lives

PRELUDE: "I Would Be True"

CALL TO WORSHIP:

I appeal to you therefore, brethren, by the mercies of God, to present your bodies as a living sacrifice, holy and acceptable to God, which is your spiritual worship. Do not be conformed to this world but be transformed by the renewal of your mind, that you may prove what is the will of God, what is good and acceptable and perfect. Finally, brethren, whatever is true, whatever is honorable, whatever is just, whatever is pure, whatever is lovely, whatever is gracious, if there is any excellence, if there is anything worthy of praise, think about these things.[1]

HYMN: "I Would Be True" or "Jesus Calls Us"

PRAYER POEM:

> Just as I am, Thine own to be,
> Friend of the young, who lovest me,
> To consecrate myself to Thee,
> O Jesus Christ, I come.
>
> In the glad morning of my day,
> My life to give, my vows to pay,
> With no reserve and no delay,
> With all my heart I come.
>
> I would live ever in the light,
> I would work ever for the right,

I would serve Thee with all my might,
Therefore, to Thee, I come.

Just as I am, young, strong and free,
To be the best that I can be
For truth, and righteousness, and Thee,
Lord of my life, I come.[2]
—MARIANNE HEARN

INTRODUCTION BY THE LEADER [3]

What is the meaning of conversion? Following the Second World War newspapers and magazines told about the conversion of industrial plants from wartime to peacetime production. A tremendous change took place in the industrial life of our nation. Machinery was adapted, adjusted, or changed entirely. Workers were shifted and reorganized. The products of industry were transformed—from guns and tanks to refrigerators and automobiles.

Conversion in the spiritual realm is a tremendous change in the life of an individual. It is a turn-about-face. It is a complete reorganization of one's thoughts and attitudes. An individual, before conversion, walks along the pathway of his own sinful, selfish desires. When his mind is illumined by the light of the gospel, he turns about and, with his eyes upon his Guide, walks the path of Christian discipleship.

What about the "products" of one's life? That is the real proof of conversion! The products of life are transformed—from selfishness, pride, and resentment to unselfishness, humility, and lovingkindness. Jesus said, "You will know them by their fruits."

Conversion is a personal experience in which an individual meets Jesus Christ in a vital, tranforming way. Although its essential meaning is always the same, conversion can happen in different ways and in different places. We shall listen to several important characters from God's Word and let them tell us about the experience that changed their lives.

I. *THE CONVERSION OF PETER*

Simon was my original name. The fact that you know me by the name of Peter is an indication of the tremendous change that took place in my life. I want to tell you about that change.

My brother Andrew and I lived in Bethsaida, a village near the north shore of the Sea of Galilee. We owned a thriving fishing business. Andrew and I heard a great deal about a man called John the Baptist who was preaching by the Jordan River. We traveled southward to the Jordan and, along with many others, listened to the stirring messages of this great preacher.

One day Andrew ran toward me in great haste. "Simon," he exclaimed, "we have found the Messiah." He hurried me along the path to a shady nook among the tamarisk and poplar trees. There I saw for the first time the Man who changed my life. John the Baptist had introduced him to Andrew as "the Lamb of God, who takes away the sin of the world." I soon discovered that his name was Jesus.

Jesus looked at me with eyes that seemed to see my inmost thoughts. "So you are Simon the son of John," he said. "You shall be called Peter."

Peter! Why, that means "a rock"! I had always been an impulsive fellow. I was amazed that this Stranger would think of calling me a rock! I couldn't get his strange statement out of my mind. Every time a group of people gathered about Jesus I slipped into the crowd and listened to what he had to say.

Andrew and I decided that we should not leave our fishing business any longer. We followed the twists and turns of the Jordan River until we came once more to the Sea of Galilee and our own village of Bethsaida. As we lowered our large nets into the sea and pulled the load of fish onto the boat, thoughts of Jesus kept coming into my mind—the radiance of his face, the deep light that shone from his eyes, and especially the words he had said to me with such certainty, "You shall be called Peter."

And then one day we saw him again! I knew it was he the moment I saw him walking along the rocky shore of the Sea of Galilee. Andrew and I were near the shore, lowering a net into the water. When he came near to us, the Master spoke to us words of great challenge and significance. "Follow me," he said, "and I will make you become fishers of men."

In that moment I realized that my life was different. A strange new joy took possession of me. The Master wanted me, a humble fisherman, to be his follower. He was interested in me. He felt that I could be of service in his kingdom. Life now had meaning and purpose. Andrew and I left our nets immediately, in order that we might be with Jesus.

I remember, as if it were yesterday, another experience with the Master. Andrew and I had fished all night and caught nothing, but Jesus told us that we should try once more. He enabled us to take into our nets an enormous load of fish. Realizing as never before my own insignificance, I fell to my feet before Jesus and cried, "Depart from me, for I am a sinful man, O Lord." Jesus understood my feeling of great need, and, as a result of this experience, a new peace filled my life.

Even after these life-changing experiences I miserably failed my Lord. My worst failure, of course, is known to all of you. I denied my Lord three times on the night before his crucifixion. I could not understand why it was necessary for him to die. I was disappointed, disillusioned, and terribly afraid. The day of his death was the blackest day of my life.

The Resurrection, of course, changed everything! I had another chance to pledge my loyalty to my Lord and to receive his forgiveness. I realized that Jesus was with me every moment of every day—even when his physical body had been taken from our sight. I preached on the day of Pentecost, but it was really Christ speaking through me. Three thousand persons were brought into the kingdom of God on that day. In the name of Jesus I was able to heal the lame man by the gate of the temple. In the strength of Jesus I was able to preach daily and to endure persecution with joy and thanksgiving. It was the power of the risen Christ that changed my life from Simon the sinner to Peter the rock.

II. *THE CONVERSION OF PAUL*

My name, like Peter's, is a reminder of the transformation which took place in my life. My original name was Saul—Saul the persecutor. Think of it! With fierce violence I persecuted my Lord and his followers. Then, through the power of Jesus Christ, I became Paul the preacher. I would like to tell you about the day that changed my life.

Having been trained as a strict Pharisee, I felt that belief in Jesus must be stamped out. In order to help bring this to pass, I secured permits from the high priest in Jerusalem to go to Damascus, seek out those who were followers of Jesus Christ, and bring them back to Jerusalem for trial. I was sure they would suffer the same fate as Stephen.

Now Damascus is a seven-day journey to the north of Jerusalem. As my companions and I rode on horseback toward Damascus, I had to keep forcing from my mind the thought of Stephen and the magnificent way in which he had died. The slow progress of our journey toward Damascus irritated me. I craved activity; I wanted to get on with the job of stamping out these troublesome followers of the Way.

When we had almost reached Damascus, the greatest day of my life arrived. Suddenly, without warning, a brilliant light from heaven shone about me. I fell to the ground and heard a voice saying to me, "Saul, Saul, why do you persecute me?"

I realized that someone of great authority was speaking to me. "Who are you, Lord?" I asked, not knowing who it was that had spoken.

It was then that the shattering revelation came to me. The one who had spoken said simply, "I am Jesus, whom you are persecuting."

The Lord of heaven and earth was Jesus—the very Jesus whom I was persecuting with such violence and hatred! The convictions of a lifetime, the efforts and attitudes of my entire life, tumbled to the ground beside me in a mass of ruins. It is no wonder that I could not see! Indeed, at that moment I could not think or feel!

But the Lord Jesus did not leave me without help. "Rise and enter the city," he said, "and you will be told what you are to do."

I arose immediately, and my friends led me into Damascus. What a contrast to the entrance I had planned into the city! I had intended to enter the city with a display of cruelty and power and put into subjection all the followers of the Way. Instead, I was led into the city, humble and without sight, and in complete subjection to the Author of the Way, Jesus Christ.

My companions took me to the home of Judas on a street named Straight. My mind was in a turmoil; it was necessary for me to reorganize my thinking about God, about Jesus, about life itself. Once again my Lord provided guidance and help. He spoke to a humble disciple by the name of Ananias. Man of faith that he was,

Ananias was willing to minister to me, the most feared persecutor of the church!

"Brother Saul," Ananias said, "the Lord Jesus who appeared to you on the road by which you came, has sent me that you may regain your sight and be filled with the Holy Spirit."

Immediately something like scales seemed to fall from my eyes and once again I could see. My mind was beginning to understand the meaning of my experience along the Damascus Road. I knew now, because of the example of Ananias, that a vision of Christ could be translated into human experience. Ananias had given me my first practical lesson in Christian discipleship, and I was now ready to go forth as a follower of the Way. I was baptized immediately and began proclaiming in the synagogues that Jesus is the Son of God. Because of my experience with Jesus Christ on that memorable day along the Damascus Road, I became Paul the preacher.

III. *THE CONVERSION OF THE SAMARITAN WOMAN*

I, too, had an experience with Jesus Christ that changed my life. My experience of conversion was not quite as sudden or as dramatic as Paul's, but it was genuine and real.

My home was in the little village of Sychar in the central part of Samaria. My people, the Samaritans, and the Jews were enemies and had no dealings with each other. Just outside my village was a well called Jacob's Well, because it was located near the field which Jacob gave many centuries ago to his son Joseph.

One day, about noon, I walked toward Jacob's Well, carrying my heavy water jar. I was in desperate need of a Saviour that day as I trudged along the dusty path, for I had lived a very sinful life. I was surprised to find a Stranger resting on a bench beside the cool stone wall around the well. The Man was a Jew, but, strangely enough, he smiled at me and asked me if I would give him a drink.

I could not hide my astonishment. "How is it," I asked, "that you, a Jew, ask a drink of me, a woman of Samaria?"

"If you knew who it is," the stranger said, "that is asking you for a drink, you would ask him, and he would give you living water." My mind and heart were strangely stirred by these words. I knew the words held great significance for me, but I did not perceive their true meaning.

The Master led me one step nearer the realm of spiritual truth by giving this never-to-be-forgotten challenge: "Every one who drinks of this water [physical water] will thirst again, but whoever drinks of the water that I shall give him will never thirst; the water that I shall give him will become in him a spring of water welling up to eternal life."

Jesus was aware of my great need for forgiveness. He knew about the great burden of sin which I carried in my heart and mind. He referred to my sin; quietly, yet forcefully, he stated the terrible fact of it.

"Sir, I perceive that you are a prophet," I exclaimed with a growing realization of who he really was. Under his loving guidance I was another step nearer the kingdom of God.

This wonderful Stranger had aroused within me long-forgotten hopes of the promised Messiah. "I know that Messiah is coming," I said with a feeling of great wistfulness.

The Master answered my longing with one brief statement: "I who speak to you am he."

That was the final step—the great revelation—that brought me into a vital relationship with my Saviour and Lord. That was the moment which transformed my life.

SHARING SESSION (optional):

1. In what ways were the conversion experiences of Peter, Paul, and the Samaritan woman similar? In what ways were they different?

2. Think of the experience of Peter. In what ways was the conversion of Peter a gradual process? Do you think that this type of conversion can be as real and vital as the sudden type? What evidences do we find in the life of Peter that his conversion was genuine?

3. Paul's conversion is an example of the sudden, dramatic type of experience. Do you think that Paul's experience on the Damascus Road was as sudden as it seemed to be? Did Paul have any preparation for this experience? Do you think that the death of Stephen played a part in Paul's conversion? (See Acts 7:54–8:1.) In what way? What evidences do we find in the life of Paul that his conversion was genuine?

4. Do people in our day ever have sudden, dramatic conversion experiences? Is the gradual type of conversion more common? Why?

5. The conversion of the Samaritan woman was the result of an interview with another person. In her case the interview was with Jesus Christ himself. Jesus began the interview by referring to the activity in which the woman was engaged—drawing water from the well. He then led her step by step to the point where she realized who he was and humbly received his forgiveness and peace. What are some of the important steps which led to the conversion of this woman? Do we find evidences in the life of the Samaritan woman that her conversion was genuine? (See John 4:28-30, 39-42.)

6. Is it necessary for us to know the exact moment when conversion takes place in our lives? Is it possible for us to know with assurance that such an experience has taken place? What is the test of a genuine conversion? What did Jesus mean when he said, "By their fruits you shall know them"?

7. Does an initial experience of conversion mean that growth in the Christian life will follow automatically? Why is it important that we should think of the Christian life as a process of growth and development?

LEADER:

Young people today can have a genuine experience of conversion. Their lives can be transformed by the power of the living Christ. This experience comes to youth in different ways and at different places. The important thing is that the experience be genuine and that young people know Jesus Christ as their Saviour, Friend, and Guide.

Let us make sure that we know the meaning of Christian discipleship and that we have had a transforming experience of fellowship with Jesus Christ. We can be sure by dedicating our lives anew to him right now and by humbly receiving into our minds and souls his forgiveness, peace, and power.

POEM:

> Have Thine own way, Lord!
> Have Thine own way!
> Thou art the Potter;

I am the clay.
Mould me and make me
After Thy will,
While I am waiting,
Yielded and still.[4]
                    —ADELAIDE A. POLLARD

PERIOD OF SILENT PRAYER AND DEDICATION (as the pianist plays softly "Have Thine Own Way, Lord")

CLOSING PRAYER:
Come into our lives, O Christ, with thy radiant, transforming power. Forgive our sinful ways and help us to demonstrate in our daily lives the fruits of the Christian life. May we radiate love, joy, patience, and kindness in all of our activities and experiences. AMEN.

14. The Mission of the Church

A medium-sized table and the following white candles will be needed for this service: 1 eighteen-inch candle, 6 twelve-inch candles, and sufficient small candles for the audience. The eighteen-inch candle, with 3 twelve-inch candles on each side, should be arranged in candle-holders on the table. The tall center candle should be lighted before the service begins. The other candles may be lighted from the center candle at the appropriate times during the service.

The first candlelighter will stand behind the table to the right of the center candle and will be responsible for lighting the 3 twelve-inch candles to the right of the center candle. The second candlelighter will stand behind the table to the left of the center candle and will light the 3 twelve-inch candles to the left of the center candle. The leader may stand immediately behind the tall center candle.

Prelude: "The Church's One Foundation"

Call to Worship:
>
> Our church proclaims God's love and care
> To all who work and worship there,
> Who sing together hymns of praise,
> And prayers of glad thanksgiving raise.
>
> Her hands reach out in service through
> Kind, helpful deeds that Christians do,
> To show God's children of every land
> The world of love that he has planned.

Gladly we come our praise to sing,
And gifts of friendly service bring;
We, too, would know God's love and care,
And work and joy with others share.[1]
—MABEL NEIDERMEYER

PRAYER:

We thank thee, O God, for thy church where we can sing together our hymns of praise and join in prayers of glad thanksgiving. We are thankful for the joys and blessings which come to us as we worship and serve thee in thy church. We pray for the local church where we worship and for all churches that faithfully proclaim thy message of salvation. Guide us as we think together about the mission of the church in the world today. We pray in the name of Christ, the Foundation and Cornerstone of every true church. AMEN.

LEADER:

For no other foundation can anyone lay than that which is laid, which is Jesus Christ.[2]

RESPONSE (to be sung by the entire group): First stanza of "The Church's One Foundation"

LEADER:

There is one body and one Spirit, just as you were called to the one hope that belongs to your call, one Lord, one faith, one baptism, one God and Father of us all, who is above all and through all and in all.[3]

RESPONSE: Second stanza of "The Church's One Foundation"

LEADER:

Come to me, all who labor and are heavy-laden, and I will give you rest. Take my yoke upon you, and learn from me; for I am gentle and lowly in heart, and you will find rest for your souls.[4]

RESPONSE: Third stanza of "The Church's One Foundation"

LEADER:

Christ loved the church and gave himself up for her, that he might sanctify her, having cleansed her by the washing of water with the

100

word, that the church might be presented before him in splendor, without spot or wrinkle or any such thing, that she might be holy and without blemish.[5]

RESPONSE: Fourth stanza of "The Church's One Foundation"

LEADER:

Jesus Christ is the Head of the church. We look to him as our Leader and Guide as we strive to fulfill the high and holy mission of the church. Christ established the church as the instrument for carrying on his work in the world. The apostle Paul declares that Christ is the head of the body, which is the church. As Christians, we are the body of Christ. We are his hands, his feet, his voice. We have been given the tremendous challenge of proclaiming the message of Christ and extending his kingdom upon the earth. Paul also reminds us that Christ loved the church and gave his life for it.

This tall, glowing candle represents Jesus Christ, the Leader and Lord of the church. We must look to him for guidance as we consider the church's mission.

FIRST CANDLELIGHTER:

The central mission of the church was stated with crystal clarity by our Lord: "Go therefore," he said, "and make disciples of all nations." We call these words the Great Commission. They are the marching orders of the church, uttered shortly before Christ completed his earthly ministry. Our Lord is depending on his followers, the members of his church, to proclaim his message of salvation to all minkind. (Lights first twelve-inch candle to the right of the center candle.)

This radiant candle represents the most important mission of the church, that of introducing men, women, and youth to Jesus Christ and helping them know him as the Saviour and Lord of their lives. "Ye shall be my witnesses," Jesus said, "in Jerusalem and in all Judea and Samaria and to the end of the earth." That is our mission—our supreme task. We are to share our faith in Christ with those about us and with men and women around the world.

HYMN: "O Zion, Haste" or "Jesus Shall Reign Where'er the Sun"

SECOND CANDLELIGHTER:

The latter part of the Great Commission emphasizes another important mission of the church. Jesus said that after winning men to his kingdom, we are to teach them to observe all the things which he has commanded. That's a mighty big order! We must know and observe the commands of Christ ourselves, before effectively teaching them to others. We must study and ponder the teachings of Jesus until they become a basic part of our thinking and living. Then we must find ways of helping others to know and practice the commands of Christ. This is the teaching ministry of the church. It is a never-ending ministry which begins with small children and continues through all age groups and all stages of maturity. As we continue to win new converts to Christ, we must give them friendly encouragement and help them grow and develop in the Chrisitan life. (Lights first twelve-inch candle to the left of the center candle.)

This lighted candle represents the second great mission of the church, that of helping Christians develop in Christian understanding and maturity. None of us ever arrives at the end of Christian growth and development. The Christian life is a never-ending experience of adventure and discovery. There are always new horizons and new heights of understanding that beckon us onward and upward. The apostle Paul spoke of the length and breadth and height and depth of the gospel. The church must have a great teaching ministry in order to help men, women, and youth receive new insight and new understanding of the meaning of Christian discipleship.

SOLO: "Lord, Speak to Me, That I May Speak"

FIRST CANDLELIGHTER:

Another important mission of the church is to encourage Christians to meet together regularly for the worship of God. A vital part of the church's ministry is to provide worship services that are inspiring and meaningful. Group worship brings warmth and vitality to the spiritual life of all who participate. There are values and blessings in group worship that are not received by those who feel they can worship God outside the fellowship and associations of the church. When Christians come together for times of prayer and meditation and for the singing of hymns of praise, their faith in God is strengthened and their lives are fortified and enriched. (Lights second twelve-inch candle to the right of the center candle.)

This glowing candle represents the light of worship. Each one of us should realize the importance of attending each week the worship services of our church. We should also encourage our friends and associates to discover the rich blessings that come from joining with others in the regular worship of God.

HYMN: "O Worship the King" or "Joyful, Joyful We Adore Thee"

SECOND CANDLELIGHTER:

Jesus frequently stressed another vital mission of the church. The members of a church should demonstrate the love of God by the spirit of love which they manifest in their own lives. "Love one another," Jesus said, "as I have loved you. By this all men will know that you are my disciples, if you have love for one another." The church should provide many opportunities for vital Christian fellowship. The members of a church should demonstrate a spirit of oneness and togetherness, as they come together frequently to work, worship, and witness in the Master's name. (Lights second twelve-inch candle to the left of the center candle.)

This candle represents the warmth and light of Christian fellowship. We read in the book of Acts that the early Christians "continued steadfastly in fellowship." Christians are joined to one another in a close-knit fellowship because of their common love and loyalty to Jesus Christ. It is one of the church's important missions to encourage this spirit of fellowship and love among all Christians.

HYMN: "Blest Be the Tie That Binds"

FIRST CANDLELIGHTER:

Another important mission of the church is to provide opportunities for service for all its members. One of the church's vital functions is to unite the talents, energy, and resources of many Christians, thus enabling them to serve mankind effectively in the name and spirit of Christ. Christians, working unitedly under the leadership of Jesus Christ, can overcome many of the evils which are rampant in the world. They can minister to all the needs of mankind by presenting to men a Saviour who is interested in every area of life. (Lights third twelve-inch candle to the right of the center candle.)

This candle symbolizes the light of Christian service. Jesus said, "Whoever would be great among you must be your servant." He also said, "As you did it to one of the least of these my brethren, you did it to me." The church should provide avenues of service to men of all races, classes, and nations.

SOLO: "O Master, Let Me Walk with Thee"

SECOND CANDLELIGHTER:

The church is a unique institution. Its ministry is world wide in scope; its message is eternal in significance. The church, with Jesus Christ as its Leader, binds together men of all races and nations. When the church is true to its divine mission, it leaps across all barriers of race and class. (Lights third twelve-inch candle to the left of the center candle.)

This candle represents the radiant light of Christian brotherhood. Christ's message of love and good will is the only hope of lasting peace in the world. It is the church's mission to proclaim this message to the end of the earth, thus bringing together in one great fellowship of love men of all tribes and nations.

SOLO: "In Christ There Is No East or West"

LEADER:

As we light our individual candles from the tall white candle representing Christ, let us rededicate our lives to Jesus Christ. May we determine to serve Christ more loyally through the church, thus helping the church fulfill its great mission upon the earth. (The young people light their individual candles from the center candle and form a circle of light around the room. As the young people light their candles, the pianist may play softly "O Master, Let Me Walk with Thee.")

CLOSING PRAYER: (The pianist may continue playing the hymn very softly.)

Our Father, we thank thee for the church and for the encouragement and inspiration it gives to our lives. We thank thee for the church's important mission which challenges us to take thy message of hope and salvation to those about us and to all nations of the world. Help us, as we hold these lighted candles, to rededicate our lives to Christ and to the work of his church. May our lives be glowing lights for thee as we strive, with thy help, to carry out the church's great mission. In the name of Christ, our Saviour and Lord. AMEN.

(The leader may suggest that the young people leave quietly as the pianist continues to play the consecration hymn. The candles should be put out as the young people leave the door of the room.)

15. The Hope of Immortality

PRELUDE: "Crown Him with Many Crowns"

CALL TO WORSHIP:

> I know not how that Bethlehem's Babe
> Could in the God-head be;
> I only know the Manger Child
> Has brought God's life to me.
>
> I know not how that Calvary's cross
> A world from sin could free:
> I only know its matchless love
> Has brought God's love to me.
>
> I know not how that Joseph's tomb
> Could solve death's mystery:
> I only know a living Christ,
> Our immortality.[1]
> —HARRY WEBB FARRINGTON

PRAYER:

We are thankful, O Christ, for the hope of eternal life which you have brought to mankind. Help us to walk in closer fellowship with you and thus experience a deeper faith and a more steadfast hope in the life everlasting. AMEN.

HYMN: "Crown Him with Many Crowns" or "He Lives"

LEADER:

Through the ages men and women of all races have believed in some type of future life. The writings, paintings, and burial customs

106

of people throughout history have indicated a universal belief in immortality. Such a belief seems deeply implanted in the human mind and is a strong indication of the reality of a future life. Immortality is one of the basic truths of life—otherwise, man's conception of eternity would be higher than God's. Reason and experience affirm that the Creator of this vast universe has a plan for his children that is far more comprehensive and enduring than man's finite mind can hope or imagine.

We live in a reasonable universe guided by physical laws that are dependable and trustworthy. These laws make wise use of the physical resources of the universe. The elements which make up the physical universe change their form, but they are not destroyed. The spiritual laws of the universe are also rational and dependable; they take into account the spiritual resources and capabilities of man—the highest of God's creations. Man has unlimited capacities, many of which cannot be developed and utilized in this life. Immortality is logical and reasonable. The spiritual qualities of man will not be wasted or discarded by death. Man's spiritual nature is eternal and will not be destroyed by the transition which we call death. Human personality is God's most priceless creation. It, above all else, will survive.

> If in the cycle of the earth
> No atom of that earth can die—
> The soul, which is of nobler birth,
> Must live,—and live eternally.[2]
> —JOHN BOWRING

Although the rational arguments in favor of immortality are convincing, an intimate knowledge of God gives us the one completely satisfying hope of eternal life. The Christian's true hope of immortality is based on a personal experience of fellowship with God as he has revealed himself in Jesus Christ.

READER I:

Beloved, let us love one another; for love is of God, and he who loves is born of God and knows God. He who does not love does not know God; for God is love. In this the love of God was made manifest among us, that God sent his only Son into the world, so that we might live through him.[3]

READER II:

God is love. He loved the world so much that he sent his Son to show us what his love is like. Jesus taught us that God is a loving, heavenly Father who is interested in each one of his children. We see the love of God demonstrated in the life and death of our Lord. God's compelling love is one of the foundation stones of our hope in eternal life. Since God is all wise and all loving, we can depend on him to have a plan for the future that will be best for us, his children.

READER I:

Who shall separate us from the love of Christ? Shall tribulation, or distress, or persecution, or famine, or nakedness, or peril, or sword? No, in all these things we are more than conquerors through him who loved us. For I am sure that neither death, nor life, nor angels, nor principalities, nor things present, nor things to come, nor powers, nor height, nor depth, nor anything else in all creation, will be able to separate us from the love of God in Christ Jesus our Lord.[4]

READER II:

Not only do we see the love of God demonstrated in Jesus, but we can also experience God's love in our own lives. Through Christ we can know God and have fellowship with him. Christian belief in immortality is based on our experience of fellowship with God in this present life. God's power sustains us in this life and will sustain us in the life to come. When our experience of fellowship with God is vital and real, we are confident that nothing can disrupt that fellowship— not even the experience of death. The character of God—as revealed in Jesus Christ—is the guarantee of eternal life. We have learned to know God and depend on him in this life. We therefore know that we can depend on him through all time and eternity.

READER I:

Jesus said to her, "I am the resurrection and the life; he who believes in me, though he die, yet shall he live, and whoever lives and believes in me shall never die. Let not your hearts be troubled; believe in God, believe also in me. In my Father's house are many rooms; if it were not so, would I have told you that I go to prepare a place for you? And when I go and prepare a place for you, I will come again and will take you to myself, that where I am you may be also. Yet a little while, and the world will see me no more, but you will see me; because I live, you will live also." [5]

READER II:

Throughout his ministry upon the earth Jesus stressed the reality of eternal life. "I go and prepare a place for you," he said, "that where I am you may be also." Jesus promised his disciples that he would always be with them—even when they could no longer see his physical body. His words had the ring of authority, and as he spoke, eternal life became real and understandable. His life, as well as his words, demonstrated the reality of immortality. Jesus manifested such power and vitality in his daily living that men and women were aware of the eternal quality of his life.

READER I:

Now after the sabbath, toward the dawn of the first day of the week, Mary Magdalene and the other Mary went to see the sepulchre. And behold, there was a great earthquake; for an angel of the Lord descended from heaven and came and rolled back the stone, and sat upon it. His appearance was like lightning, and his raiment white as snow. And for fear of him the guards trembled and became like dead men. But the angel said to the women, "Do not be afraid; for I know that you seek Jesus who was crucified. He is not here; for he has risen, as he said. Come, see the place where he lay. Then go quickly and tell his disciples that he has risen from the dead, and behold, he is going before you to Galilee; there you will see him. Lo, I have told you." [6]

READER II:

Although Jesus' life and teachings inspire faith in immortality, it is his resurrection which is the cornerstone of our belief in eternal life. The empty tomb is the most significant symbol of our Christian faith. It gives meaning to the Cross and to all other aspects of our Saviour's life upon the earth. We trust and serve a living Lord who overcame the forces of sin and death. "Because I live," Jesus said, "you shall live also." This is the basis of our confidence and faith in eternal life. It is the foundation of our steadfast hope in immortality.

READER I:

This Jesus God raised up, and of that we all are witnesses. Let all the house of Israel therefore know assuredly that God has made him both Lord and Christ, this Jesus whom you crucified. And with great power the apostles gave their testimony to the resurrection of the Lord Jesus, and great grace was upon them all.[7]

READER II:

The early disciples were filled with despair and bewilderment when Jesus was put to death on the cross. Their Leader was gone. Their hopes were shattered. Fearful and dejected, they deserted their Lord in his hour of greatest need.

Christ's resurrection changed everything. The lives of the disciples were transformed by their belief in the risen Christ. Their fear turned to faith. Their cowardice was changed to courage. Their sorrow became a song of joy. Fearful, timid men became bold proclaimers of the message of salvation. The book of Acts declares: "With great power the apostles gave their testimony of the resurrection of the Lord Jesus."

The living Christ transformed the lives of his first disciples. He has continued to empower and transform men, women, and youth through the centuries. He is able to give us new hope, new power, and new insight today. Since Christ provides strength and courage for this life, we know we can depend on him to care for us throughout eternity. Eternal life is real to us because Christ is real, and we have discovered his forgiveness, his presence, and his peace.

STORY:

DISCOVERING THE PRESENCE OF JESUS

Jack Allen, one of the most popular pupils at Mapletown High School, appeared unexpectedly at Mr. Henderson's church-school class on Easter Sunday morning. The members of the class greeted Jack cordially, trying not to reveal their surprise at his unannounced arrival. They had a vague feeling that he would be bored with their discussion of the Easter lesson. To their amazement Jack was the first to ask a question after Mr. Henderson's brief introductory remarks.

"I'm interested in science," Jack said. "Is it possible for a scientific person to believe in life after death?"

"That's a good question," Mr. Henderson said. "Who has an answer?"

"Many scientists do believe in life after death," Bill Hunt suggested. "Mr. Wood, our science teacher at high school, says there are many truths which cannot be proved by scientific methods."

"I've heard him say that," Jack agreed, "but if life after death can't be proved by science, how can it be proved?"

"That's too much for me," Bill exclaimed. "I guess Mr. Henderson will have to answer that one."

"Let's think for a moment about the ocean tides and the stars in their orbits," Mr. Henderson suggested. "How can we explain the wonders of the universe?"

"There must be a Creator responsible for these natural laws," Jack said, to the surprise of the other young people. "I think most scientists believe in God as the Creator of the universe."

"That's very well stated," Mr. Henderson agreed. "Now that we're thinking of God as the Creator, what is God's greatest and highest creation?"

"A human being is God's greatest creation," Ralph Benton said. "Man is more than a physical being. He has spiritual qualities as well."

"You're right, Ralph," Mr. Henderson said. "God has formed oceans and mountains and solar systems which have lasted thousands of years. Will he allow his highest creation to be blotted out after a few brief years?"

"That makes the future life seem mighty reasonable," Ralph said with real earnestness.

"But does it actually prove there is such a life?" Jack asked with a trace of wistfulness in his voice. "No one has ever visited that other life and returned to tell us about it."

"I'm wondering," Mr. Henderson said slowly. "Hasn't anyone ever visited that other realm and returned to tell men about it?"

Martha Allison, contrary to her usual manner, had been sitting quietly through all the discussion. Suddenly she jumped to her feet. "Why, of course, we have proof," she exclaimed. "Of course, someone visited that other life and returned. It's the Easter message! Jesus died and rose again! I never realized its importance before!"

All the pupils were impressed by Martha's important discovery! There were a few moments of complete silence.

"I've believed in God for a long time," Jack Allen said at last. "But I've never known much about Jesus. What did he do after he rose from the dead?"

"There are many accounts in the Bible of Jesus' meeting with various people after his resurrection," Mr. Henderson explained. "He convinced them that he was the same Jesus who had been put to death on the cross. On one occasion he met with more than five hundred people and proved his identity to them."

"That was sufficient proof for the people of that day," Jack said with the same wistfulness in his voice, "but how can we know that Jesus is still alive today?"

"That's another excellent question!" Mr. Henderson declared. "Who has an answer to Jack's question?"

"Many people through the centuries have continued to believe in Jesus," Joyce Johnson suggested.

"Many people in our own day believe in him and receive help and guidance from him," Bill added.

"We have felt the presence of Jesus right here in our class," Ralph said earnestly. "He guides us as we think together about these important matters."

"Even I have felt his nearness," Martha added in a spirit of real earnestness. "Especially today I have realized as never before that Jesus is here with us in this very room."

"I guess you're right," Jack Allen said slowly. "I, too, had the feeling just now that Jesus was very near." [8]

SOLO: "I Know That My Redeemer Lives" (tune: "Bradford," C. M.)
> I know that my Redeemer lives;
> He lives, who once was dead;
> To me in grief He comfort gives;
> With peace He crowns my head.

He lives triumphant o'er the grave,
At God's right hand on high,
My ransomed soul to keep and save,
To bless and glorify.

He lives, that I may also live,
And now His grace proclaim;
He lives, that I may honor give
To His most holy Name.

Let strains of heavenly music rise,
While all their anthem sing
To Christ, my precious Sacrifice,
And everliving King.
—CHARLES WESLEY

CLOSING PRAYER:

We are filled with gratitude, O God, as we think of thy love and of the eternal life which thou hast provided for us, thy children. Help us to experience this abundant, eternal life now, as we walk in daily fellowship with thee. May we have a more complete and steadfast assurance that this life of fellowship with thee continues through the ages of eternity. In the name of Christ, who abolished death and brought life and immortality to light through the gospel. AMEN.

16. The Final Triumph of Christ's Kingdom

PRELUDE: "All Hail the Power of Jesus' Name"

CALL TO WORSHIP:

Therefore God has highly exalted him and bestowed on him the name which is above every name, that at the name of Jesus every knee should bow, in heaven and on earth and under the earth, and every tongue confess that Jesus Christ is Lord, to the glory of God the Father.[1]

HYMN: "All Hail the Power of Jesus' Name" or "Ye Servants of God, Your Master Proclaim"

PRAYER:

We praise thee, O Christ, for thy majesty and power. Help us to rely on thy strength and guidance to overcome selfish motives and sinful thoughts and habits. We pray that we may be worthy of witnessing for thee and of helping to advance the work of thy kingdom. Increase our allegiance to thee and our faith in the power of righteousness and truth. May we have a confident assurance of the final triumph of thy kingdom over all the forces of evil. In thy name we pray. AMEN.

POEM:

How shall come the kingdom holy,
In which all the earth is blest,
That shall lift on high the lowly,
And to weary souls give rest?
Not with trumpet call of legions

114

> Bursting through the upper sky,
> Waking earth thro' all its regions
> With their heav'n-descending cry.
>
> Not with dash or sudden sally,
> Swooping down with rushing wing;
> But, as, creeping up a valley,
> Come the grasses in the spring;
> First one blade and then another,
> Still advancing are they seen,
> Rank on rank, each by its brother,
> Till each inch of ground is green.
>
> Through the weary days of sowing,
> Burning sun and drenching show'r,
> Day by day, so slowly growing,
> Comes the waited harvest hour.
> So the kingdom cometh ever,
> Though it seems so far away;
> Each high thought and true endeavor
> Hastens on the blessed day.[2]
> —MINOT JUDSON SAVAGE

SCRIPTURE:

Now after John was arrested, Jesus came into Galilee, preaching the gospel of God, and saying, "The time is fulfilled, and the kingdom of God is at hand; repent, and believe in the gospel."

Being asked by the Pharisees when the kingdom of God was coming, he answered them, "The kingdom of God is not coming with signs to be observed; nor will they say, 'Lo, here it is!' or 'There!' for behold, the kingdom of God is in the midst of you." [3]

TALK I:

THE MEANING OF THE KINGDOM

The kingdom of God, the kingdom of heaven, and the kingdom of Christ have the same meaning. The use of these phrases in the Scriptures indicates clearly that the words are used interchangeably and that the meaning of all three expressions is the same. It should also be kept in mind that the *true church* (composed of all earnest Christians of all ages) is identical with the kingdom of God.

The kingdom of God is the family of God. It is the company of all earnest Christians who have accepted the leadership and kingship of Jesus Christ. The kingdom of God is composed of all people who have, in humility and faith, accepted God's gracious rule over their individual lives.

The kingdom of God is a *present reality*. Jesus established the Kingdom when he began his public ministry upon the earth. At the beginning of his ministry he declared, "The time is fulfilled, and the kingdom of God is at hand; repent, and believe in the gospel."

The Pharisees asked Jesus when the kingdom of God would be established. Jesus made it very plain that the Kingdom was a present reality. "The kingdom of God," he told them plainly, "is in the midst of you." The Kingdom is "in the midst of you" whenever there are earnest Christians proclaiming the message of salvation. Not all accept, but the Kingdom is there, and whoever repents of his sins and believes the gospel may enter.

The kingdom of God is a *future hope*. In spite of the tremendous growth of the Kingdom, there are multitudes in every generation who do not accept the lordship of Jesus Christ. Vast sections of the world still have little or no knowledge of the gospel. Many who claim to be followers of the Master do not work for the advancement of Christ's kingdom. Although the complete triumph of the Kingdom has not yet taken place, as followers of the living Christ, we have the confident assurance that eventually his kingdom will cover the earth as waters cover the sea.

The kingdom of God is an *inner faith*. Although Christ's kingdom is present and at work in the world today, it is neither an earthly nor a political kingdom. It is spiritual, and the conditions for entering the Kingdom are spiritual. We cannot buy our way into the Kingdom, nor pay anyone to pray us or our loved ones into it. When Jesus announced that the kingdom of God was at hand, he gave the condition for entering that kingdom: "Repent, and believe in the gospel."

There are two translations of Luke 17:21: "The kingdom of God is *in the midst of you"* (R.S.V.), and "The kingdom of God is *within you"* (K.J.V.). Both ideas are accurate and true. When a person responds to Jesus Christ with an earnest, inner faith, then one can say with assurance to him: "The kingdom of God is within you."

The kingdom of God is a *way of life*. When we make Jesus Christ the Saviour and King of our lives, we have the kingdom of God within us, and we have the presence and power of Christ in our lives. Because we have Christ within us, every aspect of life is changed—our thoughts, motives, goals, actions—everything! The kingdom of God cannot be locked within the heart. It shines forth. It becomes a way of life which influences those around us. If we have *inner faith* in Jesus Christ, we will give *outward expression* of that faith in our daily lives.

HYMN: "My Life, My Love, I Give to Thee" or "Have Thine Own Way, Lord!"

SCRIPTURE:

Consider the lilies of the field, how they grow; they neither toil nor spin; yet I tell you, even Solomon in all his glory was not arrayed like one of these. But if God so clothes the grass of the field, which today is alive and tomorrow is thrown into the oven, will he not much more clothe you, O men of little faith? Therefore do not be anxious, saying, 'What shall we eat?' or 'What shall we drink?' or 'What shall we wear?' For the Gentiles seek all these things; and your heavenly Father knows that you need them all. But seek first his kingdom and his righteousness, and all these things shall be yours as well.[4]

TALK II:

SEEK FIRST THE KINGDOM

A person cannot get in a car and drive the car in all directions at the same time. Neither can a person put many different things first in his life. When young people try to give their allegiance to various interests and loyalties, they are trying to accomplish the impossible. Only one thing can actually be first in our lives. What shall it be? This is youth's all-important decision.

Jesus gave a clear-cut answer to the question: What shall I place first in my life? "Seek first the kingdom of God," he said, "and everything you need shall be yours as well." When we place God's kingdom first, all other activities and interests find their places in a harmonious, well-balanced pattern of living.

When young people seek first the kingdom of God, they develop a new attitude toward fun and social activities. Having a good time is no longer the chief goal in life. Discovering and doing the will of God becomes all important, and young people have a lot of fun as they make new discoveries regarding his will. A young man called one evening in the homes of several young people who were prospects for the church. He had very interesting and worth-while visits with all these prospects. As soon as he had completed his calls, he hurried to the home of his pastor. Without waiting for preliminary greetings, he exclaimed: "I had a wonderful time in every home I visited. No kidding! I never had so much fun in all my life!" Needless to say, this young man has continued to find great joy in reaching young people for Christ and the church—even though he does not always receive the enthusiastic welcome that he received on that first night of calling.

Seeking first the kingdom of God is fun of the highest and best type. Parties and other social activities are occasions for joyous and meaningful Christian fellowship. They are also opportunities for helping other young people discover the joy of being a part of Christ's kingdom.

Placing the kingdom of God first in one's life makes a difference in home and family relationships. A high-school girl whose parents were not church members made these interesting comments to her pastor: "I really have to watch my step at home. My father said he had noticed an improvement in my behavior since I became a Christian. In fact, he said he might attend the church membership class if I continue to behave better at home. I've got to stop quarreling with my little brother, because I want my mother and father to attend the class and find out what it means to be a Christian." This girl was beginning to realize that even daily actions at home have something to do with the extension of God's kingdom upon the earth.

Seeking first the kingdom of God has an influence on a young person's attitude toward schoolwork and the gaining of an education.

If we earnestly seek God's plan for our lives, we realize that we need a thorough and well-rounded education in order to be of greatest service and usefulness to the kingdom of God. When viewed in this light, an education has increased meaning and purpose for our lives. The choosing of our life vocation also takes on added significance. An earnest Christian desires to choose a vocation in which he can do his part to advance the kingdom of God throughout the world.

Placing God's kingdom first has an effect on the way in which we use our time, our talents, and our money. It makes a difference in our attitude toward people of other races and nationalities. In short, every area of our lives is influenced by our sincere desire to "seek first the kingdom of God and his righteousness."

HYMN: "I Love Thy Kingdom, Lord" or "How Lovely Is Thy Dwelling Place"

SCRIPTURE:

Another parable he put before them, saying, "The kingdom of heaven may be compared to a man who sowed good seed in his field; but while men were sleeping, his enemy came and sowed weeds among the wheat, and went away. So when the plants came up and bore grain, then the weeds appeared also. And the servants of the householder came and said to him, 'Sir, did you not sow good seed in your field? How then has it weeds?' He said to them, 'An enemy has done this.' The servants said to him, 'Then do you want us to go and gather them?' But he said, 'No; lest in gathering the weeds you root up the wheat along wtih them. Let both grow together until the harvest; and at harvest time I will tell the reapers, Gather the weeds first and bind them in bundles to be burned, but gather the wheat into my barn.' "

Another parable he put before them, saying, "The kingdom of heaven is like a grain of mustard seed which a man took and sowed in his field; it is the smallest of all seeds, but when it has grown it is the greatest of shrubs and becomes a tree, so that the birds of the air come and make nests in its branches." [5]

Talk III:
THE FINAL TRIUMPH OF THE KINGDOM

By means of parables or stories Jesus, during his earthly ministry, taught many important truths about his kingdom. Almost all of these parables give a clear indication of the final triumph of the kingdom of God.

The parable about the wheat and the weeds is a definite promise of the ultimate triumph of righteousness. As the Kingdom grows, evil will be present along with the good, until the time comes for God to separate the evil from the good. This indicates that the time will come when the Kingdom will be triumphant over the forces of evil.

The parable of the mustard seed predicts the triumphant growth of the Kingdom. It teaches that although Christ's kingdom began on a very small scale with only a handful of disciples, it will grow until it becomes a mighty force for righteousness.

The Lord's Prayer also suggests the final triumph of Christ's kingdom. Jesus taught his followers to pray for the time when God's will is to be done on earth as it is done in heaven. The kingdom of God is present in the world today, but it will come to its full fruition in the future.

There are many references in the writings of Paul that indicate the complete and final victory of Christ and his kingdom. Paul declared that the time will come when "at the name of Jesus every knee should bow, . . . and every tongue confess that Jesus Christ is Lord, to the glory of God the Father."

When we think of the culmination of Christ's kingdom, we think of the triumphant reign of Christ and his return to earth in power and glory. There are many passages in the New Testament which point clearly to Christ's personal return to the earth. When the disciples stood on the Mount of Olives at the time of Christ's ascension, two angels spoke to them: "Men of Galilee, why do you stand looking into heaven? This Jesus, who was taken up from you into heaven, will come in the same way as you saw him go into heaven."

When the second coming of Christ is to take place we cannot know. Jesus said, "But of that day and hour no one knows, . . . watch therefore, for you do not know on what day your Lord is coming." Our task is to be faithful servants of Christ, obedient to his command to carry on the work of his kingdom. We should be ready at all times for his return, working faithfully to extend his kingdom upon the earth.

We should think of Christ, not as our King in some far-distant future, but as the Leader and Lord of our lives in the present. We should renew our allegiance to him as he leads and guides us in the experiences of everyday living. We should think of him, not only as our Friend and Companion, but also as our living, triumphant King.

HYMN OF DEDICATION: "Lead On, O King Eternal"

CLOSING PRAYER AND BENEDICTION:

We dedicate our lives to thee, O Christ. We acknowledge thee as our Saviour, Lord, and King. We pray for strength to follow thy leadership in our daily experiences. Grant that we may have courage and wisdom as we strive to extend thy kingdom upon the earth.

"Now unto the King eternal, immortal, invisible, the only God, be honor and glory for ever and ever." AMEN.[6]

Growth in Christian Discipleship

17. Prayer Makes a Difference[1]

PRELUDE: "Come, Thou Almighty King"

CALL TO WORSHIP:

O come, let us sing to the Lord; let us make a joyful noise to the rock of our salvation! Let us come into his presence with thanksgiving; let us make a joyful noise to him with songs and praise! For the Lord is a great God, and a great King above all gods. In his hand are the depths of the earth; the heights of the mountains are his also. The sea is his, for he made it; for his hands formed the dry land. O come, let us worship and bow down, let us kneel before the Lord, our Maker! [2]

PRAYER:

We bow before thee, our Father, in reverence and humility. Help us to be aware of thy greatness and of our deep and abiding need of thee. We earnestly desire to know thee better and to have fellowship with thee. May each one of us feel thy presence in our midst as we think together about the importance of prayer and communion with thee. AMEN.

HYMN: "Come, Thou Almighty King" or "We Gather Together"

LEADER:

A dozen young people in an eastern city meet regularly for prayer, Christian fellowship, and the sharing of Christian experiences. On one occasion several of these young people told, spontaneously, what prayer meant to them.

"In recent weeks," said a graduate nurse, "prayer has taken on new

123

meaning for me. I have been getting up each morning in time for a period of prayer and meditation. This quiet time in the early morning has become a source of great help and inspiration. It has made it far easier for me to pray when I face problems and decisions. It has enabled me to carry more of the spirit of prayer into my busy schedule at the hospital."

Then a young man spoke eagerly: "I've made the same discovery—that I can take prayer with me to my work. I come in contact with many types of people each day. Many of them used to annoy me. Now I find myself praying for them. This has made a great improvement in my own disposition, and I'm sure it has also been helpful to several of them."

A college student then told of the help which she had received from prayer during several very strenuous months on a large university campus. A young man told about his concern for several of his friends and gave evidences that his prayers for them were being answered.

These are normal, enthusiastic, energetic American youth, and they are discovering that prayer works in a twentieth-century setting. Many earnest Christians are making this same discovery. Many of them are humble disciples who have discovered the secret of true prayer and who live each day in intimate fellowship with God. There are also many great Christian leaders in our day who are demonstrating in their lives the power of prayer.

Impersonations of two outstanding men who live by prayer will be presented. The first impersonation will portray Dr. Frank C. Laubach. Dr. Laubach was for many years a missionary in the Philippines. In more recent years he has gone to many remote sections of the world with his remarkable phonetic system which teaches large numbers of people to read and write in a very short time. Dr. Laubach not only stresses a literacy program, but through the years he has also emphasized the power of prayer. In the following interview Dr. Laubach will be interviewed by Helen, a typical member of a Christian youth fellowship.

IMPERSONATION OF DR. FRANK C. LAUBACH [3]

(The two young people taking part in this impersonation enter and sit down together informally.)

HELEN: I'm glad for this opportunity to talk to you about prayer,

Dr. Laubach. I am sure I haven't yet discovered its real meaning. How can prayer become more vital and meaningful in my life?

DR. LAUBACH: Perhaps I can answer that question best by telling you about an experiment which I began in my life a number of years ago. I determined to live all my waking moments in conscious listening to the inner voice, asking without ceasing, "What, Father, do you desire said? What, Father, do you desire done this minute?" I discovered that my task is to live each hour in continuous inner conversation with God and in perfect responsiveness to his will. This is all I need do in order to make each hour gloriously rich. The most wonderful discovery that has ever come to me is that I do not have to wait until some future time for the glorious hour. I need not sing, "O that will be glory for me," and wait for my grave. *This hour* can be heaven. Any hour for anybody can be as rich as God!

HELEN: You've given me a brand new idea about prayer, Dr. Laubach. How can a young person attain this sense of vital fellowship with God?

DR. LAUBACH: Precisely as any friendship is achieved; that is, by doing things together. The depth and intensity of a friendship depend upon the variety and extent of the things friends do and enjoy together. Friendship with God is the friendship of child with parent. As an ideal son grows daily into closer relationship with his father, so we may grow into closer fellowship with God by widening into his interests, thinking his thoughts, and sharing his enterprises.

HELEN: Does this friendship with God affect our relationship to our fellow men?

DR. LAUBACH: Very definitely! God is constantly pointing me to some dull, dead soul which he has never reached, and wistfully urging me to help him reach that stolid, tight-shut mind. All day I see souls, dead to God, look sadly out of hungry eyes. I want them to know my discovery—that any minute can be paradise, that any place can be heaven! That any person can have God! That every person does have God the moment he speaks to God or listens for him!

HELEN: Would you say, then, that prayer is vitally connected with life and with our everyday relationships with people about us?

DR. LAUBACH: Exactly! We should pray with pencil and paper at hand.

When God sends a thought, we should write it down and keep it visible until it can be carried into action. Vital prayers aways suggest things to be done. Indeed, prayer and action must be mates, or both are weak. The mightiest men and women on earth are strong in prayer and strong in deeds. This is the only unbeatable combination.

HELEN: Do you have any special word for young people about prayer?

DR. LAUBACH: A progressive American educator said: "Instead of teaching young people to listen to long prayers and longer sermons on Sunday morning, teach them to make brief sentence prayers many times a day; teach them that prayer is the best way to meet every need and every task." Youth has a thousand times more mental and physical energy than Protestant churches have helped them use creatively. If young people are taught that by praying for leaders they actually mold world history, they pray with all the reckless abandon of youth. This sense that they can do something vital rescues them from cynicism, enlarges their world view, creates interest in really important affairs, keeps them close to God, makes them ambitious to serve, gives them a sense of mission, and saves them from throwing their lives away in cheap sin. American youth need a powerful cause and a program they can undertake at once. Prayer for everybody is one such program, and saving our age is the cause!

HELEN: Thank you, Dr. Laubach, for your inspiring thoughts about prayer.

DR. LAUBACH: My thanks to you for this pleasant time of fellowship, and may you experience in greater measure the power and vitality of prayer.

LEADER:

Our second impersonation will depict Dr. E. Stanley Jones, well-known missionary, author, and lecturer, and a great man of prayer. Dr. Jones will be interviewed by Ralph, a typical twentieth-century Christian youth.

IMPERSONATION OF DR. E. STANLEY JONES [4]

(*The young person impersonating* DR. JONES *is seated at a table, reading a book.* RALPH *enters.*)

RALPH: Excuse me for interrupting, Dr. Jones.

DR. JONES: Interruptions are often God-given opportunities. Won't you sit down?

RALPH: Thank you. I have a few questions I'd like to ask you about prayer.

DR. JONES: I'm always very happy when a young person wants to talk to me about prayer. What questions do you have?

RALPH: I'm interested in knowing what prayer means to you and whether or not it actually works. How important is prayer to you personally?

DR. JONES: For me, prayer is all important. I'm better or worse as I pray more or less. If my prayer life sags, the rest of my life sags with it. When I pray, I'm like an electric bulb fastened in a socket. I'm full of light and power. When I do not pray, I'm like a bulb out of the socket. I am without light and power.

RALPH: What prayer plan or procedure do you follow, Dr. Jones?

DR. JONES: When I was a student in college, I set aside for prayer and meditation one half hour in the morning, one half hour at noon, and one half hour in the evening. I have followed this plan through the years, except that I have combined the noon hour with the evening one. My morning prayer time lasts from thirty to forty-five minutes. Part of this time I spend with my Bible. When I read the Bible, it clarifies my vision of what I need, so that, having steeped myself in God's Word, I ask for the right things. In the evening I spend a full hour alone with God. I sit and absorb the love and power of God directly, without using the Bible. God speaks through his Word, but he also speaks to us directly. I find that when the evening prayer hour is observed at sunset, it tones me up for the entire evening.

RALPH: How can prayer work, Dr. Jones, in a universe governed by laws already set in motion?

DR. JONES: I believe this is an open and unfinished universe. As some things are left undone in the universe, contingent on our acting, so I believe that some things are left undone in the universe, contingent on our praying. There are things that will not be done until we pray.

RALPH: I had never thought of prayer in that way. How does prayer work in an individual life—in your life and mine?

DR. JONES: Prayer has become as natural in my life as breathing. In breathing, I breathe out the bad air and breathe in the good. In prayer I do much the same thing. I breathe out sin, weakness, and confusion and breathe in God's forgiveness, strength, and certainty. Prayer is surrender to and co-operation with God. All our powers are heightened when we co-operate with God. There is a plus added to life. When we align ourselves, through prayer, to God's purposes, God can do things through us that we could not possibly do in our own strength.

RALPH: Many of us, as Christian young people, desire to experience the power of prayer in our daily lives. Do you have any suggestions that will serve as a guide for us to follow?

DR. JONES: Here are some suggestions for the quiet time of prayer which all Christians should observe each day:

1. Decide on the time you ought to give to the quiet time. Hold to it. Don't make it a matter of debate each day. Pray by the clock, whether you feel like it or not. Organize the day around the quiet time.

2. Come to the quiet time with expectancy. Direct your faith toward God and draw upon his resources.

3. Before you pray, get your thoughts and feelings directed by God's Word.

4. During the reading of God's Word, take the attitude of lowly listening.

5. Have a pen or pencil ready to write down the thoughts that come to you from God.

6. Let your mind circle around a verse of scripture that has a special message for you.

7. After you have read a portion of the Bible, relax and say, "Father, what have you to say to me?"

8. Then, say to God what you have to say. Your prayers have been cleansed and directed by the steps taken so far.

9. After you have said what you have to say, surrender it into the hands of God.

10. Thank God for the answer to your prayers, whatever the answer may be.

11. If your mind wanders during the quiet time, make the thing to which the mind wanders an object of prayer or a means of prayer.

12. Make the quiet time the high point of each day.

RALPH: I'm going to put these suggestions into practice, Dr. Jones. Tomorrow morning I will start observing the quiet time of prayer.

DR. JONES: Good for you, Ralph! I shall be praying that your first observance of the quiet hour may be a glorious success.

PERIOD OF GUIDED PRAYER (give time for silent prayer between each prayer request.)

Let us pray that each one of us will make use of the suggestions which have been made regarding prayer.

Let us pray that those of our group who have already started a daily prayer time may be more earnest and faithful in the observance of it.

Let us pray that those of our group who have not yet started a daily prayer time will begin today.

Let us pray that Christians around the world may experience in greater measure the meaning and power of prayer.

PRAYER HYMN (to be sung softly by the entire group): First stanza of "What a Friend We Have in Jesus"

CLOSING PRAYER:

We thank thee, our Father, for thy Son Jesus Christ, who, by his life upon the earth, taught us the value of prayer. We are thankful that he is our Friend and that we can have fellowship with him by means of prayer. We are grateful, too, for Christians of the past and of the present who have discovered the power and purposes of prayer. May we be inspired by their example and profit from their experiences. Help us to carry out our earnest resolves to spend more time each day in quiet communion with thee. May prayer "make a difference" in our lives at this very moment and throughout each day of the future. AMEN.

18. Discovering the Meaning of Prayer

Prelude: "Sweet Hour of Prayer"

Call to Worship:

> 'Mid all the traffic of the ways,
> Turmoils without, within,
> Make in my heart a quiet place,
> And come and dwell therein:
>
> A little shrine of quietness,
> All sacred to Thyself,
> Where Thou shalt all my soul possess,
> And I may find myself:
>
> A little shelter from life's stress,
> Where I may lay me prone,
> And bare my soul in loneliness,
> And know as I am known:
>
> A little place of mystic grace,
> Of self and sin swept bare,
> Where I may look upon Thy face,
> And talk with Thee in prayer.[1]
>
> —John Oxenham

Response: First stanza of "Sweet Hour of Prayer"

Prayer:

May these moments of meditation, O God, be a "sweet hour of prayer" for each one of us. Guide us as we discuss the meaning and

130

significance of prayer. May prayer become more meaningful to us and occupy a more vital place in our daily experiences. AMEN.

HYMN: "Take Time to Be Holy" or " 'Tis the Blessed Hour of Prayer"

LEADER:[2]

What does prayer mean to you? How important is it in your life? Does it have meaning and vitality for you? Does it have a vital relationship to your daily problems and experiences? Have you had evidence of its power and effectiveness in your life? Is it possible that we, as Christian young people, are often disappointed in our attempts at prayer, because we fail to understand its real purpose? Let's try to discover from the Bible something of the true meaning and significance of prayer.

READER I:

He also told this parable to some who trusted in themselves that they were righteous and despised others: "Two men went up into the temple to pray, one a Pharisee and the other a tax collector. The Pharisee stood and prayed thus with himself, 'God, I thank thee that I am not like other men, extortioners, unjust, adulterers, or even like this tax collector. I fast twice a week, I give tithes of all that I get.' But the tax collector, standing far off, would not even lift up his eyes to heaven, but beat his breast, saying, 'God, be merciful to me a sinner!' I tell you, this man went down to his house justified rather than the other; for every one who exalts himself will be humbled, but he who humbles himself will be exalted." [3]

READER II:

This story by the master Teacher gives us a startling lesson about prayer. Two men went into the temple to pray—a Pharisee, one of the religious leaders of Jesus' day, and a tax collector. Jesus said that the Pharisee "prayed thus with himself." This proud, arrogant man was not really praying. He was merely talking to himself! He was patting himself on the back, reminding himself what a fine, religious, law-abiding fellow he was!

Surprisingly enough, the tax collector, who was despised by the Pharisee and by his other fellow countrymen, actually experienced the reality of prayer. He prayed, not mere words, but an earnest prayer of repentance that brought him into a vital relationship with the living God. What was his prayer? "God, be merciful to me a sinner." God heard that simple prayer. He was able to forgive the man because of the man's humility.

Jesus stated an important principle at the close of this story: He that exalts himself shall be humbled, but he that humbles himself shall be exalted. Earnestness, sincerity, humility—these are some of the major characteristics of true prayer. Do we have a humble, repentant spirit when we come to God in prayer? Do we earnestly feel our need of his forgiveness and guidance? Are we just talking to ourselves when we pray, like the Pharisee of old, or do we actually talk to our heavenly Father?

READER I:

"And when you pray, you must not be like the hypocrites; for they love to stand and pray in the synagogues and at the street corners, that they may be seen by men. Truly, I say to you, they have their reward. But when you pray, go into your room and shut the door and pray to your Father who is in secret; and your Father who sees in secret will reward you.

"And in praying do not heap up empty phrases as the Gentiles do; for they think that they will be heard for their many words. Do not be like them, for your Father knows what you need before you ask him." [4]

READER II:

This is one of Jesus' teachings that calls forth the hearty assent of youth. Most young people have little patience with the hypocrite—the person who "puts on airs" and pretends to be something he is not. Let's be sure that we apply this insistence on sincerity to our prayer life. Let's have no pretending there, of all places! We must be sure that we're not just going through the motions of praying, that we are not just saying empty, meaningless words. Jesus warns us not to use vain repetitions when we pray. He also urges us to go into our own private room, shut the door, and pray to our heavenly Father. Why this emphasis on secrecy? Simply this: Prayer, in its basic essence, is *friendship with God*. We must spend time alone with God in order to nurture and cultivate our friendship with him.

We may also think of prayer as conversation with God. Prayer is a two-way proposition: it is listening to God as well as talking to him. It is the quiet sharing and mutual understanding of true friends. Public prayers and group prayers are important, but back of them and supporting them, like the girders and foundation stones of a great bridge, must be the quiet day-by-day companionship of individual Christians with the living God. Are we, as Christian young people, living in daily fellowship with God? Do we spend time each day in quiet communion with him?

READER I:

"Blessed are those who hunger and thirst for righteousness, for they shall be satisfied." "Ask, and it will be given you; seek and you will find; knock, and it will be opened to you. For every one who asks receives, and he who seeks finds, and to him who knocks it will be opened. Or what man of you, if his son asks him for a loaf, will give him a stone? Or if he asks for a fish, will give him a serpent? If you then, who are evil, know how to give good gifts to your children, how much more will your Father who is in heaven give good things to those who ask him?" [5]

READER II:

Ask—seek—knock. These are vivid words, and they tell us a great deal about prayer. Prayer is an attitude of earnest seeking after God. It is hunger and thirst after righteousness.

Parents know how to give good gifts to their children. How much more shall our Father in heaven give good things to those who ask him! Why does he withhold these blessings until we seek them? Simply because we are not in a condition to receive and appreciate God's greatest gifts until we have a seeking mind, a humble spirit, an eager faith.

True prayer is yielding our lives to the will and purposes of God. It is an attitude of complete trust in God. Prayer is giving God a chance to do for us what he cannot do until we are ready to receive his strength and guidance. Real prayer is turning our lives over to God and saying: "Here, Lord, take complete control of my life. Use me according to thy purpose, and guide me in every experience of life."

The basic spirit of all our prayers should not be "give me," but "guide me."

READER I:

And after he had dismissed the crowds, he went up into the hills by himself to pray. When evening came, he was there alone. And in the morning, a great while before day, he rose and went out to a lonely place, and there he prayed. In these days he went out into the hills to pray; and all night he continued in prayer to God. And when it was day, he called his disciples, and chose from them twelve, whom he named apostles.

Then Jesus went with them to a place called Gethsemane, and he said to his disciples, "Sit here, while I go yonder and pray." And taking with him Peter and the two sons of Zebedee, he began to be sorrowful and troubled. Then he said to them, "My soul is very sorrowful, even to death; remain here, and watch with me." And going a little farther he fell on his face and prayed, "My Father, if it be possible, let this cup pass from me; nevertheless, not as I will, but as thou wilt." And he came to the disciples and found them sleeping; and he said to Peter, "So, could you not watch with me one hour? Watch and pray that you may not enter into temptation; the spirit indeed is willing, but the flesh is weak." [6]

READER II:

The prayer life of Jesus, as it is recorded in the New Testament, gives us further enlightenment on the meaning and purpose of prayer.

First of all, Jesus prayed in order that he might remain in constant fellowship and contact with his Father. Prayer, for him, was a way of life—a life of communion with God. Mark records a busy Sabbath day which Jesus spent in Capernaum—a day of teaching, healing, and ministering to the needs of great crowds of people. And then Mark tells us that on the next morning, a great while before day, Jesus went to a desert place to pray. Prayer was the source of Jesus' strength for the strenuous days of activity and service which were an important part of his ministry upon the earth. Matthew records that on another occasion, after Jesus had sent the multitudes away, he went to a mountain alone to pray. Jesus withdrew from the crowds, from the noise and confusion of everyday living, in order that he might be alone with God.

Jesus also prayed at times of great crisis and decision in order to receive illumination and guidance from the Father. Luke tells us that Jesus went up to a mountain to pray and that he continued all night in prayer to God. It was after this night of prayer that he chose the twelve disciples, who were eventually to be entrusted with the work of his kingdom.

Our Lord prayed in agony at Gethsemane. The Cross loomed just ahead. "If it be possible," he cried, "let this cup pass from me; nevertheless, not as I will, but as thou wilt." Jesus came from the Garden, with a calm power that awed the mob which had come to seize him. Where did he get that inner poise and power? It was prayer that fortified and strengthened him in body, mind, and soul.

Jesus was able to draw upon the power and resources of God in times of crisis because he lived in constant fellowship with the Father in the everyday experiences of life. Is it possible that we cannot find God in times of great need because we do not live in close fellowship with him each day? For many of us prayer has not yet become a way of life, a life of daily companionship with God as he is revealed in Jesus Christ.

SHARING SESSION (questions that will encourage the young people to share their ideas, experiences, and problems regarding prayer) :

1. What is the basic meaning of prayer as revealed in the life of Jesus?

2. Can young people today actually experience vital fellowship with God? In what ways?

3. On what specific occasions have you been aware of the presence of God?

4. How can prayer be more meaningful to us as individual young people?

5. What is the most helpful method of daily prayer and Bible-study that you have used?

6. How can prayer be more meaningful to us as a group?

7. In what specific ways can we improve the worship experiences of our youth department?

LEADER:

We learn to pray, not by discussing prayer, but by actually praying. May we experience the reality of prayer during these closing moments of quiet meditation.

POEM:

> Prayer is the soul's sincere desire,
>   Uttered or unexpressed;
> The motion of a hidden fire,
>   That trembles in the breast.
>
> Prayer is the burden of a sigh,
>   The falling of a tear;
> The upward glancing of an eye,
>   When none but God is near.
>
> .   .   .   .
>
> Prayer is the Christian's vital breath,
>   The Christian's native air;
> His watchword at the gate of death—
>   He enters heaven with prayer.
>
> .   .   .   .
>
> O Thou by whom we come to God—
>   The Life, the Truth, the Way!
> The path of prayer Thyself hast trod;
>   Lord, teach us how to pray! [7]
>   —JAMES MONTGOMERY

SILENT PRAYER (As each one waits silently before God and listens for the "still, small voice" of God)

PRAYER HYMN (to be sung softly by a soloist or by the entire group): "More Love to Thee, O Christ" or "Dear Lord and Father of Mankind"

CLOSING PRAYER:

We know that you are very near to us, O Lord, for we have felt your presence in our midst, and we have heard your voice within our inmost being. We can never be the same, for we have felt the touch of your Spirit upon our lives. We have experienced a little more of the real meaning of prayer, and we desire above all else to continue this experience of prayer in our daily lives. Help us to live a life of prayer tomorrow and on each succeeding tomorrow. AMEN.

19. Experiencing the Reality of Prayer

PRELUDE: "Draw Thou My Soul, O Christ"

CALL TO WORSHIP:

"Ask, and it will be given you; seek and you will find; knock, and it will be opened to you. For every one who asks receives, and he who seeks finds, and to him who knocks it will be opened." [1]

PRAYER:

Our Father in heaven, help us to hunger and thirst after thee and the things of thy kingdom. May we have eager, seeking minds, earnestly desiring to discover more of the meaning and challenge of Christian discipleship. We thank thee that when we ask, seek and knock, we are able to receive thy guidance and to experience more of thy love and power. In the name of Christ we pray. Amen.

HYMN: "Draw Thou My Soul, O Christ" or "What a Friend We Have in Jesus"

POEM:

> I name Thy hallowed name,
> I bring Thee a new day;
> Lord, keep my life from sin and shame,
> And teach me how to pray.
>
> Thy kingdom come to me,
> And build within my heart
> A shrine for me, a throne for Thee,
> A temple set apart.

138

> Thy will be done by me
> In little things, close by,
> That so my home on earth may be
> More like Thy heaven on high.
>
> Give me my bread today,
> Enough to keep me strong,
> Enough to share; and help me pray
> For those who do me wrong.
>
> If any tempt me, lead
> To purer air above;
> Thy power is gentle in my need,
> Thy glory is Thy love.[2]
>
> —Louis F. Benson

Scripture:

He was praying in a certain place, and when he ceased, one of his disciples said to him, "Lord, teach us to pray, as John taught his disciples." And he said to them, "When you pray, say: 'Father, hallowed be thy name. Thy kingdom come. Give us each day our daily bread; and forgive us our sins, for we ourselves forgive every one who is indebted to us; and lead us not into temptation.' " [3]

Leader: [4]

The disciples came to Jesus with a very practical request about prayer. They had observed the significant place of prayer in the life of Jesus. They had the feeling that prayer was the secret of his power. And so they came to Jesus with the simple, practical request, "Lord, teach us to pray."

As twentieth-century disciples, we have the same earnest desire to experience the reality of prayer. We have heard prayer extolled as the mightiest force in the universe. As we have studied God's Word, particularly the life of our Lord, we've sensed the importance of prayer. There have been brief moments when we have felt the nearness of God. But we desire to live in close fellowship with God each day; we desire to experience the power of prayer in our daily lives.

A dramatic presentation, "Prayer Comes Alive," will give us help at this point. In the first scene we discover Jim and Dick at a Christian youth camp. In scene II prayer is beginning to come alive for them at camp. In scene III Jim and Dick are back home, sharing their camp experiences with a few of their friends.

DRAMATIC PRESENTATION:

PRAYER COMES ALIVE

SCENE I: (DICK *and* JIM *enter, dressed in typical camp attire, and sit down together in a leisurely, informal manner.*)

DICK: Did you ever get up real early in the morning just to see what things are like out of doors?

JIM: I've never been especially interested in seeing nature at the break of day. Too early for me, I guess. Why do you ask?

DICK: That speaker at camp worship this morning hit me between the eyes when he told about the need for a quiet time with God each day.

JIM: Me too. But what does that have to do with nature in the early morning?

DICK: I was just thinking about getting up early each morning, taking a hike to a scenic spot, and having a quiet prayer time out of doors.

JIM: Not a bad idea—except that it comes so early in the day!

DICK: Why don't you go along with me?

JIM: Breakfast comes early enough at this camp, without getting up in time for a hike and a prayer meeting before breakfast! I can hardly roll out when the third bugle call sounds!

DICK: I'll roll you out of that upper bunk of yours! Come on, let's try it for one morning anyway.

JIM: Okay! I'll try anything once. What time do we start?

DICK: About 5:30 tomorrow morning.

JIM: Five thirty! That really is getting up before breakfast! How did I ever get myself into this? Rolling me out of that upper bunk at 5:30 A.M. may be more of a job than you bargained for!

DICK: Don't worry about that! I'll see that you make it!

(*Exit* DICK *and* JIM.)

SCENE II: (DICK and JIM *enter, talking.*)

JIM: Let's go to that same spot by the gnarled oak.

DICK: Okay. Here we are. There are other swell views here at camp, but this one beats them all. (DICK *and* JIM *sit informally upon the floor or a bench.*)

JIM: I agree. We've been here four mornings at the noble hour of 5:30 A.M. No wonder we appreciate the view! Seriously, Dick, this idea of yours has been tops. I've never gotten much out of Bible-reading and prayer before.

DICK: Neither had I, Jim. We'll have to continue this early morning prayer habit when we get back home.

JIM: It'll be hard, Dick, not having you to roll me out of bed!

DICK: I'll miss that part of it too! It's your turn to read from the Bible, Jim. Aren't we ready for the last chapter of Philippians?

JIM: That's right. (*Turns to the passage in his Bible.*) Here it is! (*Reads Phil. 4:1-13.*) Let's stop at the thirteenth verse, Dick: "I can do all things in him who strengthens me." Isn't that a swell motto for a Christian?

DICK: It really is, Jim. That would be a good verse for us to repeat each morning at the beginning of our quiet time.

JIM: There are other good verses in this chapter—just meant for young people, it seems to me. Notice the fourth verse: "Rejoice in the Lord always; again I will say, Rejoice." Young people like to do that! And there's the sixth verse: "Have no anxiety about anything, but in everything by prayer and supplication with thanksgiving let your requests be made known to God." We need Someone to whom we can take our problems. This verse says to take everything to God. I like that thought and also the promise in the seventh verse: "And the peace of God, which passes all understanding, will keep your hearts and your minds in Christ Jesus."

Verse 8 is another important verse: "Whatever is true, whatever is honorable, whatever is just, whatever is pure, whatever is lovely, whatever is gracious, . . . think about these things." That's a good motto for a young person too.

DICK: That's great, Jim! I didn't dream there was so much in one

141

short chapter for young people. Let's have our time of silent prayer while we think about these great truths.

SILENT PRAYER (*as* JIM *and* DICK *reverently bow their heads in prayer*)

PRAYER (*by* DICK): Dear God, thank you for the beauty of this place and for the important truths we have discovered in your Word. We are glad that prayer and Bible-reading have become more meaningful to us. When camp is over, help us to continue our quiet prayer time each morning. May we share with other young people what we have learned about prayer. Help us to be courageous Christians and to remember that we can do all things through Christ who strengthens us. AMEN.
(*Exit* JIM *and* DICK.)

SCENE III: (JIM *is reading a book in the living room of his own home. He goes to the door to greet* DICK.)

JIM: Come in, Dick. It's good to see you.
DICK: The feeling is mutual, my friend. This was a good idea of yours, Jim, to get some of the gang together, so we can tell them about camp.
JIM: Only three of them can come tonight, Dick. We can talk things over with them and later pass it on to the rest. Here they are now.
(JANE, MARTHA *and* BILL *enter. They are greeted cordially by* JIM *and* DICK. *They all sit down informally.*)
DICK: Jim and I had a lot of fun at camp; but, surprisingly enough, we've also come back with a serious idea or two!
JANE: This is surprising news! Come to think of it, Jim did sound rather serious when he invited us to come over this evening.
JIM: Dick and I heard a lot at camp about having a prayer time each day. We had heard that sort of thing before and had never taken it very seriously. This time we tried it out and discovered that it isn't just a lot of talk. It really works. I should add that we tried it, because Dick persistently rolled me out of bed at 5:30 every morning!
MARTHA: Five thirty! This is almost more than we can take!
JIM: I'll admit it sounds unbelievable! Dick will tell you more about it. It was his idea in the first place.

142

DICK: There isn't much more to tell. We went to the same spot every morning—a little clearing by an old, gnarled oak. We read a chapter each day from Philippians and talked about the important verses in the chapter. Then we had a time of silent prayer and a spoken prayer. It sounds very simple, but it did something to us.

BILL: It sounds like a good idea to me. I, for one, feel the need of it.

JIM: Good for you, Bill! Dick and I have been doing this same thing individually since we came home, and we're still getting a lot of help from it. That's why we wanted to tell you about it.

JANE: I've heard of other young people trying this sort of thing, but it never seemed very practical before. Why couldn't all of us give it a try?

DICK: We were hoping you'd want to try it. Why couldn't we have our individual prayer time at about the same hour each morning?

MARTHA: If you mean at 5:30 A.M.—that's too early for me!

DICK: We'll compromise and make it seven o'clock! The exact time makes very little difference. The important thing is to have a quiet time for Bible-reading and prayer before the day's activities begin.

BILL: Wouldn't it be a good idea for all of us to read the same scripture passage each day? What are you fellows reading now?

JIM: We haven't decided on another book yet, but one of the camp leaders suggested that we read Mark and then Acts.

JANE: That sounds like a good plan. Let's read a chapter each day. And let's jot down in a notebook the verses that are most helpful to us, as well as other good ideas that come to us as we read the Bible and pray. Why don't we get together every week or so and share our ideas?

DICK: That's a swell suggestion, Jane! We can memorize the most helpful verses which we jot down in our notebook. Jim and I have already memorized one verse which we repeat each morning at the beginning of our prayer time: "I can do all things in him who strengthens me."

MARTHA: That's a grand way to begin the prayer time, Dick. Reading a stanza or two of a devotional hymn is also helpful.

JANE: I'm anxious to try out these ideas tomorrow morning!

DICK: I'm looking forward to the first sharing session when we talk

143

over our experiences. There are young people in many parts of the country who have formed discipleship groups which meet regularly for prayer, Christian fellowship, and the sharing of experiences. Perhaps our sharing sessions will develop into a real discipleship group.

BILL: I'm all for it, Dick. Let's meet next week at this same time and tell about the results of our daily Bible-reading and prayer.

JIM: That'll be fine. Same time—same place! Meanwhile let's talk to other members of our youth fellowship and invite them to share in our prayer experiment.

MARTHA: I've made many resolutions to read the Bible and pray daily— all of which have gone the way of most resolutions. But this is the first time I've ever been really enthusiastic about the idea. I think that prayer has "come alive" for me!

DICK: That expresses the feelings of all of us, Martha. I'm sure that our "prayer experiment" will not fail. We are looking to Jesus for guidance, remembering that we can do all things through him who strengthens us.

(*Exit all the young people.*)

TIME FOR DECISION AND DISCUSSION:

1. Each young person must discover his own personal prayer plan. Prayer must "come alive" for each individual. Encourage each young person to decide upon a definite prayer plan which, with God's help, he will carry out during the days ahead.

2. The group may decide upon a suggested time for a daily prayer period. They may also decide upon a book of the Bible which all the young people would read during their daily prayer period for a specified time, such as a week or two weeks. (Philippians or Mark are good "starters" for such a plan.)

3. Members of the group may suggest other devotional helps for the daily prayer time, such as a book of poems, a daily devotional booklet, a Bible commentary, or a Bible dictionary.

4. The group may also decide to meet a week later (or at another time) for the purpose of sharing experiences that the young people will have as a result of their observance of the quiet time.

5. The young people may be interested in making plans for a disciple-

ship group (sometimes known as a cell group) which will meet regularly, at a time other than the youth fellowship hour, for the specific purpose of prayer, discussion of important aspects of the Christian life, and the sharing of vital Christian experiences.

PERIOD OF SILENT PRAYER AND DEDICATION (as a soloist sings "Have Thine Own Way, Lord")

CLOSING PRAYER:

Help us, our Father, to discover the prayer plan that will make prayer come alive for each one of us. We thank thee for Jesus, our Redeemer and Friend. May we look to him for guidance and strength as we make plans for our daily quiet time of prayer. May we experience the reality of prayer during these moments of meditation and throughout each day of our lives. AMEN.

20. The Importance of Sharing Our Faith[1]

CALL TO WORSHIP:

And Jesus came and said to them, "All authority in heaven and on earth has been given to me. Go therefore and make disciples of all nations, baptizing them in the name of the Father and of the Son and of the Holy Spirit, teaching them to observe all that I have commanded you; and lo, I am with you always, to the close of the age." [2]

HYMN: "We've a Story to Tell to the Nations" or "Christ for the World We Sing"

PRAYER:

We thank thee, Lord, that ours is the glorious challenge of carrying thy message to those about us and to the ends of the earth. We are grateful that we can be colaborers with thee and that thy redemptive message has been entrusted to us. We praise thee for the privilege of sharing in work that is world wide in scope and eternal in significance. We praise thee, too, for the meaning and purpose which Christian discipleship gives to our daily experiences. AMEN.

DOXOLOGY: "Praise God from Whom All Blessings Flow"

LEADER:

Why should we share our faith in Christ with others? Why should every Christian be an evangelist? We'll try to answer these important questions by means of two rather unique interviews. One of our members will act as a representative of all Christian youth of our day and do the interviewing for us. He will interview two biblical evangelists—Peter and John. "Let's pretend" used to be a popular pastime

146

when we were children. Let's pretend at this time that these two distinguished persons leave their celestial heights to have a brief visit with us. Listen carefully to their message, for what they have to say comes directly from God's Word.

FIRST INTERVIEW

(*Christian* YOUTH *may be seated at a table with an empty chair beside him. He looks nervously at his watch.*)

YOUTH: I must be a little nervous about these two interviews that are scheduled for today. I guess that's to be expected. One doesn't entertain heavenly visitors every day! I'm glad they're coming one at a time and that Peter will be the first one. As I remember from my Sunday-school lessons, he was a pretty human sort of person during his lifetime. Here he comes now. (YOUTH *rises to greet* PETER *and offer him a chair.*) Welcome, Peter, to twentieth-century America!

PETER (*looking about him*): It's a privilege to return to the earth for a brief visit, although I must admit it is a bit of a letdown after so many years in the celestial kingdom. But I well remember that life on this earth was full of worth-while adventure. I'm glad to be here.

YOUTH: You were a fearless Christian leader in your day, Peter. As Christian youth, we desire to be worthy followers of the Master. Tell us how we can recapture the spirit of courage and enthusiasm which you and the other early disciples had.

PETER: I was not always fearless. I remember yet, to my shame, how I denied my Lord. It was only his grace and power that gave me courage.

YOUTH: What were some of the outstanding experiences that you had as a follower of Jesus?

PETER: The day of Pentecost remains in my memory as though it were but yesterday. On that day we received the gift of the Holy Spirit, as Jesus had promised. The Holy Spirit enabled us to give our testimony with power and to win three thousand people to the Lord Jesus.

I remember, too, the day that John and I healed the lame beggar, as we were on our way to the temple. The crowds gathered around us as though we had healed the man by our own strength. I set their minds straight in a hurry. "Why fasten your eyes on us," I asked them, "as though by our own power we have made him walk? God has glorified his servant, Jesus. And by faith in his name has this man been made strong."

Soon there were five thousand Christian believers, then the number grew so rapidly that we lost count. The chief priests and scribes were afraid of losing their positions of authority. They had us imprisoned and beaten with stripes; they charged us not to speak in the name of Jesus. "We must obey God rather than men," we told them, and every day in the temple and at home we ceased not to teach and to preach Jesus as the Christ.

I'm sure you've read about these events in your New Testament in the book of Acts.

YOUTH: I have, but they've never before seemed so real to me. And I never realized how much you early disciples shared your faith with others.

PETER: Every Christian believer must be an evangelist. This, above all else, is the primary responsibility of every follower of the Master.

YOUTH: I'd never thought of it just that way. Why is it so important, Peter, for every Christian to be an evangelist?

PETER: There are many reasons, my young friend. Let me give you a few that seem of special importance to me. First of all, *Jesus has done so much for his followers, that they dare not keep their blessings to themselves.* They would be the most selfish of all people on earth if they did not share their Christian faith.

Christ arose from the dead and appeared to us, his first disciples. That gave us the faith and certainty that life continues beyond the grave. This faith in eternal life is the priceless possession of every Christian believer. How can any Christian keep it to himself?

Christ is our hope of eternal life. He is our Redeemer, who has made possible the forgiveness of our sins. He has redeemed us, not with silver or gold, but by his own precious blood. He bore our sins in his own body upon the cross, that we might live unto righteousness. By his stripes we are healed. He suffered and died, the righteous for the unrighteous, that he might bring us to God.

YOUTH: I do not understand these great Christian teachings as I should, and I have never before realized how important they are.

PETER: I have referred to all these great truths in one of my letters, which you will find in your Bible by the name of First Peter. It might pay you to read that brief letter, as well as other parts of your New Testament.

YOUTH: I'm going to read that letter of yours, Peter, and the rest of my New Testament more seriously than I have ever done before.

PETER: Here is another reason why every true Christian must be an evangelist: *Our Lord commanded it.* "Go ye into all the world," he said, "and preach the gospel to every creature." This was his final command, his last directive to his disciples, uttered just before his ascension into heaven. How can his followers ever forget these words?

YOUTH: I'm afraid most of his twentieth-century followers have forgotten them. Thank you for bringing them to our attention.

PETER: I must be going. I have been away too long from my celestial home. Yours is the tremendous challenge of taking the gospel message around the world and seeing lives transformed by its dynamic power. Much as I would enjoy sharing in that thrilling adventure, I long for the clear, pure atmosphere of the Eternal City. The blessing of our Lord and Saviour be with you forevermore.

(*Exit* PETER.)

SOLO (*as* YOUTH *remains seated in quiet contemplation*): "Jesus, Thy Boundless Love to Me" or "Saviour, Thy Dying Love"

SECOND INTERVIEW:

JOHN (*Enters quietly*): I am John, a humble disciple of the Lord Jesus Christ. I'm sorry to interrupt your reverie, but I believe you have a few questions to ask me during my brief leave of absence from the Celestial City.

YOUTH (*stands to greet* JOHN *and offer him a chair*): You are most welcome, John. It was a real privilege to talk with your friend Peter, but there are several questions which I am anxious to ask you. There are many who feel, after reading the books you have written in our New Testament, that you understand the Christian life better than any other human being who ever lived. What do you think are the most important requirements of Christian discipleship?

JOHN: There are two all-important requirements: We must have faith in Jesus Christ and love for our fellow men. This is God's commandment, that we believe in the name of his Son, Jesus Christ, and love one another. If you want to remember this twofold commandment, you will find it stated in my little epistle called First John. "Faith" and "love" are the two greatest words in the Christian's vocabulary. Both of these words are mentioned again and again in your New Testament.

YOUTH: I've already determined to study the New Testament with renewed earnestness, John, and to urge my friends to do the same. Here's another question: What is the greatest task or responsibility of a Christian?

JOHN: Jesus said to his followers, "Ye shall be my witnesses." That is the primary task of every Christian. It is important to remember that a Christian must witness for Christ by his life as well as by his lips.

YOUTH: You are very much in agreement with your friend Peter— only he used the word "evangelist" instead of "witness." Let me ask you the same question that I asked Peter. Why is it important for every Christian to be an evangelist or witness for Christ?

JOHN: I think I know how Peter answered that question. I'll suggest a few additional reasons why it is imperative that every Christian be an evangelist. *Men, women, and youth have no hope of eternal life unless they are won to a vital, saving faith in Jesus Christ.* "For God so loved the world, that he gave his only begotten Son, that whosoever believeth in him should not perish, but have everlasting life. He that believeth on the Son hath everlasting life: and he that believeth not the Son shall not see life; but the wrath of God abideth on him."

YOUTH: I've read those words many times in your Gospel, John, but I never realized their real significance before. What a responsibility this places upon those of us who are followers of Christ!

JOHN: You're right, my friend. Christ is central in God's plan of salvation. There is no other way. Jesus himself said: "I am the way, and the truth, and the life: no one comes to the Father, but by me."

Here's another reason why every Christian should share his faith: *Men need Jesus in order to live an abundant, satisfying life on earth.* The eternal life which Christ offers is not a promised blessing for the distant future. It is a practical way of life for the twentieth century, in which you and your friends are living. This truth has special significance for young people. Most of their earthly life is still before them. Through a vital faith in Jesus Christ they can discover the thrill and adventure of the abundant life.

Let me mention one more reason for sharing the Christian message. *A Christian must tell the story of Christ to others in order that his own faith may grow and continue to be vital and meaningful.* People who fail to share their faith gradually lose the radiance and vitality of their Christian discipleship. Our Lord repeatedly stated this basic law of life: "He that saveth his life shall lose it; and he that loseth his life for my sake shall find it." This is my final word before I quickly make my way to the Eternal City: lose yourself in serving others and in sharing your faith, and you will find life—life at its glorious best! (JOHN *leaves quickly.*)

YOUTH: He is gone! Before I could even thank him! (*Thoughtfully*) Evangelism! I never dreamed it was so important! Sharing with others! I have plenty to share now, that's certain! I'll get started right now at this business of being an evangelist! (*Exit* YOUTH.)

HYMN: "O Zion, Haste" or "Fling Out the Banner! Let It Float"

PERIOD OF SILENT PRAYER (as the young people dedicate their lives to the all-important task of being witnesses for Christ)

CLOSING PRAYER AND BENEDICTION:

O God, help us to feel within the innermost depths of our being, the urgency and importance of sharing the Christian message with others. May we realize that our Christian faith is a priceless possession and that we dare not withhold it selfishly from other people. Implant within our minds the truth that men are without hope of eternal life unless they hear and accept thy message of salvation. Increase our faith, O God, and enable us to share the good news of the abundant life with those about us and with men and women of other lands.

"Now may the God of peace who brought again from the dead our Lord Jesus, the great shepherd of the sheep, by the blood of the eternal covenant, equip you with everything good that you may do his will, working in you that which is pleasing in his sight, through Jesus Christ; to whom be glory for ever and ever." AMEN.[3]

21. Reaching Others for Christ

Prelude: "I Love to Tell the Story"

Call to Worship:

> The voice of God is calling
>   Its summons unto men;
> As once He spake in Zion,
>   So now He speaks again.
> Whom shall I send to succor
>   My people in their need?
> Whom shall I send to loosen
>   The bonds of shame and greed?
>
> I hear my people crying
>   In cot and mine and slum;
> No field or mart is silent,
>   No city street is dumb.
> I see my people falling
>   In darkness and despair.
> Whom shall I send to shatter
>   The fetters which they bear?
>
> We heed, O Lord, Thy summons,
>   And answer: Here are we!
> Send us upon Thine errand,
>   Let us Thy servants be.
> Our strength is dust and ashes
>   Our years a passing hour:
> But Thou canst use our weakness
>   To magnify Thy power.

> From ease and plenty save us;
>   From pride of place absolve;
> Purge us of low desire;
>   Lift us to high resolve;
> Take us, and make us holy;
>   Teach us Thy will and way.
> Speak, and behold! we answer;
>   Command, and we obey! [1]
>   —JOHN HAYNES HOLMES

PRAYER:

May each one of us, our Father, hear thy clear call to service in thy kingdom. Make us aware of the needs of men, women, and youth in our own land and in other parts of the world. Help us to show our concern for those who are hungry and homeless by sharing with them a part of our own abundance. Above all, may we feel a sense of responsibility toward those who have not experienced thy forgiveness and thy comforting presence in their lives. Show us ways in which we can make known thy message of love to others. AMEN.

HYMN: "Ye Servants of God, Your Master Proclaim" or "I Love to Tell the Story"

SCRIPTURE:

And Jesus went about all the cities and villages, teaching in their synagogues and preaching the gospel of the kingdom, and healing every disease and every infirmity. When he saw the crowds, he had compassion for them, because they were harassed and helpless, like sheep without a shepherd. Then he said to his disciples, "The harvest is plentiful, but the laborers are few; pray therefore the Lord of the harvest to send out laborers into his harvest." [2]

POEM: (As the poem is read, the pianist may play softly "O Master, Let Me Walk with Thee.")

> Use me, God, in Thy great harvest field,
> Which stretcheth far and wide like a wide sea;
> The gatherers are so few; I fear the precious yield

153

Will suffer loss. Oh, find a place for me!
A place where best the strength I have will tell:
It may be one the older toilers shun;
Be it a wide or narrow place, 'tis well
So that the work it holds be only done.[3]

—CHRISTINA ROSSETTI

HYMN: "O Master, Let Me Walk with Thee" or "Hark, the Voice of Jesus Calling"

LEADER: [4]

Many of us, as Christian young people, feel that it is important to share our faith with others, but we don't know how to go about it. We don't know what methods to use or what plan to follow. It is possible for young people to find the Christian life so joyous and challenging that it becomes a natural and important part of their conversation with their friends. Someone has said that if young people desire to win other youth to Christ, they must be natural, enthusiastic, persistent, and kind. We will see these qualities demonstrated in an informal skit. In the first scene we discover three Christian young people— Bill, Dick, and Jane—talking together informally at Jane's house on a certain Sunday afternoon. The second scene also takes place at Jane's house, exactly a week later. The third scene is the same; the time is about a month later.

DRAMATIC PRESENTATION:

AN EVANGELISTIC EXPERIMENT

SCENE I:
BILL: That was a real sermon we heard in church this morning.
DICK: Well, yes, if you mean by a real sermon, the kind that bothers your conscience the rest of the day.
JANE: Those are my sentiments, too, Dick. When Mr. Thomas told about a small group of young people winning fourteen other young people to Christ—well, I began to realize we haven't been taking our Christian discipleship very seriously.
BILL: You're right, Jane. We have a swell youth group. Most of them

will come out for our meeting tonight, and we'll have fun together. But it's almost exactly the same group that we had a year ago. I don't think we've won a single young person to Christ all year.

DICK: A few young people have united with the church as a result of Mr. Thomas' efforts.

JANE: Yes, but they haven't come to many of our youth activities, and we haven't gone out of our way to make them feel welcome. I'm afraid we're a pretty self-centered bunch, interested chiefly in having a good time.

BILL: I have an idea. Why couldn't the three of us demonstrate the importance of youth evangelism?

DICK: How can we do it?

BILL: By each one of us winning a friend to Christ.

JANE: It's a good idea, Bill, but I wouldn't know how to begin.

DICK: I think it's worth a try anyway. I'm all for it, Bill.

BILL: I'm going to try to win Jack Johnson. We've played basketball together, and I know him well. I heard him say he didn't go to any church.

DICK: That'll be great, Bill. He'll be a swell new member for our group. I'll try to win Ralph Green. He's had a rough time of it this past year since his father was in that auto accident.

JANE: You fellows are getting a head start on me! I can't think of a single prospect right off, but I'll find one!

BILL: By the way, we're having a youth fellowship social next Friday evening. Wouldn't that be a good time to help our prospects get acquainted with the rest of the gang?

DICK: A swell idea! How about it, Jane?

JANE: I'll have my prospect there! And, listen, what do you think of this? I'm on the committee to plan the social. Why couldn't we sing some hymns at the close of the party and have several young people tell what Christ and the church mean to them—a sharing session like we had at camp last summer?

DICK: That sounds great, Jane. We'll have to take our prospects to the church services next Sunday too. Hearing Mr. Thomas will help them understand the meaning of the Christian life.

BILL: I think I'll drop around and see Jack this afternoon. He might be able to go to church with me this evening.

DICK: A good idea, Bill! I'll look up Ralph this afternoon too.

JANE: You two are determined to get ahead of me in this project. But I'll catch up with you! I'll have a good prospect out for the party Friday night.

DICK: A good-looking prospect, did you say?

JANE: Dick, I'm surprised at you! Outward appearances are strictly secondary—especially in an evangelistic endeavor!

DICK: (*as he and* BILL *rise to leave*): I know it, Jane, but it's still not such a bad idea—your bringing a good-looking prospect, I mean!

JANE: I'll see what I can do for you!

DICK *and* BILL: So long. We'll see you tonight at church.

JANE: Bye, now.

SCENE II (*one week later*):

JANE (*rises to greet* BILL *and* DICK): I sort of thought you'd drop around so we could talk over our evangelistic experiment. We've gotten off to a good start, haven't we?

BILL: Having three new young people at the party Friday helped to make the evening a success.

DICK: Jane's prospect helped especially! You were very obliging, Jane, in the prospect you chose! Seriously, I think it was the best social we've ever had. The sharing session at the end was tops.

JANE: I thought you'd appreciate Kathy. She has the "outward appearances" and a lot of inner worth besides.

DICK: You're right, Jane. She seems very interested in the church too. You'll probably be the first to win your prospect after all.

JANE: I had a wonderful talk with Kathy yesterday. It's the first time I ever really shared my Christian faith with anyone. It was a grand experience, and my own faith means more to me than ever before.

BILL: I know what you mean, Jane. I had a good talk with Jack after the social. He was impressed by the testimonies that were given Friday night, but I'm afraid he feels rather self-conscious in our group. He told me that he had never attended church regularly and that he knew very little about the Bible or Christian teachings. I tried to tell him about our Christian beliefs. I don't know whether it helped him much, but it really gave me a lift to share what little I know.

DICK: You two are really going to town with your prospects. I tried to talk to Ralph about the Christian life, but he had very little to say. He said he had a good time at the party, but added that he was afraid he didn't exactly "fit in" with the group.

JANE: Maybe he felt self-conscious too—for a different reason than Jack. His family has been very hard pressed financially, and perhaps he doesn't realize that in a group of Christian young people, clothes and cars and television sets are not all-important. We'll have to help both of these fellows realize that they have a real contribution to make to our group.

DICK: You've given me an idea, Jane. Ralph makes swell posters. I'm going to ask him to make a few to advertise our youth banquet next month. I'm in charge of publicity for the banquet, and he could help me a lot. In fact, I'm going over to see him about it right now.

BILL: I'll go along with you, Dick. So long, Jane. See you tonight.

JANE: So long. And good luck with Ralph!

SCENE III (*about a month later*):

JANE (*rises to greet* BILL): Come in, Bill. Sunday afternoon seems to be a good time to check up on our evangelistic experiment. Where's Dick?

BILL: I don't know. I stopped by his house, but he wasn't at home. This experiment, as you call it, is one of the most worth-while experiences I've ever had.

JANE: That goes for me, too, Bill. Wasn't it a thrill this morning when Kathy and Jack went forward at the close of the service? I'm so glad you thought of this idea, Bill. It isn't nearly as difficult as I thought it would be. In fact, it's been such fun winning one, that I've already spoken to several other girls about coming to our church.

BILL: The idea is working out far better than I had dared to hope, but I'm afraid Dick is getting discouraged about Ralph. Ralph was in church this morning—for the first time in several weeks.

JANE: He made the posters for the youth banquet, though, and they're really good. I heard several young people tell him this morning how nice the posters are. Maybe he's beginning to realize that we need him in our group.

BILL: Have you noticed, Jane, that the members of our youth department are getting more friendly and more interested in other young

157

people? Several of them have started bringing friends of theirs to church.

JANE: I've noticed it, Bill. I think our evangelistic experiment is bringing new life to the entire group. There's someone at the door. Maybe it's Dick. (*She starts to the door.*)

DICK (*hurrying in excitedly*): I have good news for you! I've just been at Ralph's home and had a wonderful talk with him. It's the first time he's been willing to talk about the Christian life. He said he feels sure now that we really want him in our group. He also told me that he wants to be a Christian and a member of our church.

BILL: That's great news, Dick! Jane and I were just talking about our evangelistic experiment, as she calls it. This makes it a hundred per cent success in its initial tryout, but, of course, this is only the beginning.

DICK: That's right, Bill. There's no stopping now! Ralph was just telling me about his cousin whom he is sure we can win to Christ and the church. I've also thought of several other prospects.

BILL: Mr. Thomas told me this morning that he'd be glad to lead a series of discussions for our entire group on how to reach young people for Christ.

JANE: That would help all of us, Bill. After receiving instructions from Mr. Thomas, perhaps our whole group can go out in teams of two to do evangelistic visitation. I'd like for our entire gang to get in on this experiment of ours.

DICK: That should be our goal, Jane. Let's pray and work that it may be realized.

BILL: I'm glad you mentioned prayer, Dick. It seems to me that if our evangelistic experiment continues to be successful, we must spend more time in prayer.

JANE: I've been thinking of the same thing. It's almost time for us to go to church. Before we go, why don't we spend a few minutes in prayer for all the members of our youth fellowship and for all the young people outside the church whom we should win to Christ.

SOLO: "Saviour, Thy Dying Love" (Use the "Amen" at the end.)
(*During the solo* JANE, BILL, *and* DICK *bow their heads in silent prayer.*)

CLOSING PRAYER AND BENEDICTION (by the leader):

Our Father, help us to be eager to share our knowledge of Christ with our friends and with others who do not know the joys of Christian discipleship. May we be friendly to those who are lonely, patient with those who are thoughtless, kind to those who are discouraged and distressed. Grant that we may be humble and teachable, realizing that we enjoy the blessings of the Christian life, not because of our own merit, but because of thy love and compassion for us.

"Now may our Lord Jesus Christ himself, and God our Father, who loved us and gave us eternal comfort and good hope through grace, comfort your hearts and establish them in every good work and word." AMEN.[5]

22. Discovering Our Lifework

To the Leader:

This meeting on vocations makes use of three check lists which are to be filled out by the young people who are present. Prepare enough copies of the check lists so that each young person will have a copy of each one. Be sure to have sufficient pencils available. These check lists are not to be signed or given to the leader. They are for the use of the individuals who check them. No one else will read them. Make this plain to the young people, and they will be more willing to check the lists accurately and honestly.

Prelude: "Give of Your Best to the Master"

Call to Worship:

> Let me but do my work from day to day
>> In field or forest, at the desk or loom,
>> In roaring market-place or tranquil room;
> Let me but find it in my heart to say,
> When vagrant wishes beckon me astray,
>> "This is my work; my blessing, not my doom;
>> Of all who live, I am the one by whom
> This work can best be done in the right way."
>
> Then shall I see it not too great, nor small,
>> To suit my spirit and to prove my powers;
>> Then shall I cheerful greet the labouring hours,
> And cheerful turn, when the long shadows fall
> At eventide, to play and love and rest,
> Because I know for me my work is best.[1]
>> —Henry van Dyke

PRAYER:

We are grateful, our Father, for the health of body and mind which enables us to work. We are thankful for the talents and abilities which you have given to each one of us. Help us to discover and develop these abilities and to use them in the type of work in which we can be of greatest service to mankind. In the name of Christ, our Master and Lord. AMEN.

HYMN: "Give of Your Best to the Master" or "God of Grace and God of Glory"

LEADER:

The choice of a vocation is one of the most important decisions any of us will make throughout our span of life. This decision determines the way in which we will spend approximately one third of the hours of each day for the remainder of our lives. This decision determines to a large extent the contribution which each one of us will make to society and to the world. The choice of a vocation has a great influence upon the contacts we will have with our fellow men. It has a great influence upon the attitudes, habits, and personality traits we will develop during our lifetime.

Because of the unusual importance of choosing a life vocation, young people should give much earnest thought to this decision. A helpful way to begin is for each young person to discover and analyze his own mental and physical assets. (Distribute a copy of the check list on mental and physical assets to each young person. Allow time for the young people to check the desired information.)

DISCOVERING OUR MENTAL AND PHYSICAL ASSETS:
(Check the answers which apply to you.)

I. Mental Assets
   1. Through the years have your grades in school been: Fair ——— Good ——— Very Good ———
   2. Do you like to read: Comics ——— Light fiction ——— Biography ——— Travel books ——— Scientific books ——— Great literary classics ———
   3. Through the years has your interets in schoolwork been: Slight ——— Average ——— Very great ———

4. Do you enjoy study, writing, research, or other concentrated mental effort: Occasionally ———— Quite frequently ———— Very frequently ————

II. Physical Assets   Yes   No

1. Do you have plenty of energy for work and play?   ———— ————

2. Are you reasonably free from headaches, nervous tension, and feelings of fatigue?   ———— ————

3. Are your eyes in good condition?   ———— ————

4. Is your hearing good?   ———— ————

5. Is your speech free from defect?   ———— ————

6. Can you distinguish between various colors?   ———— ————

LEADER:

Several comments should be made regarding mental and physical qualifications for various jobs. As a rule, only those capable of concentrated mental effort should consider the following vocations: medicine, ministry, law, teaching, journalism, physics, astronomy, scientific research, and diplomatic service. There are certain vocations, such as the following, which demand robust health and physical endurance: nursing, medicine, missionary work, journalism, dramatics, aviation, mining, forestry. Certain jobs require excellent eyesight: library work, research, engraving, drafting, dressmaking. In other jobs, hearing is of great importance: telephone operating, stenographic work, music, etc. In still other vocations, speech is of utmost importance: ministry, teaching, law, dramatics, politics, diplomatic service, salesmanship. The accurate discerning of colors is important in interior decorating, dress-designing, painting, and other forms of art work.

A serious consideration of our mental and physical assets will give us valuable guidance as we make decisions regarding our lifework. Another way of obtaining help in choosing a vocation is to discover our interests and aptitudes.

(Distribute copies of the following check list. Allow time for the young people to write the desired information.)

DISCOVERING OUR INTERESTS AND APTITUDES

(Rate the following interests and aptitudes 1-10, according to your personal interest in them. Place "1" before the item in which you are most interested, "2" before the item which rates second in interest to you, etc.)

  a. Artistic aptitudes (painting, dramatics, music, etc.)
  b. Domestic science (cooking, sewing, interior decorating, etc.)
  c. Social aptitudes (interest in working with people)
  d. Public speaking (before either small or large groups)
  e. Mechanical aptitudes (ability to work with one's hands)
  f. Mathematics
  g. Science (geology, chemistry, biology, etc.)
  h. Literary aptitudes (writing, journalism, etc.)
  i. Agriculture (farming, soils, conservation, etc.)
  j. Business (salesmanship, business management, etc.)

LEADER:

The interests that you have rated highest represent the areas that you should investigate carefully for vocational ideas. You should remember, however, that you undoubtedly have hidden aptitudes that you have not yet discovered. It would probably be wise to investigate several vocational fields in addition to the ones which you have rated highest on your list. You may watch your own rating as vocational possibilities are suggested for each of these areas of interest.

(The leader may desire to have the following vocational suggestions written on a blackboard and to read the lists from the board.)

Artistic aptitudes: Only those with outstanding artistic abilities should aspire to become professional artists. There are related vocations, however, which provide many openings for young people with ability along artistic lines: photography; industrial designing; teaching in various artistic fields; administrative work in the field of music, dramatics, etc.

Domestic science: There are many job possibilities for young people interested in domestic science: teaching in this field, dietetics, dress-designing, dressmaking, selling, advertising and buying of clothing, selling and advertising of foods, interior decorating, domestic service. Interest and training in this field provide help for the all-important task of homemaking.

Social aptitudes: Here are a few of the job possibilities for young people interested in working with people: teaching (from preschool to college), social work, nursing, missionary work, Christian education, ministry, personnel work, medicine, dentistry, salesmanship, political or diplomatic service, advertising, working in a store or shop.

Public speaking: Interest in public speaking points toward the following vocations: ministry, law, teaching, political or diplomatic career.

Mechanical aptitudes: Many vocations are open to young people with mechanical ability: engineering; work in a machine shop, inventor's laboratory, garage, or repair shop; work as a carpenter, mason, or other skilled craftsman; operating machine tools; drafting.

Mathematics: If young people are interested in mathematics, they should investigate the following vocations: engineering, surveying, astronomy, banking, insurance, bookkeeping, accounting, statistical work, market research, or business administration.

Science: Here are a few of the vocational possibilities for young people with scientific interest and ability: medicine, physics, biology, botany, geology, chemistry, scientific research, laboratory technician, teaching in any of these fields.

Literary aptitudes: Young people with literary aptitudes should investigate the following vocational opportunities: library work, writing (including writing for religious publishing houses), editorial work, secretarial work, journalism, teaching literature or composition.

Agriculture: Interest in agriculture suggests the following vocational opportunities: farming, dairying, agricultural experimentation and research, landscape gardening, forestry, conservation, government work in the field of agriculture.

Business: Interest in the field of business points toward the following job opportunities: salesmanship, advertising, store management, buying, wholesaling, manufacturing, executive jobs in business.

LEADER:

In addition to analyzing our mental and physical assets and our interests and aptitudes, it is helpful to discover our attitudes toward vocations in general. What are your attitudes toward getting a job? What factors are most important to you in the choice of your lifework? (Distribute copies of the following list. Allow time for the young people to write the desired information.)

DISCOVERING OUR ATTITUDES TOWARD VOCATIONS

(Rate the following factors according to their importance in the choice of a vocation. Rate the factor which you consider most important "1," the next most important factor "2," etc.)

    a. One's interest in and enthusiasm for a particular vocation
    b. One's aptitude or qualifications for a particular vocation
    c. The amount of money one can earn
    d. The nearness of the job to parents and friends
    e. The advice of trained Christian counselors
    f. The earnest seeking of God's will
    g. The supply of trained workers in various vocations
    h. The service one can render to humanity
    i. The wishes and suggestions of one's family
    j. The prestige and honor that a vocation offers
    k. The type of people with whom one will be associated
    l. The length of working hours
    m. The surroundings and working conditions of the vocation

LEADER:

What factors do you think are most important in the choosing of a vocation? Why? What factors are of least importance? Why?

One group of young people marked this list and discussed the importance of the various factors. They decided that "a," "b," "f," and "h" are the factors that are most important in the choice of a vocation. They felt that factors "c," "e," "g," "k," and "m" are next in importance, and that "d," "i," "j," and "l" are of least importance.

How do the conclusions of the above group compare with your own ratings? In what ways do you agree with these young people? In what ways do you disagree?

SCRIPTURE: Matt. 20:25-28; 7:7-8

LEADER:

These scripture passages give us help and inspiration as we make decisions regarding the choice of a vocation. God's Word tells us plainly that those who are truly great are the ones who serve their fellow men. Jesus said, "Whoever would be great among you must be your servant. . . . Even as the Son of man came not to be served but to serve, and to give his life as a ransom for many." Jesus also said, "Ask, and it shall be given you; seek, and you shall find." Let us earnestly seek the will of God in the important decisions we must make regarding our life-work. Let us pray that each one of us may discover God's will and way for our lives.

PERIOD OF SILENT PRAYER (During the period of silent prayer the pianist may play softly "Have Thine Own Way, Lord.")

CLOSING PRAYER:

Dear God, may we open our hearts and minds to receive your guidance during these moments of quiet meditation. Give us insight and wisdom regarding the choice of our vocations. May we desire above all else to choose that type of work whereby we can be of greatest help in advancing your kingdom upon the earth. We pray in the name of Christ, our Leader and Lord. AMEN.

23. Using Our Lives for Christ
(Life Vocations)

PRELUDE: "Finlandia" by Sibelius

CALL TO WORSHIP:

> Our faith is in the Christ who walks
>> With men today, in street and mart;
> The constant Friend who thinks and talks
>> With those who seek him with the heart.

> His gospel calls for living men
>> With singing blood and minds alert;
> Strong men, who fall to rise again,
>> Who strive and bleed, with courage girt.

> We serve no God whose work is done,
>> Who rests within his firmament:
> Our God, his labors but begun,
>> Toils evermore, with power unspent.

> God was and is and e'er shall be;
>> Christ lived and loved—and loves us still;
> And man goes forward, proud and free,
>> God's present purpose to fulfill.[1]
>> —THOMAS CURTIS CLARK

PRAYER:

Our earnest desire, O God, is to discover your plan and purpose for our lives. We need your help and guidance as we choose our lifework.

Lead us along the path you would have us follow, and may the decisions we make each day be in accordance with your will. In the name of Christ. AMEN.

HYMN: "Who Is on the Lord's Side?" or "Stand Up, Stand Up for Jesus"

SCRIPTURE:

Blessed are those who are persecuted for righteousness' sake, for theirs is the kingdom of heaven. Blessed are you when men revile you and persecute you and utter all kinds of evil against you falsely on my account. Rejoice and be glad, for your reward is great in heaven, for so men persecuted the prophets who were before you.[2]

POEM:

God hath not promised
Skies always blue,
Flower-strewn pathways
All our lives through;
God hath not promised
Sun without rain,
Joy without sorrow,
Peace without pain.
But God hath promised
Strength for the day,
Rest for the labor,
Light for the way,
Grace for the trials,
Help from above,
Unfailing sympathy,
Undying love.[3]
—ANNIE JOHNSON FLINT

SCRIPTURE:

He who loves father or mother more than me is not worthy of me; and he who loves son or daughter more than me is not worthy of me;

[3] "What God Hath Promised." Copyright. Reproduced by permission. Evangelical Publishers, Toronto, Canada.

and he who does not take his cross and follow me is not worthy of me. He who finds his life will lose it, and he who loses his life for my sake will find it.[4]

POEM:

Purge me, O God
With Thy refining fires!
Nor heavy rest Thy blame,
When flesh shrinks from the flame!

Sweep my soul clean
By cleansing winds!
Nor let me fret at storm and stress,
Whose purpose is to bless!

Give me a task too big,
Too hard for human hands.
Then I shall come at length
To lean on Thee;
And leaning, find my strength.[5]
—WILBUR HUMPHREY FOWLER

LEADER:

Give me a task too big,
Too hard for human hands.

These two lines express the spirit of Christian discipleship. A true follower of the Master does not look for the easy job, the snap course, the meaningless honor. He is not interested in short cuts, in following the line of least resistance, in getting something for nothing. The Christian disciple is eager and alert. He is asking, seeking, knocking at the doors of opportunity and service. He is interested in expanding his mind so that it may take in more of truth and knowledge. He is eager to enlarge his soul in order that it may contain more love, more courage, more vision.

Christian discipleship is no easy, sugar-coated experience. It is a life of high endeavor and daring adventure. It is not a pastime for timid souls. The Christian life demands all that we have of faith, courage, loyalty, and allegiance. It demands more than we have in our own strength. Christ has called us to tasks that are far beyond our human power of accomplishment. But with each task he gives sufficient strength for those who are ready to draw upon his unlimited resources. We must earnestly seek Christ's plan for our lives and follow his leadership each step of the way as we strive to fulfill his lofty purposes in our daily experiences.

HYMN: "Rise Up, O Man of God" or "Faith of Our Fathers"

A TRUE STORY:

MAKING EACH DAY COUNT FOR GOD

When William Borden enrolled as a student at Yale University, his friends knew that he came from a wealthy family, but they did not realize the extent of his wealth. The year before he entered the university, Bill's parents had given him a trip around the world. Although only sixteen years of age, he, accompanied by a young man several years older, spent an entire year visiting many countries, including Japan, China, India, Egypt, Palestine, Greece, Italy, France, and England. During this journey Bill dedicated his life to God as a missionary.

Bill Borden entered Yale University with a determination to begin active service for Christ immediately. Charles Campbell became his closest friend at the university, and these two young men spent time praying together in Bill's room each morning before breakfast. They invited other fellows to join them, and before long the group became so large that it had to be divided. As a result of this demonstration of the importance of prayer, other prayer groups were started among the students.

From the time that he entered Yale University, Bill Borden quietly and humbly tried to win fellow students to a belief in Christ. At first it was difficult for him, but Bill felt that if he was to be Christ's missionary, he should begin sharing his faith on the college campus. He decided to have a Bible-study group in his room each Tuesday evening. To this group he invited many of his friends who were not Christians.

A large number of them, even those who had once openly opposed Christianity, became earnest followers of Christ.

Bill Borden was a sociable person who made friends easily. He was also a very good student. During his junior year at college he was elected president of the Yale chapter of Phi Beta Kappa, the highest scholastic organization in America. He was interested in all types of sports, especially football, wrestling, and track. Sailing was one of his favorite hobbies, and during summer vacations he took many friends for long trips on his sailboat. Even during these pleasure trips, Bill gathered his friends together each morning for Bible-study and prayer.

In spite of all these many interests and activities, Bill Borden discovered other tasks to do for God. He went to the poor section of New Haven and established the Yale Hope Mission, where men could learn about the love of God and get a new start in life. He not only paid the expenses, but also gave much time and thought to the work and program of the mission. Frequently he spoke at the evening services, telling in simple words what Christ meant to his life. He loved the destitute men who came to the mission, and often stayed after the service to talk and pray with them in order that they might know Christ and walk in the Christian way of life.

After graduating from Yale, William Borden went to Princeton Seminary. He had studied carefully the needs on the various mission fields of the world and had decided to be a missionary among the Mohammedans in northwest China. This was perhaps the most remote and difficult field of missionary service. Practically none of the people in this area of China had heard the gospel message.

In addition to his studies at the seminary and numerous Christian activities and projects, Bill Borden had much of the responsibility of looking after the business interests of his family, especially after his father's death. He exercised great care in the way he spent his money, spending very little on himself, but giving generously to dozens of missionary projects and other Christian enterprises. He felt that not only his time but also his money was an important trust that should be used for God's glory.

After graduating from the seminary, he made arrangements to go to Cairo, Egypt, for language-study before beginning his missionary efforts in China. The last three months in this country he spent not with his family and close friends, but at thirty different colleges, challenging hundreds of students with the need for recruits for foreign-mission service. He was able to secure passage for Egypt on a ship leaving December 17. Not even waiting to spend the Christmas vacation at home, he sailed for Egypt one week after completing his tour of the colleges. Using each day for God was all important to William Borden. He had a divine sense of urgency about proclaiming the message of Christ and advancing his kingdom upon the earth.

Arriving in Cairo, Bill immediately began intensive study of the Arabic language. He helped spread the message of Christ by handing out tracts to the Mohammedans and other non-Christians of Cairo. He organized and supervised the distribution of tracts in the Arabic language to the 800,000 inhabitants of Cairo. Such a project had never been carried out before, but Bill Borden accomplished it several weeks after arriving in the city.

How wise William Borden was to spend every day in significant service for God! If he had waited until he was fully trained to accomplish his great work for the kingdom of God, he would never have done it at all. He had been in Egypt only three months when he contracted a serious disease and died. He lived only twenty-five years, but he filled those brief years with such unselfish service for Christ that he has been a blessing to millions of people. The story of his life, translated into many languages, has made its way around the world.

It was only after Bill's death that his friends realized that he was a millionaire. His will provided that every dollar of his money should be given to Christian work in America and abroad. One of his Princeton classmates made this significant statement about him: "No one would have known from Borden's life . . . that he was a millionaire, but no one could have helped knowing that he was a Christian." [6]

LEADER:

We should desire above all else to make each day of our lives count for God. Not one of us has a lease on life. We do not know how many days we will have in which to make our contribution to mankind. We should seek God's guidance as we face the tasks and responsibilities of everyday living. We should also look to him for leadership as we choose our life vocation, praying definitely for his help as we make this important decision. As Christian youth, we should give special consideration to the wide variety of church vocations which are now open to young people. Full-time Christian workers are needed today in many fields, including medicine, nursing, teaching, preaching, agriculture, journalism, art, music, secretarial work, administrative work, chaplaincy, youth work, as well as many other vocational opportunities.

No one with your exact combination of capabilities has ever lived before or will ever live after you. You can do a work for Christ that no one else can do and that will never be done unless you do it. God has a plan for your life which will use your talents and abilities for the advancement of his kingdom. Let us pray that each one of us will discover God's plan and purpose for our lives.

POEM:

> Lord, let me not die until I've done for Thee
> My earthly work, whatever it may be.
> Call me not hence with mission unfulfilled;
> Let me not leave my space of ground untilled;
> Impress this truth upon me that not one
> Can do my portion that I leave undone.
>
> —ANONYMOUS

SOLO: "We Would Be Building" (tune: "Finlandia" by Sibelius)

> We would be building; temples still undone
> O'er crumbling walls their crosses scarcely lift
> Waiting till love can raise the broken stone,
> And hearts creative bridge the human rift;
> We would be building, Master, let Thy plan
> Reveal the life that God would give to man.
>
> Teach us to build; upon the solid rock
> We set the dream that hardens into deed,
> Ribbed with the steel that time and change doth mock,
> Th' unfailing purpose of our noblest creed;
> Teach us to build; O Master, lend us sight
> To see the towers gleaming in the light.

173

O keep us building, Master; may our hands
  Ne'er falter when the dream is in our hearts,
When to our ears there come divine commands
  And all the pride of sinful will departs;
We build with Thee, O grant enduring worth
  Until the heav'nly Kingdom comes on earth.[7]

—PURD E. DEITZ

CLOSING PRAYER:

We are thankful, O Christ, for the challenge of working with you in the building of your kingdom on earth. May we perform our daily tasks faithfully, even though we do not know your complete plan for our lives. If you desire any of us to enter full-time Christian service, may we have the insight to hear your call and the courage to answer it without delay. Help us to make each day count for you and for the advancement of your kingdom, realizing that no one else can do the work that we leave undone. AMEN.

24. The Meaning of Christian Friendship

PRELUDE: "Rejoice, Ye Pure in Heart"

CALL TO WORSHIP:

> Thou God of all whose spirit moves
>> From pole to silent pole;
> Whose purpose binds the starry spheres
>> In one stupendous whole;
> Whose life, like light, is freely poured
>> On all men 'neath the sun;
> To Thee we lift our hearts, and pray
>> That Thou wilt make us one.
>
> One in the patient company
>> Of those who heed Thy will,
> And stedfastly pursue the way
>> Of Thy commandments still;
> One in the holy fellowship
>> Of those who challenge wrong,
> And lift the spirit's sword to shield
>> The weak against the strong.
>
> One in the truth that makes men free,
>> The faith that makes men brave;
> One in the love that suffers long
>> To seek, and serve, and save;
> One in the vision of Thy peace,
>> The kingdom yet to be—

When Thou shalt be the God of all,
And all be one in Thee.[1]
　　　—JOHN HAYNES HOLMES

HYMN: "In Christ There Is No East or West" or "Lift up Our Hearts, O King of Kings"

PRAYER:
Our Father, we thank thee that Christian friendship surmounts the barriers of race, class, and nationality. Help us to experience the joy of fellowship with thee and with friends who share our love for thee. Refine our attitudes and purify our motives so that we may understand more clearly than ever before the real meaning of friendship. In the name of Christ, the great Friend of all mankind. AMEN.

READER I:
Christian friendship has as its foundation a common love and loyalty to Jesus Christ. A love of Jesus, mutually shared, always brings friends closer to one another. When young people work and worship together in the church, their friendships become more worth while and meaningful. Friends of Jesus are better friends of one another because of their friendship with the Master.

READER II:
You are my friends if you do what I command you. No longer do I call you servants, for the servant does not know what his master is doing; but I have called you friends, for all that I have heard from my Father I have made known to you.[2]

READER I:
Christianity sets high standards for friendship. Christian love, which is a feeling of genuine appreciation and good will toward another person, is the most important aspect of friendship. Jesus taught that his own love for us should be the standard of our love for others.

READER II:
A new commandment I give to you, that you love one another; even as I have loved you, that you also love one another. By this all men will know that you are my disciples, if you have love for one another.[3]

READER I:

Christian friendship thrives on a spirit of humility and forgiveness. Christian young people feel their need of help and forgiveness from Christ and are therefore charitable and forgiving toward one another. They do not return evil for evil, but constantly try to overcome evil with good.

READER II:

Then Peter came up and said to him, "Lord, how often shall my brother sin against me, and I forgive him? As many as seven times?" Jesus said to him, "I do not say to you seven times, but seventy times seven."

For if you forgive men their trespasses, your heavenly Father also will forgive you; but if you do not forgive men their trespasses, neither will your Father forgive your trespasses.[4]

READER I:

A Christian friend is not overbearing and conceited. He does not set himself up as a judge of others. He is aware of his own faults and does not magnify the weaknesses of his friends. He does not gossip about the real or imagined sins of other people.

READER II:

"Judge not, that you be not judged. For with the judgment you pronounce you will be judged, and the measure you give will be the measure you get. Why do you see the speck that is in your brother's eye, but do not notice the log that is in your own eye? Or how can you say to your brother, 'Let me take the speck out of your eye,' when there is the log in your own eye? You hypocrite, first take the log out of your own eye, and then you will see clearly to take the speck out of your brother's eye."[5]

READER I:

A Christian friend is dependable and trustworthy. He is loyal to his friends at all times and under all circumstances. A true friend is not "two faced"; he does not talk about a person when his back is turned. He is not a fair-weather friend, forgetting to be of help when problems and difficulties arise. A Christian friend rejoices when joy or honor comes to another; he is genuinely concerned when others experience sorrow or failure.

READER II:

Let love be genuine; hate what is evil, hold fast to what is good; love one another with brotherly affection; outdo one another in showing honor. Bless those who persecute you; bless and do not curse them. Rejoice with those who rejoice, weep with those who weep. Do not be overcome by evil, but overcome evil with good.[6]

READER I:

Christian friendship is enhanced and enriched by thoughts that are uplifting, lofty, and beautiful. A Christian friend realizes that he has the responsibility of keeping his mind and body pure and clean.

READER II:

Do you not know that your body is a temple of the Holy Spirit within you, which you have from God? You are not your own; you were bought with a price. So glorify God in your body. Finally, brethren, whatever is true, whatever is honorable, whatever is just, whatever is pure, whatever is lovely, whatever is gracious, if there is any excellence, if there is anything worthy of praise, think about these things.[7]

READER I:

Christian friendship is stimulating and worth while. It results in more "honest-to-goodness" fun than any other type of friendship. And the fun that Christian young people experience together is still fun when it is discussed at school or work the next day. There are no hangovers and no regrets. Christian friendship is one of life's most joyous experiences because it is based on fellowship—not only with human friends, but also with Christ.

READER II:

If you keep my commandments, you will abide in my love, just as I have kept my Father's commandments and abide in his love. These things I have spoken to you, that my joy may be in you, and that your joy may be full.[8]

DRAMATIC PRESENTATION:
MARY MAKES A DISCOVERY [9]

(MARY *and* BILL *are seated in living-room chairs, talking together informally.*)

BILL (*thoughtfully*): I've been thinking a lot lately—about friendship.

MARY (*surprised*): Friendship? Rather an unusual subject for contemplation, isn't it?

BILL: I don't know that it is. I don't see anything unusual about it.

MARY: Oh, Bill, you're always up in the clouds! Why don't you stick to practical matters?

BILL: This is a practical matter. We have a lot of friends, don't we? And they aren't up in the clouds either!

MARY: That's for certain! I haven't noticed any of them sprouting wings as yet! (*More seriously*) Of course, we have friends, Bill, but why give it so much thought?

BILL: Well, we might be able to do more for our friends if we gave a little consideration to the real meaning of friendship.

MARY: You're always thinking about doing more for other people, Bill. Why don't you think about yourself once in a while? If you don't look out for yourself, no one else will!

BILL: Is that really your idea of friendship, Mary?

MARY: Well, I don't know. To be honest, I'm afraid I've thought pretty much in terms of what I could get out of my friends, rather than what I could give to them. I'm really terrible as a friend.

BILL: Don't be too hard on yourself. I don't think any of us in our crowd have discovered the true meaning of friendship. We haven't paid enough attention to what the Bible says about friends. It's been a long time since I've read the chapter on Christian love in First Corinthians.

MARY: The Bible? I've never thought of the Bible as having much to do with friendship!

BILL: I really didn't intend for this to be a sermon, Mary. I won't bore you with my ideas any longer. I've got to run along anyway—have a theme to write tonight.

MARY: You may get up in the clouds, Bill, but you're definitely not a bore! Stop in again.

BILL: Thanks, Mary. I will. So long! (*Exit* BILL.)

MARY (*thoughtfully*): I wonder what the Bible does say about friendship. (*Picks up a Bible from a table nearby and leafs through it.*) What did Bill say about a chapter on Christian love? Was it in First Corinthians? (*With greater interest.*) This must be it! I'm sure it is —the thirteenth chapter. (MARY *begins reading silently and thoughtfully.*)

Reader (concealed behind a screen or curtain, the reader reads slowly and with great meaning I Cor. 13):

"If I speak in the tongues of men and of angels, but have not love, I am a noisy gong or a clanging cymbal. And if I have prophetic powers, and understand all mysteries and all knowledge, and if I have all faith, so as to remove mountains, but have not love, I am nothing. If I give away all I have, and if I deliver my body to be burned, but have not love, I gain nothing.

"Love is patient and kind; love is not jealous or boastful; it is not arrogant or rude. Love does not insist on its own way; it is not irritable or resentful; it does not rejoice at wrong, but rejoices in the right. Love bears all things, believes all things, hopes all things, endures all things.

"Love never ends; as for prophecy, it will pass away; as for tongues, they will cease; as for knowledge, it will pass away. For our knowledge is imperfect and our prophecy is imperfect; but when the perfect comes, the imperfect will pass away. When I was a child, I spoke like a child, I thought like a child, I reasoned like a child; when I became a man, I gave up childish ways. For now we see in a mirror dimly, but then face to face. Now I know in part; then I shall understand fully, even as I have been fully understood. So faith, hope, love abide, these three; but the greatest of these is love."

MARY (*eagerly*): What a message! I didn't know the Bible was like that! It *does* have something to say about friendship. Why, I believe I could substitute the word "friend" in part of this. Let's see, what did it say? (*She glances through the chapter and then reads the following very slowly.*)

"A friend is patient and kind; a friend is not jealous or boastful; he is not arrogant or rude. A friend does not insist on his own way;

180

he is not irritable or resentful; he does not rejoice at wrong, but rejoices in the right. A friend bears all things, believes all things, hopes all things, endures all things. Friendship never ends."

MARY (*enthusiastically*): This is the Christian idea of friendship as clear as crystal! I must give Bill a ring and tell him about my discovery! (*Exit* MARY.)

LEADER:

This skit has given us a glimpse of the real essence of friendship, which is unselfish love. Jesus is our supreme example of Christian love. His ministry upon the earth provides in tangible form a picture of friendship on the highest level. Although Jesus' friends failed him on many occasions, he never wavered in his attitude of love and concern for them. Even as he faced the Cross, he was thinking, not of his own suffering, but of his friends and their need for comfort and strength.

Christ not only gives us an example of friendship at its best, he also empowers us to live according to the ideals of Christian friendship and to experience friendship on its highest level. There is a special glow and radiance to Christian friendship because of the beauty and presence of our Master and Friend. He gives the friendships of life their deepest meaning and their most cherished joys and satisfactions. In order to experience the true meaning of friendship, we must know Jesus Christ as our divine Companion and Friend.

HYMN (by the entire group or as a solo): First stanza of "What a Friend We Have in Jesus"

CLOSING PRAYER:

Dear God, we thank thee for Jesus, the Friend who gives guidance and motivation to our everyday experiences. We are thankful, too, for human friends and for the joys which they bring to our lives. Help us to be better persons, more dependable, loyal, and unselfish, in order that we may experience more fully the real meaning of friendship. May we be more grateful than ever before for the tie that binds our hearts in Christian love. In the name of Christ, who gives friendship its true meaning and significance. AMEN.

FRIENDSHIP CIRCLE

(The young people may quietly form a friendship circle and sing the first stanza of "Blest Be the Tie That Binds.")

BENEDICTION:

The Lord bless you and keep you: The Lord make his face to shine upon you, and be gracious to you: The Lord lift up his countenance upon you, and give you peace. AMEN.[10]

25. Preparing for Christian Marriage

PRELUDE: "Love Divine, All Loves Excelling"

CALL TO WORSHIP:

Put on then, as God's chosen ones, holy and beloved, compassion, kindness, lowliness, meekness, and patience, forbearing one another and, if one has a complaint against another, forgiving each other; as the Lord has forgiven you, so you also must forgive. And above all these put on love, which binds everything together in perfect harmony.[1]

PRAYER:

We are thankful, our Father, that love, rather than force, is the greatest thing in the world. We are grateful for thy redeeming love and for the love of our families and friends. Help us to be more worthy of the love that has been showered upon us throughout our lives, and may we manifest a spirit of love in our words and deeds each day. AMEN.

HYMN: "Love Divine, All Loves Excelling" or "O Happy Home, Where Thou Art Loved the Dearest"

LEADER:

Young people should realize that preparation for marriage should take place in the immediate present. In fact, this preparation actually began many years ago, for our attitudes toward marriage have been influenced through the years by our parents and teachers, by our friends and associates, and by what we have read, observed, and experienced.

The important thing is to do what we can in the present and the future to develop Christian attitudes and ideals regarding marriage.

183

With God's help we should strengthen the moral and spiritual foundation of our lives, thus striving to make ourselves worthy of Christian marriage and capable of establishing an enduring Christian home.

TALK I:

THE SECRET OF WINNING FRIENDS

One of the ways of preparing for Christian marriage is to realize the importance of worth-while friends. If we have an abundance of friends and frequent times of happy fellowship with them, we will have opportunities of discovering the "one and only" with whom we eventually desire to share a lifetime of happiness. Furthermore, if we discover the secret of winning friends and enjoying their companionship, we will receive valuable help in developing our ability to get along with people.

1. DEVELOP A GENUINE INTEREST IN OTHERS

One of the basic principles that will be of help to us in making friends is developing a genuine interest in people. Our Christian faith is important in this connection. As we respond to the love of God as it is revealed to us in Christ, we will have a greater love for others. As we study God's Word, we will gradually realize the tremendous worth of human personality. We will develop a new appreciation for ourselves and others and will discover numerous admirable traits of character in the people about us.

We should spend time in wholesome activities with young people of our own age. We should be active members of the youth fellowship of our church, attend meetings regularly, and also participate in the programs and projects of the group. As young people play together, plan together, and pray together, they discover the rich meanings and true values of Christian friendship.

We should show an interest in young people who are quiet and retiring. As we help them develop hidden resources and abilities, we will discover that they have a vital contribution to make to our group and to our individual lives. We should listen to what other young people have to say, rather than try to monopolize the conversation ourselves. We should ask questions of others in order to learn about their ideas and interests.

2. ANALYZE YOURSELF

In learning the secret of winning friends, it is important to analyze ourselves. We should face our weaknesses and shortcomings honestly. It is helpful to make a list of the undesirable characteristics in our lives and try to correct them. Our Christian faith will be of great help to us in this endeavor. The Bible tells us to confess our sins to Christ and seek his forgiveness. We do not need to carry with us the burden of our past failures and mistakes. We have the assurance from God's Word that Christ will forgive us. If we try to live each day in close fellowship with Christ, he will help us develop the qualities of daily living that are important in the making of worth-while friendships.

3. DEVELOP CHRISTIAN CHARACTERISTICS

One of the most important ways of getting along with people is to learn to be pleasant and agreeable. The best place to begin the practice of these attributes is in the home. If we develop a congenial spirit in our own family group, it will be easy to carry this same spirit into other relationships. This does not mean that we should agree with everything someone else says or does. It is important to have our own ideas and convictions, but it is also important to learn how to disagree with others in a graceful, considerate manner. We should not acquire the habit of hunting for opportunities to disagree with other people. On the contrary, we should constantly look for points of agreement and magnify them rather than the differences of opinion. We should not try to force our viewpoints on others, but be willing to learn constructive ideas from those who have opinions that are different from our own. Above all, we should not get into the unbearable habit of taking the opposite point of view every time someone else expresses an opinion. This unfortunate practice of constantly trying to correct and improve the words and conduct of other people drives away more friends than almost any other habit. We must look for the best in our friends, and by commending their best efforts, continually bring to light wonderful new facets of their personalities.

By thinking of others and looking for the best in them, we will forget ourselves and our own selfish desires. We will develop a genuine concern for others and find ways of showing that concern by actions that are gracious, pleasing, and Christlike. The attention that we show to others will not be forced and artificial. Our interest in them will be genuine, and our personality will be joyous, radiant, and contagious.

TALK II:

THE PROBLEMS OF DATING AND COURTSHIP

Dating and courtship are a normal part of the process of preparing for Christian marriage. Young people should be interested in experiencing courtship at its finest and best. They should be interested in overcoming the problems that stand in the way of discovering the true joys and values of dating and courtship.

1. PERSONAL APPEARANCE

The importance of personal appearance can scarcely be overemphasized. Handsome features and expensive clothes are not essentials, but neatness and cleanliness, which are available to everyone, are absolutely imperative. Great care should be taken to guard against body odor and bad breath. Personal cleanliness has a direct relationship to the feeling of respect which we have for ourselves and for others. If we have a wholesome respect for ourselves and for other people, we will do all we can to make ourselves neat, clean, and attractive. This simple principle has a direct bearing on whether or not we earn the respect of others and experience the joys of dating and courtship.

2. CONSIDERATION FOR OTHERS

Consideration for others is another important principle which applies to the problems of dating and courtship. Such simple things as being on time and not keeping the other person waiting are important. It is also important to consider the interests and desires of the person with whom one has a date. It is wise to think of each date as an important event, to forget social affairs one has attended in the past, and concentrate on making the present occasion joyous and worth while.

There are various ways of helping to make each social experience pleasant and rewarding. Do all you can to make your partner and others who are present feel at ease and included in the festivities. Do not neglect the person with whom you have a date by spending most of the evening in the company of others. Contribute your share of fun and gaity to the occasion, but do not monopolize either the conversation or the entertainment. Successful dating comes more often to those who have about them an element of quiet depth and reserve than to those who are loud, boisterous, and lack self-control.

3. A JOYOUS EXPERIENCE

Every date should be bubbling over with happiness and good cheer. If the occasion is to attain this goal, both the fellow and the girl must be cheerful and optimistic. Do not whine or fret or complain. Forget petty annoyances and fill every moment with a joyous spirit of fun and fellowship. Be a good listener. It is better to say too little than too much. Be generous with sincere compliments, but leave unsaid all biting criticism and unkind remarks. Be a good sport and enter into wholesome activities with animation and enthusiasm. As a Christian, however, you should refrain from doing anything that is cheap, vulgar, or harmful to yourself or others. You will be respected in the long run for remaining true to Christian principles and convictions. Each date should be an experience that is fun to think about the following day. There should be no unpleasant memories and no regrets.

TALK III:

THE CHOICE OF A LIFE MATE

Having experiences of fun and fellowship with many different friends will be of help to us in making the choice of a life mate. It is helpful to date a number of different persons, especially during the teen-age years, rather than to "go steady" with the first person with whom we have a date. This will give us much needed knowledge and understanding regarding different types of personalities and will enable us to discover a life mate who will have many interests and ideals that are similar to our own. Teen-age love is genuine and has its place in preparing a person for later decisions regarding marriage. These experiences of early youth should not be belittled and discounted as "puppy love." Teen-age love can be as sincere as love at twenty-five, but it is not based on the same degree of experience and understanding. Teen-age young people should remember this and give themselves the opportunity of enjoying the companionship of many young people.

There are many tests of true or abiding love which will help young people as they make decisions regarding the choice of a life mate.

1. COMRADESHIP

Two people who are really in love have a sense of comradeship that is deeply satisfying to both. There is a feeling of great delight when they are together and a feeling of great loss when they must be apart. This spirit of comradeship is not based entirely on physical attraction; it is a mental, emotional, and spiritual relationship as well. This feeling of comradeship is present when the couple is worshiping in church in the company of many others. It is present at a hilarious party or in a crowded store. True comradeship expresses itself when two persons talk quietly for long periods of time about their hopes and aspirations for the future. Or, when both are silent, there is a sense of comradeship that conveys thoughts that words can never express. There may be times when physical caresses are very meaningful, but true comradeship is not dependent on physical expressions of endearment.

2. ADMIRATION

When two are in love, they have a deep feeling of respect and admiration for the ideals and attitudes of each other. There may be differences of opinion on minor issues, but each has respect for the other person's point of view. Each has the feeling that the other is completely worthy of admiration. Both have complete confidence in the trustworthiness and integrity of the other. Each person is attractive to the other, not only in physical appearance, but in numerous charming and lovable personality traits as well. Each one has such great admiration for the other that he takes great delight in introducing his beloved to his family and friends.

3. AFFECTION

A genuine feeling of affection characterizes two people who are in love. Affection expresses itself in acts and words of tenderness, kindness, and thoughtfulness. Real love is never cold and impersonal. It is never rough, harsh, and inconsiderate. True love between a man and a woman is radiant, affectionate, and gentle.

4. UNSELFISHNESS

One of the most important tests of true love is whether it is motivated by selfishness or unselfishness. The spirit of genuine love is, "What can I do for the other person?" True love never asks, "What can I get from this relationship?" Love forgets self and thinks in terms of bringing abiding joys and satisfaction to the one who is beloved.

This high standard of unselfish love can scarcely be achieved by human effort. Young people should study the example of Christ as it is recorded in the Gospels and, with the help of Christ, strive to make their lives worthy of experiencing love at its highest and best. A self-centered person, who thinks in terms of gratifying his own whims and desires, is incapable of noble, unselfish love and is unworthy of receiving such love from another.

5. IDEALISM

True love between a man and woman inspires and ennobles the lives of both persons. When love is experienced, there is a heightening of idealism and of hopes and aspirations. Religion and love are bound closely together, and as two people are drawn close to one another by the bonds of love, they come into closer contact with God.

Self-restraint and discipline are a necessary part of the idealism of true love. It is easy for a young person to fail to measure up to the ideals of purity that he cherishes for himself and for the one he eventually hopes to marry. Self-control gives way to harmful self-indulgence unless young people are aware of the temptations and dangers involved. Sexual excesses before marriage mar the idealism of the relationship and are an indication that the couple has not yet discovered the full meaning and significance of genuine love. Such excesses make more difficult the experiencing through the years of a love that is increasingly inspiring and meaningful.

One of the tests of true love is whether or not it has spiritual depth and Christian idealism closely associated with it. Christian young people who are in love will encourage one another to deepen and develop the spiritual aspects of life. They will feel that God has enabled them to experience the joys of true love, that marriage is a sacred relationship, and that a worthy Christian home must be built on spiritual foundations. Christian couples will pray together and study the Bible diligently. They will be eager to take God into every experience and relationship and will earnestly seek his guidance in every decision.

POEM:

> I love you,
> Not only for what you are,
> But for what I am
> When I am with you.
> I love you,
> Not only for what
> You have made of yourself,
> But for what
> You are making of me.
>
> I love you
> For the part of me
> That you bring out;
> I love you
> For putting your hand
> Into my heaped-up heart
> And passing over
> All the foolish, weak things
> That you can't help
> Dimly seeing there,
> And for drawing out
> Into the light
> All the beautiful belongings

That no one else had looked
Quite far enough to find.

I love you because you
Are helping me to make
Of the lumber of my life
Not a tavern
But a temple;
Out of the works
Of my every day
Not a reproach
But a song. . . .
—Anonymous

Hymn: "I Would Be True" or "Happy the Home"

Closing Prayer:

Our Father, help us to realize that unselfish love is the only sure foundation for Christian marriage. We thank thee for thy love for us and for the revelation of thy love which we find in Jesus Christ. May we realize that as we respond to thy love, we will have a greater love for those who are near and dear to us. May we prepare for Christian marriage by being more unselfish and loving in our daily contacts and experiences. Teach us the joy of forgetting self and expending our energy in loving service for others. In the name of Christ, who loved us and gave his life for us. Amen.

26. There's My Ideal

PRELUDE: "I Need Thee Every Hour"

CALL TO WORSHIP:

> Give me a dream and a day,
> Lord of my reaching heart;
> Life gives so much away,
> I must return a part.
>
> Far calls the lure of the task,
> Oceanward plunges the stream,
> Fit me for life, I ask,
> Give me a day and a dream.
> —ANONYMOUS

PRAYER:

We are thankful, O God, for the dreams and aspirations which you have placed within our souls. We know that we are unable to realize these dreams in our own strength. Flood our minds with thy truth, strengthen our wills with thy power, and illumine our pathway with thy radiance and light. We pray in the name of Christ. AMEN.

HYMN (by the entire group or as a solo. Tune: "Hursley" L. M.)

> Dear Master, in whose life I see
> All that I would, but fail to be;
> Let Thy clear light for ever shine,
> To shame and guide this life of mine.
>
> Though what I dream and what I do
> In my weak days are always two,

192

Help me, oppressed by things undone,
O Thou, whose deeds and dreams were one.[1]
—JOHN HUNTER

LEADER: [2]

Personality is the combination of qualities or characteristics which makes each individual different from every other indvidual. Personality is the impact a person makes on his friends and associates. If the impact is pleasant or favorable, we say that individual has a pleasing personality. If the impact is unpleasant or irritating, we say that person has a negative personality.

What are the characteristics of Christian personality? Are there distinct traits of character which indicate that a person is a Christian? Can one tell the difference between a Christian and a non-Christian? Is the standard for Christian personality different from the personality standard for society as a whole? Should a Christian young person make a pleasing and positive impression on other people?

These are some of the questions which we will try to answer during this program on "There's My Ideal." Several informal skits will be presented to help us find the answers to these questions.

SKIT I:

LEADER: Peggy and Janet attend the same college. They are both from prominent, well-to-do families, but they have entirely different attitudes and viewpoints. Peggy is busy with her homework when Janet drops in for a brief visit.

PEGGY: Come in, Janet. You're just in time to help with these algebra problems. I suppose you have yours all done.

JANET: I certainly do not, and, what's more, I don't intend to do them. Why in the world do you spend every evening slaving on homework? I get by all right without studying. The teachers all know my father. He's a big shot, you know, and that helps my grades at school.

PEGGY: Most of the teachers know my father, too, but why should we take advantage of that? It isn't fair to the others.

JANET: Why worry about everyone else, Peggy? Look out for yourself— that's my motto! Anyway, most of the members of our class are as poor as church mice. Their parents have no influence or position in the community. Why worry about them?

PEGGY: I can't see that money and social position make much difference.

JANET: I never could understand your ideas, Peggy. Your family is very prominent in this town. You ought to be glad you're better than the common crowd.

PEGGY: We are not better than others, Janet, because our parents are wealthy and well known. In fact, those who are really great are interested in all types of people and are eager to be of service to others. Some of my very best friends are from the "common crowd," as you call it.

JANET: I know that very well, and that's just the reason I don't chum around with you as much as I used to do. I don't care to stoop to the common level. I guess I'd better be running along. (*With sarcasm*) I'm afraid I'm keeping you from those all-important algebra problems! (JANET *exits hurriedly*.)

PEGGY: Well, I guess I really got told! Now that I think of it, Janet hasn't been coming over as often as usual. It's funny I hadn't missed her! Guess I've been too busy having a good time with my friends from the "common crowd"! (*Exit*.)

SHARING OUR IDEAS:

1. What Christian character traits are illustrated in this skit?

2. What non-Christian traits are illustrated?

3. Several young people may read the following scripture passages: Luke 18:9-14; I Pet. 5:5-6; Phil. 2:2-3; Gal. 3:28.

4. What Christian personality traits are emphasized in these scripture verses?

5. After a consideration of these scripture passages and of Skit I, list on a large chart or on a blackboard several distinct characteristics of Christian personality. (Suggestions: humility, unselfishness, democratic spirit, willingness to serve.)

SKIT II:

LEADER: Dick and Ralph are good friends and are active members of the same church. They are talking together when Jack, the popular captain of the college football team, stops to talk to them.

JACK: Hi, fellows! What do you know?

DICK: Not much of anything. We were just talking about next Saturday's game.

RALPH: We were also talking about our youth fellowship meeting next Sunday evening.

JACK: Youth fellowship meeting! What in the world is that?

RALPH: It's the youth organization of our church.

JACK: Oh, that! Must be sort of a tame affair!

RALPH: Not exactly! We have a swell gang and a lot of fun. Why don't you visit our group Sunday evening?

DICK: Listen, Ralph. I'm sure Jack is more interested in Saturday's game than in what our gang is doing on Sunday.

JACK: You're right, Dick. I haven't much time for girls' stuff.

RALPH: It isn't girls' stuff, Jack. You'd be surprised how many fellows attend. It isn't just a social affair either. We talk over important problems, and we find the answers to a lot of them too.

JACK (*with a slight show of interest*): What kind of problems?

RALPH: The everyday problems of young people, as well as questions that all of us have about life, death, sin, war, and a lot of other things.

JACK (*with surprise*): You don't find the answers to problems like that, do you?

RALPH: Not the complete answers, but we do learn a lot.

JACK: Who gives you these answers?

RALPH: We get help from the Bible, Jack, and from other books about the Christian life. We also pray about these problems.

DICK: Just a minute, Ralph! Didn't you hear Jack say that he wasn't interested in this sort of thing? You'll be preaching him a sermon if you aren't careful!

JACK (*good-naturedly*): Maybe that's what I need! I probably need your youth fellowship too. Tell me more about it some other time, Ralph. I've got to run along now. (*Exit* JACK.)

RALPH: Did you hear what Jack said? He wants to find out more about our youth meetings!

DICK: I could hardly believe my ears! I was sure he'd make fun of what you were telling him. You had more nerve than I did, Ralph. Next time I'll try to do better. (*Exit* DICK *and* RALPH.)

SHARING OUR IDEAS:

1. What Christian personality traits are illustrated in this skit?

2. What non-Christian traits are illustrated?

3. Why did Dick discourage Ralph in his attempt to interest the football captain in youth fellowship meetings?

4. Several young people may read the following scripture passages: Acts 5:40-42; I Cor. 15:58; 16:13; II Tim. 2:3.

5. After discussing these scripture verses and Skit II, place on your chart or on the blackboard one or more additional Christian personality traits. (Suggestions: courage, loyalty to Christ, enthusiasm, persistence.)

SKIT III:

LEADER: Mary and Barbara are spending Sunday afternoon at Barbara's home. They are in charge of the youth fellowship program that evening and are making final plans for the meeting when Beth telephones, inviting them to go to a neighboring town for the evening. Mary and Barbara are discussing what they should do.

MARY: Why didn't you tell Beth that we have charge of the program at church this evening?

BARBARA: I thought you'd want to go to Milltown with her. She has a lot of friends there, and they've probably planned a big party for tonight.

MARY: It would be fun to go, Barbara, but what about our program?

BARBARA: We can get someone else to lead it. We can take our material to them and let them use what we planned to use.

MARY: But, Barbara, it's just an hour until time for the meeting. Who would want to give the program on such short notice? I'm afraid no one else could read my scribbling anyway!

BARBARA: Oh, Mary, you're exasperating! Of course someone else could do it! Beth will never ask us to go to Milltown again, if we turn her down!

MARY: Why not ask Beth to go with us to church tonight? She may not have anything special planned at Milltown. In fact, she probably decided to go at the last minute because she didn't have anything else to do. Why don't you call her and ask her to come with us?

BARBARA (*indignantly*): I wouldn't think of asking her to go to a dull youth fellowship meeting after she has invited us to go to Milltown with her! She never goes to church anyway and would probably be bored to death if she went with us.

MARY: I don't think this meeting will be as boring as that! Besides, if she never goes to church, that's all the more reason you should invite her!

BARBARA: Why is it so terribly important, Mary, that we lead this meeting? There'll be plenty of other times that we can help with programs!

MARY: But we promised to take charge of the meeting tonight. They're counting on us.

BARBARA (*impatiently*): All right, if you think it's that important, you can lead the meeting by yourself! I'm going to Milltown with Beth!

MARY (*showing no anger*): Well, that's up to you, Barbara. It's about time for me to be going to church. Come on. We can walk together as far as the church.

(*Exit* MARY *and* BARBARA.)

SHARING OUR IDEAS:

1. What Christian character traits are illustrated in this skit?

2. What non-Christian traits are illustrated?

3. What attitude did Barbara show toward a task she had promised to do? Toward the youth fellowship meeting? Toward Mary, who was her guest?

4. A young person may read the following scripture passages: Luke 16:10; Phil. 4:8.

5. Place on the chart or blackboard one or more additional Christian personality traits. (Suggestions: honesty, dependability, faithfulness.)

SKIT IV:

LEADER: Jim and Bob are active members of the same church. They are good students at school, and both made the football team in their sophomore year at college. Joe, who failed to make the football team, began a "smear" campaign against Jim and Bob, saying that the teachers and coaches were partial to them because they were goody-goodies and had an overdose of religion. Jim and Bob have just heard about this gossip and are discussing what they should do about it.

Jim: I'll tell you one thing! Joe is going to pay for all these lies he's been telling about us! He doesn't have many friends, but I'll see to it that he loses the ones he has!

Bob: What do you mean, Jim?

Jim: Just what I said! Joe has to pay for this! I know a lot of dirt about him, and I'm going to get some real gossip started on its way.

Bob: That sounds pretty vicious, Jim.

Jim: It will be vicious! Just you wait and see!

Bob: I'm not very happy about Joe's "smear" campaign either, but I don't think we should use the same tactics.

Jim: Do you mean to say that you're going to keep still and do nothing? Are you going to let him get away with this?

Bob: Why, sure! Why get hot and bothered when there's no truth to what he's saying?

Jim: How can we get him to stop talking if we don't get even with him?

Bob: We might invite him to church! Maybe he'd get a better outlook on life.

Jim: Of all the crazy ideas! We don't want him in our church! Where in the world did you get that idea?

Bob: At church last Sunday morning! If I hadn't remembered that sermon on forgiveness, I'd probably be as excited as you are, Jim! Rise above resentments and return good for evil. Wasn't that the main idea of that sermon?

Jim: I guess you're right, Bob! I hadn't thought of it that way. I suppose this is a chance for us to put that sermon into practice. Do you think this method will work with Joe?

Bob: We can at least give it a try. Let's look around for Joe now, and see how he reacts to an invitation to attend church with us next Sunday!

(*Exit* Jim *and* Bob.)

Sharing Our Ideas:

1. What Christian personality traits are illustrated in this skit?

2. What non-Christian traits are illustrated?

3. Several young people may read the following scripture passages: Matt. 18:21-22; Mark 11:25; Luke 6:27-28; Rom. 12:17-21.

4. What is the meaning of Christian love? Is it possible to love someone who has wronged us?

5. Place on the chart or blackboard one or more additional Christian personality traits. (Suggestions: Christian love, forgiving spirit, kindness, compassion.)

LEADER:

We have discovered from God's Word that there are distinct personality traits which characterize a true Christian. The challenge that now confronts us is to achieve these character traits in our own personal lives. It can be done! When we earnestly follow Jesus Christ as Saviour and Lord, he will give us the guidance and strength to live according to Christian standards. We cannot attain the Christian ideal by our own strength. It is impossible for us to love our enemies and to return good for evil, apart from the empowerment that comes from Christ. The Christian personality, with all its distinct characteristics, can be achieved only by those who have a repentant spirit and a humble faith in Jesus Christ.

HYMN: "God Who Touchest Earth with Beauty" or "I Need Thee Every Hour"

CLOSING PRAYER:

Our Father in heaven, help us to look to Jesus as our Ideal. May we also look to him as our Saviour and Guide and seek strength from him to live according to Christian standards. Forgive us for our failures, and enable us to have a more perfect faith in thee. AMEN.

27. Right Attitudes Toward Money

PRELUDE: "Lead On, O King Eternal"

CALL TO WORSHIP:

> I thank Thee, Lord, for strength of arm
> To win my bread,
> And that, beyond my need is meat
> For friend unfed:
> I thank Thee much for bread to live,
> I thank Thee more for bread to give.
>
> I thank Thee for my quiet home,
> 'Mid cold and storm,
> And that, beyond my need, is room
> For friend forlorn:
> I thank Thee much for place to rest,
> But more for shelter for my guest.
>
> I thank Thee, Lord, for lavish love
> On me bestowed,
> Enough to share with loveless folk
> To ease their load:
> Thy love to me I ill could spare,
> Yet dearer is Thy love I share.[1]
>
> —ROBERT DAVIS

PRAYER:

We pray, our Father, that we may develop Christian attitudes toward money and toward all of our material possessions. May we discover in our daily experiences that it is more blessed to give than to receive.

May nothing that we possess or desire stand in the way of a glad and full surrender to thee. Help us to realize that money dedicated to thee can play an important part in the advancement of thy kingdom throughout the world. AMEN.

HYMN: "Lead On, O King Eternal" or "Soldiers of Christ Arise"

SCRIPTURE:

And behold, one came up to him, saying, "Teacher, what good deed must I do, to have eternal life?" And he said to him, "Why do you ask me about what is good? One there is who is good. If you would enter life, keep the commandments." He said to him, "Which?" And Jesus said, "You shall not kill. You shall not commit adultery, You shall not steal, You shall not bear false witness, Honor your father and mother, and, You shall love your neighbor as yourself." The young man said to him, "All these I have observed; what do I still lack?" Jesus said to him, "If you would be perfect, go, sell what you possess and give to the poor, and you will have treasure in heaven; and come, follow me." When the young man heard this he went away sorrowful; for he had great possessions.[2]

LEADER:

When the Rich Young Ruler told Jesus that he had observed all the commandments from his youth, he was not indulging in idle boasting. He had tried in all sincerity to obey God's commands, and yet he was not satisfied with his life. In spite of his earnest keeping of God's law, he knew there was something lacking in his life.

Jesus looked upon this earnest, seeking youth and loved him. Although he longed to have him as an intimate disciple, Jesus did not offer the rich young man a short cut into the kingdom of God. He did not belittle the cost of discipleship. "You lack one thing," the Master said. "Go, sell what you have and give to the poor; and come, follow me."

Jesus knew that this young man's possessions were at the very center of his life. He knew that true discipleship demands that the kingdom of God be placed above all else. With infinite yearning the Master waited as the rich young man made his choice between gold and God. Unfortunately, the young man's courage failed him. He

201

clung to his possessions and turned away sorrowfully from the One who could have filled to overflowing the great emptiness in his life.

Many of us today, like the Rich Young Ruler of old, turn away from Christ and from the challenge and adventure of Christian discipleship. Too often we live within the narrow confines of a self-centered life. Too often we place comfort and material possessions above the great eternal values of the Christian way of life.

POEM:

> Dear Lord and Father of mankind,
>   Forgive our foolish ways!
> Reclothe us in our rightful mind,
> In purer lives Thy service find,
>   In deeper reverence, praise.
>
>   .   .   .   .
>
> Drop Thy still dews of quietness,
>   Till all our strivings cease;
> Take from our souls the strain and stress,
> And let our ordered lives confess
>   The beauty of Thy peace.
>
> Breathe through the heats of our desire
>   Thy coolness and Thy balm;
> Let sense be dumb, let flesh retire;
> Speak through the earthquake, wind and fire,
>   O still small voice of calm!
>   —JOHN GREENLEAF WHITTIER

STORY:

A BIG CAREER

Henry Moore managed to wave a cheerful farewell to the friends who had come to see him off, then slumped into his seat as the train pulled out of the station. A brilliant record as a medical student; visions of a splendid practice in a big city; less than a year to complete his course and start upon a successful career. Then a cold, caught at a football game, followed by pneumonia. Only one thing to do, the doctors said: Give up study for the remainder of the year, rest, and live in the open as much as possible.

"You simply can't go on, Moore," his dean had said, sympathetically and with great concern. "This disease has pulled you down a lot. It would overtax your strength to do the regular work and make up what you have lost in all these weeks. You need rest, plenty of good food, and fresh air. Go home, and come back strong. We need men like you. You know how to take care of yourself, and I trust your good sense to do it."

It was good to be home again. Father and Mother were so solicitous, so anxious to help in every way. At Henry's faintest suggestion, his father brought out the big, comfortable porch swing that had been put away for the winter and contrived a canopy for it that would shield the occupant from wind and cold. His mother prepared nourishing, appetizing food for him, and ran in and out to see that he was comfortable. Friends dropped in to cheer him.

Still he suffered intensely from boredom. Visions of New York and an office on Park Avenue, the goal of his dreams, receded farther and farther as he chafed over his enforced idleness. The tedious winter came at last. On sunny days Henry lay in the swing, well protected from cold, but unhappy because of the ever receding dream of Park Avenue and the lucrative practice he had confidently hoped to build up.

Slowly, however, Henry was regaining his strength. He had begun to enjoy his hours on the porch when spring dawned and song sparrows sang in the trees, and crocuses and daffodils began to bloom in the yard.

"Most ready for a job?" called Sam, the breadman, one beautiful morning. "I sure need a helper. No pay, but just a chance to learn the business." He laughed gaily.

"That's the only kind of job I could hold," answered Henry, good-naturedly. "I'm not worth a cent."

"Then what's the matter with going along with me?" responded Sam. "I go from here to Fontana. Nice ride on a day like this."

"Would it be all right?" asked Henry, rather interested.

"Sure. You can look after the car while I deliver the bread. I told the boss I needed a helper, because it's pretty hard to watch the car and deliver the bread at the same time, and a car needs watching these days."

"What did he say?"

Sam grinned. "He said, 'Yeah? Well, you can get all the helpers you want, just so they don't cost anything; I'm not making money enough these days to hire any more people.'"

Henry laughed. "Then I'm your man, at least for today. Wait till I get my hat and overcoat."

The ride through the country proved a pleasant one. The air was balmy, and children played along the road and on the sidewalks of the villages. Sometimes Henry talked to them while Sam delivered his bread. Sometimes, without waiting for Sam to come into the house, one would come out to the sidewalk and get the bread. Then Sam, with a grin or a teasing remark, would hand the child a cooky.

"Why can't I get out at some of the places?" Henry asked one morning. "These rides are making me feel fine, but I'd like to help a little."

"You do help," said Sam, "just being along."

"I know," laughed Henry, "but as inspiring as my society is, I'd like to be doing a little something. How about this place?"

"Oh!" protested Sam, "better let me go in here, and you take the next house."

"But," insisted Henry, "there's something about this place that interests me." He did not say that what made him wonder was the expression on Sam's face every time he came away from that house.

"If they're short of change," said Sam, "leave it anyhow." He watched Henry as he carried the loaf to the door. Then a look of surprise crossed his face. A strange woman had come to the door of the pleasant-looking little house in response to Henry's knock, had shaken her head, and pointed to the rear of the lot. Henry, after hesitating a second, had walked down the yard and knocked at the door of the chicken house, and a sweet-faced old woman had appeared and taken the bread.

"Whee-ew!" whistled Henry, in response to Sam's questioning look. "Your customer has moved into that chicken house."

Sam was genuinely distressed. "Something's got to be done about that," he said. "That old couple owns this place, but the old man lost his job and she said they'd have to do something to pay the taxes. They've hardly anything to live on. So I guess they've rented their house and gone back there."

"I saw in through the door," said Henry. "It was clean as a pin and sort of cozy. Sam, that woman is a dear old lady."

"Yeah," said Sam gravely, "there's things along this route to make you think."

They passed through a factory town. A good many idlers were on the street. The factory was working only part time. Men were becoming discouraged.

Sam stopped at a cottage. There were signs of thrift on every side— a trim garden with vegetables starting up and spring flowers in bloom along the borders.

"You might go in there," said Sam. In that house there's the cutest kid you ever saw. I call him Sunny Jim, and I always give him a cooky. Generally he comes out for the bread himself, but I guess he's playing and forgot."

Henry took the cooky and the loaf of bread and knocked at the door of the cottage, but no Sunny Jim came to the door. Instead, a worried young woman appeared, evidently Jimmy's mother. Jimmy lay on a cot, moaning with pain.

"What's the matter?" asked Henry.

"He fell and hurt his ankle," said the mother, "and I don't know just the best remedy."

"Have you had a doctor?" asked Henry.

The woman shook her head. "We've no money for doctors," she said.

"Could I see his ankle?" he asked. "I'm studying medicine. Maybe I can help him." He turned, called to Sam, "Go on, and pick me up on the way back," and then entered the clean but humble cottage.

After winning Jimmy's approval by laying the cooky beside his pillow, he examined the injured ankle carefully.

"Do you think it's broken?" quavered the anxious mother.

"Not a bit of it," said Henry, cheerfully. "Just a little sprain. He'll be all right in a few days. Just get me some hot water, an old pillowcase or something, and a Turkish towel or some flannel, if you have it. We'll fix him up in a jiffy."

In answer to the mother's timid question as to what he charged, he laughed merrily, "Nothing at all, nothing at all, ma'am. I'm not a real doctor yet, you know."

"No work there, I guess, from the looks of the woman's face," said Henry to Sam on the return trip.

"Mighty little," said Sam shortly, "for months and months."

"That kid might have had a bad ankle if we hadn't happened along," said Henry. "The mother didn't seem to know what to do."

"The ones that need to know most generally don't," sagely remarked Sam.

"Queer world," said Henry, after they had ridden a while in thoughtful silence. "Some have more than is good for them, and some have nothing."

"Uh-huh," assented Sam. "Say, Doc . . ."

Both young men laughed at the premature title.

"You know," Sam became serious, "there's a kid down here I'd like you to stop in and see. Her folks had the doctor from Lawrenceville over to see her. He wouldn't come back because they couldn't pay him. You take the bread in and say I asked about Susie. Don't collect for the bread. My boss is pretty close about help, but he won't stand for anybody going without bread when they can't pay."

"Undernourished," Henry reported to Sam a few minutes later. "From the looks of things in there, that child is half-starved. What's the matter?"

"Kid's father is no account," said Sam. "No especially bad habits, but just won't work. Mother not much better! Kid went round trying to sell gimcracks till she got sick."

"Sent to Lawrenceville for a doctor, did you say?"

"Yes. But that young whippersnapper has his eye on the dollar. He ought to go to New York, that bird, where he can charge big." Henry winced.

"He just backed out and wouldn't come," Sam continued. "Seven miles is too long a drive for his swell new car. We sure need a doctor in these parts. Since old Doc Renn has gone, there's nobody round here interested in folks that can't pay. Say, d'ye know, that old man was eighty years old when he died, and he didn't leave a cent. Traveled the country round, and never sent a bill to anybody too poor to pay. Kept himself poor as a church mouse. Well, he couldn't have taken his money where he's gone if he had any, but I guess he'd laid a good deal up there of the only thing you can take along when you're through here. But folks sure do miss him. Say, Henry, I'll buy a bottle of milk every day for Susie if you'll take it in. I don't know just how to do that."

"Good!" said Henry, earnestly. "And I'll bring some fresh eggs. I can't prescribe for her, for I'm not a full-fledged doctor. But she doesn't need medicine—just food."

"Well, Son," said the minister that night as they sat before a glowing fire, you're looking a lot better. Those rides are doing you good."

"I'm feeling fine," said Henry, heartily. "I'll be plenty strong enough by fall to go back to the university. One more year there, and I'll not need to be on your hands any longer."

The young man and the older one smiled affectionately at each other. Then the father's face sobered.

"You'll be leaving us in October," he said, "for your last year. After that, I suppose it will be New York and a busy career."

"Father," said Henry, "I've changed my mind about New York."

Mr. Moore opened his eyes in surprise. "Your one ambition, Son?" he asked.

"I'm going to locate here," Henry said simply.

"Here! There's no chance for a career here, Son."

"You preach sometimes, Father, about One who went about doing good, and it always makes me think of you. That's how you spend your life. Why shouldn't I? Park Avenue is overcrowded with doctors. Here I find a great need for one. In spite of all I've heard you say, I never realized the need among the people all around us. If I left, I could never forget them."

"You'll never make a fortune," warned the minister again, though his heart warmed within him. How he needed such a helper in ministering to his people!

"Doctor Renn didn't," answered Henry. "Sam's been telling me." [3]

SOLO:

> We give Thee but Thine own,
> Whate'er the gift may be:
> All that we have is Thine alone,
> A trust, O Lord, from Thee.

May we Thy bounties thus
As stewards true receive,
And gladly, as Thou blessest us,
To Thee our first fruits give.

. . . .

And we believe Thy word,
Though dim our faith may be,
Whate'er for Thine we do, O Lord,
We do it unto Thee.
—WILLIAM WALSHAM HOW

CLOSING PRAYER:

Help us to realize, O God, that money can never provide true happiness, and that serving thee and our fellow men is far more important than earning large sums of money. May we also realize that money, when it is dedicated to thee, can be the means of advancing thy kingdom upon the earth. We are thankful for the material blessings which have been showered so bountifully upon us. May we think of our material possessions as a trust from thee, and use them to minister to the physical and spiritual needs of mankind. In the name of Christ, who came that all men might have the abundant life. AMEN.

28. The Meaning of Christian Stewardship

PRELUDE: "Take My Life, and Let It Be"

CALL TO WORSHIP:
> One small life in God's great plan,
> How futile it seems as the ages roll,
> Do what it may, or strive how it can,
> To alter the sweep of the infinite whole!
> A single stitch in an endless web,
> A drop in the ocean's flow and ebb!
> But the pattern is rent where the stitch is lost,
> Or marred where the tangled threads have crossed;
> And each life that fails of its true intent
> Mars the perfect plan that its Maker meant.[1]
> —SUSAN COOLIDGE

PRAYER:
Our Father in heaven, guide our thoughts as we consider the meaning of Christian stewardship. Illumine our minds, as we seek our place in thy great plan for mankind. Use us and all that we possess in carrying out thy purposes for our lives. AMEN.

READER I:
Jesus said to them again, "Peace be with you. As the Father has sent me, even so I send you." "Go therefore and make disciples of all nations, baptizing them in the name of the Father and of the Son and of the Holy Spirit, teaching them to observe all that I have commanded you; and lo, I am with you always, to the close of the age." [2]

READER II:

The basis of Christian stewardship is the conviction that Christ has commissioned us to carry on his work on earth. An earnest Christian is a good steward of his time, talents, and possessions. He has a sense of mission—the feeling that God has called him to tasks that are of eternal value and significance. He serves Christ in daily situations and experiences in a spirit of earnestness and dedication. A Christian steward feels the urgency and importance of the work to which Christ has called him.

HYMN: "Jesus Calls Us" or "Master, Speak! Thy Servant Heareth"

READER I:

This is how one should regard us, as servants of Christ and stewards of the mysteries of God. Moreover it is required of stewards that they be found trustworthy.[3]

READER II:

A Christian steward realizes that life, strength, talents, and possessions have been given to him as a trust from God. A Christian is responsible for the wise use of these blessings with which he has been entrusted. God's Word declares: "It is required of stewards that they be found trustworthy." Christian stewardship is the faithful and systematic giving of time, abilities, and material possessions to God, to be used in the advancement of his kingdom upon the earth.

HYMN: "A Charge to Keep I Have" or "Am I a Soldier of the Cross?"

READER I:

And Jesus went about all the cities and villages, teaching in their synagogues and preaching the gospel of the kingdom, and healing every disease and every infirmity. When he saw the crowds, he had compassion for them, because they were harassed and helpless, like sheep without a shepherd. Then he said to his disciples, "The harvest is plentiful, but the laborers are few; pray therefore the Lord of the harvest to send out laborers into his harvest."[4]

READER II:

Christian stewardship emphasizes, not only the giving of time, talents, and possessions to God, but also the motive with which these gifts are given. Because he had a genuine feeling of love and concern for them, Christ ministered to the people who crowded about him day after day. He saw a wealth of potentialities in every human soul and had a deep desire to bring to fruition the latent capabilities of each individual. Whenever he looked up a multitude of people, "he had compassion for them, because they were harrassed and helpless, like sheep without a shepherd."

As followers of the compassionate Christ, we must look upon people —even unlovely people—and see their hidden possibilities of growth and goodness. We should see them as God's distressed and sinful children for whom Christ died. If we earnestly desire to *Christianize* our fellow men, we will look upon those about us with *Christian eyes*.

SOLO:

Lord, speak to me, that I may speak
    In living echoes of Thy tone;
As Thou hast sought, so let me seek,
    Thy erring children lost and lone.

O teach me, Lord, that I may teach
    The precious things Thou dost impart;
And wing my words, that they may reach
    The hidden depths of many a heart.

O fill me with Thy fullness, Lord,
    Until my very heart o'erflow
In kindling thought and glowing word,
    Thy love to tell, Thy praise to show.

O use me, Lord, use even me,
    Just as Thou wilt, and when, and where;
Until Thy blessed face I see,
    Thy rest, Thy joy, Thy glory share.
                                        —FRANCES HAVERGAL

READER I:

"I am the true vine, and my Father is the vinedresser. Every branch of mine that bears no fruit, he takes away, and every branch that does bear fruit he prunes, that it may bear more fruit. You are already made clean by the word which I have spoken to you. Abide in me, and I in you. As the branch cannot bear fruit by itself, unless it abides in the vine, neither can you, unless you abide in me. I am the vine, you are the branches. He who abides in me, and I in him, he it is that bears much fruit, for apart from me you can do nothing. If a man does not abide in me, he is cast forth as a branch and withers; and the branches are gathered, thrown into the fire and burned. If you abide in me, and my words abide in you, ask whatever you will, and it shall be done for you. By this my Father is glorified, that you bear much fruit, and so prove to be my disciples. As the Father has loved me, so have I loved you; abide in my love. If you keep my commandments, you will abide in my love, just as I have kept my Father's commandments and abide in his love. These things I have spoken to you, that my joy may be in you, and that your joy may be full.[5]

READER II:

A Christian steward is aware of his close relationship with Christ and of his dependence upon the Master. A Christian is in partnership with Christ, but our Lord is the motivating force that gives vitality to the partnership. He is the senior Partner; we are dependent on his strength and guidance. "I am the vine," Jesus said. "You are the branches. He who abides in me, and I in him, he it is that bears much fruit, for apart from me you can do nothing."

Jesus manifested a deep and abiding joy while he was upon the earth. The secret of his joy was his close fellowship with the Father and his conviction that he was doing his Father's work upon the earth. Jesus had no desire to keep to himself this deep-seated feeling of joy and satisfaction. He wanted each one of his followers to know the peace and joy that come from centering all the activities of one's life around the will of God. Jesus desires that his followers today have this same experience of oneness with himself and with the Father. He desires that we discover the full and satisfying joy of knowing and doing the Father's will. "These things I have spoken to you," the Master said, "that my joy may be in you, and that your joy may be full."

HYMN: "Joyful, Joyful We Adore Thee" or "My God, I Thank Thee"

READER I:

The point is this: he who sows sparingly will also reap sparingly, and he who sows bountifully will also reap bountifully. Each one must do as he has made up his mind, not reluctantly or under compulsion, for God loves a cheerful giver. And God is able to provide you with every blessing in abundance, so that you may always have enough of everything and may provide in abundance for every good work.[6]

READER II:

When a Christian steward has discovered the joy that comes from a vital companionship with Christ, he is not content to keep this thrilling discovery to himself. The whole trend of his life is, "How much can I give?" rather than, "How much can I get?" He gives eagerly, for the sheer joy of giving. He knows from experience that the words of the Lord Jesus are a basic law of life: "It is more blessed to give than to receive."

A good steward of the gospel of Christ gives himself in glad and full surrender to the Master. He gives his time and abilities to the work of Christ in his own local church. He also gives his money, realizing that in this way he can have a part in extending Christ's kingdom throughout the world. A good steward gives regularly a generous portion of his income (at least a tithe, or one tenth) to the work of Christ. A part of this tithe should be designated for the work of the local church; a part of it should be given to missionary work in our own land and in other countries of the world.

Christian stewardship is closely akin to Christian discipleship. When young people have discovered the meaning of Christian discipleship and have dedicated their lives to Jesus Christ, they will use their time, strength, talents, and possessions as good stewards of the Master.

SOLO:

> Take my life, and let it be
> Consecrated, Lord, to Thee.
> Take my moments and my days;
> Let them flow in ceaseless praise.
> Take my hands, and let them move
> At the impulse of Thy love.

Take my feet, and let them be
Swift and beautiful for Thee.

Take my voice, and let me sing,
Always, only, for my King.
Take my lips, and let them be
Filled with messages from Thee.
Take my silver and my gold;
Not a mite would I withhold.
Take my intellect, and use
Every power as Thou shalt choose.

Take my will, and make it Thine;
It shall be no longer mine,
Take my heart, it is Thine own;
It shall be Thy royal throne.
Take my love; my Lord, I pour
At Thy feet its treasure-store.
Take myself, and I will be
Ever, only, all for Thee.
—FRANCES HAVERGAL

CLOSING PRAYER:

Help us, our Father, to experience in our own lives the true meaning of Christian stewardship. May we realize that the giving of our gifts to thee is an indication of our love and loyalty to thee and to the work of thy kingdom. Enable us to discover the joy of dedicating our time, talents, and possessions to thee—to be used by thee in the advancement of thy kingdom around the world. In the name of Christ, who gave his life for us. AMEN.

29. Appreciating People of Other Races

Call to Worship:

> "Live and let live!" was the call of the Old—
> The call of the world when the world was cold—
> The call of men when they pulled apart—
> The call of the race with a chill on the heart.
>
> But "Live and help live!" is the cry of the New—
> The cry of the world with the Dream shining through—
> The cry of the Brother World rising to birth—
> The cry of the Christ for a Comrade-like earth.[1]
>
> —Edwin Markham

Prayer:

> Christ,
> Grant us this boon,
> To look with Thine eyes of pity and love
> On all men's need:
> To feel from within, with Thee,
> The bite of pain, of hunger, of wrong:
> To live wholly beyond ourselves,
> In deep and active desire of help for the needy and weak.
>
> Christ,
> Conquer the selfish greed in our hearts,
> And grant us power to act,
> To struggle, to build,
> For the coming of Thy full Kingdom,

Where no man is wronged, greed and violence vanish away,
And in all God's world true brotherhood reigns.[2]

—JOHN S. HOYLAND

HYMN: "Jesus Shall Reign Where'er the Sun" or "Where Cross the Crowded Ways of Life"

POEM:

O God of Light, break forth anew
Upon the darkness of the earth,
In the new glory of the day
When brotherhood shall come to birth;
Open our eyes that we may see
The coming of thy dawn afar,
And find the way of fellowship
The promise of thy morning star.

O God of Love, show us thy love
Forever seeking all mankind,
In eager questing of thy heart
To win and bless and heal and bind;
May thy rich mercy help us love
Our neighbour as we honour thee,
And seek his good as 'twere our own
In glad and deep fraternity.

O God of Peace, bring peace on earth
Where men and nations haste to war;
Restrain our passion and our pride
Ere thine inheritance we mar;
Spare us the guilt of brother's blood
That judgment be not our desert;
Teach us to build and not destroy,
Teach us to heal and not to hurt.

O God of Life, abundant, free,
Make known thyself to men today;
Kindle thy flame of life in us
And lead us in thy living way;

> Make us the heralds of thy word,
> And builders of thy city fair,
> That all the sons of men may hear
> The song of freedom in the air.[3]
> —R. B. Y. SCOTT

LEADER:

There is one body and one Spirit, just as you were called to the one hope that belongs to your call, one Lord, one faith, one baptism, one God and Father of us all, who is above all and through all and in all.[4]

HYMN:

> In Christ there is no East or West,
> In Him no South or North,
> But one great Fellowship of love
> Throughout the whole wide earth.

LEADER:

But now in Christ Jesus you who once were far off have been brought near in the blood of Christ. For he is our peace, who has made us both one, and has broken down the dividing wall of hostility.[5]

HYMN:

> In Him shall true hearts everywhere
> Their high communion find.
> His service is the golden cord
> Close binding all mankind.

LEADER:

And he came and preached peace to you who were far off and peace to those who were near; for through him we both have access in one Spirit to the Father. So then you are no longer strangers and sojourners, but you are fellow citizens with the saints and members of the household of God, built upon the foundation of the apostles and prophets, Christ Jesus himself being the chief cornerstone.[6]

HYMN:

> Join hands, then, Brothers of the Faith,
> Whate'er your race may be!—
> Who serves my Father as a son
> Is surely kin to me.

LEADER:

But now that faith has come, we are no longer under a custodian; for in Christ Jesus you are all sons of God, through faith. For as many of you as were baptized into Christ have put on Christ. There is neither Jew nor Greek, there is neither slave nor free, there is neither male nor female; for you are all one in Christ Jesus.[7]

HYMN:

> In Christ now meet both East and West,
> In Him meet South and North,
> All Christly souls are one in Him,
> Throughout the whole wide earth.[8]
>   —JOHN OXENHAM

LEADER:

As Christian young people, we should take advantage of opportunities of becoming well acquainted with people of other races and nationalities. We must remember that there are many different types of people who belong to other races, just as there are many types of people who belong to our own race. We should look for the best qualities in people of other nationalities and not condemn the entire group because of a few who bring discredit to it. When getting acquainted with people of other races, we should notice the basic traits of character which they have in common with us, rather than concentrating on the external characteristics which cause them to be different from us. We should also try to appreciate the music, crafts, literature, art, inventions, and other contributions which various racial and national groups have made—not only to our own country, but to the progress of mankind as a whole. Above all, we should remember that people of all races and nations are made in the image and likeness of God and that God has no favorites among his children.

The gospel of Jesus Christ is a universal message of salvation. Christ died for the redemption of every human being, regardless of his color, race, class, or nationality.

STORY:

INCREASING OUR UNDERSTANDING OF OTHERS

A sleepy little midwestern town was stirred from its absorption in its own affairs by the arrival of a D.P. family. The Garber family had come directly from Latvia and knew very little about the English language or American customs.

The five Garber children were enrolled immediately in the public school. Mara, the oldest, who was classified as a senior in high school, was determined to become a part of the American way of life as rapidly as possible. In her desire to learn the English language, she talked a little too much—and made a good many mistakes as a result. The high-school fellows and girls had the feeling that Mara was a bit too aggressive for someone who had just come to America.

One Sunday evening after church several of the high-school gang were discussing the Garber family, Mara in particular.

"Do we have to invite her to youth fellowship meetings?" Janet asked peevishly.

"I thought that was one of the purposes of our youth fellowship," Jack commented, "to help young people feel at home in our community."

"We don't have many new people in our town," Helen added. "When a young person comes all the way from Latvia, I think we should at least invite her to our group."

"Oh, I know," Janet complained, "but she talks too much. We have to answer too many of her questions at school."

"She's only trying to learn about our country," Helen said. "Everything is strange to her here."

"If we give her an inch, she'll take a mile," Janet persisted. "She'll try to run our youth fellowship."

"Maybe we should think about our responsibility to Mara and her family," Jack suggested, "rather than how we feel about her personally."

"That sounds too pious to me," Bill spoke up for the first time. "I

219

agree with Janet. Why do we have any special responsibility to the Garbers? We've let them come to this country. Now that they're here, they should be able to look out for themselves."

"I'm afraid I can't go along with you on that, Bill," Helen said quietly. "We're Christian young people. We have a responsibility to anyone who needs our help. Mara is just our age. We can help her more than anyone else. If we were more friendly and helpful to her, she wouldn't have to ask so many questions."

"Maybe we could help her with her English instead of just laughing at her mistakes," Jack added.

"I think we should try to put ourselves in her place," Helen continued. "Then we'd understand why she's trying so hard to find out about everything and to make new friends."

"You two are rather convincing," Janet admitted, "with all your ideas on Christian responsibility."

"I suppose we should try to help her," Bill agreed somewhat reluctantly.

"It might turn out," Jack added, "that she can help us as much as we can help her."

As a result of this conversation, Mara Garber was invited to attend the youth meetings at the church. Within a few months she became an active, enthusiastic member of the group.

"I have a confession to make," Janet said to Jack one day after school.

"A confession?" Jack asked. "This is so sudden—and so unusual!"

"No joking, please," Janet admonished. "I'm serious—for once." And Jack realized that she really was in earnest about something.

"You and Helen were right," Janet continued, "about inviting Mara to our youth fellowship. I think we have been able to help her, and I know she has brought new life and enthusiasm to our group."

"I'm glad you feel that way about her," Jack said. "I think that because of Mara all of us are much more interested in people of other countries."

"Mara seems more a part of the community since she joined our group," Janet added. "And she doesn't ask so many questions, does she?"

"I think we ask her more questions now than she does us," Jack said with a grin.

"Bill has changed his ideas about Mara, too," Janet continued.

"Why, yes, he has," Jack agreed. "I noticed that he was talking to Mara during most of the lunch hour this noon."

"What about Mara's younger brothers and sisters?" Janet asked. "Couldn't our group do something for them too? They haven't even started to Sunday school yet."

"We should get better acquainted with them," Jack suggested, "and maybe we could help them with clothes. Their clothes are different from the clothes our younger brothers and sisters wear. Perhaps that's one reason they haven't started to Sunday school."

"I have it!" Janet declared excitedly. "It won't be so very long until Christmas. Why can't we help the Garbers celebrate their first Christmas in America? We could decorate a Christmas tree for them and have candy and toys and some new clothes for the younger children."

"That sounds swell," Jack agreed. "And why couldn't we sing Christmas carols with them and have a brief Christmas service in their home?"

"Here comes Mara now," Janet exclaimed. "Let's see what she thinks of the idea. . . . We have an idea, Mara. Will you let our youth fellowship help your family celebrate your first Christmas in America? We could all decorate a Christmas tree together and have games and Christmas carols and the Christmas story and gifts and everything that belongs with Christmas."

Mara's eyes were shining. "All of you are too wonderful to me and my family," she said. "I never knew there was any place in the world where people have such lovely ideas as in America."

"Bill will go for our brain storm," Jack said. "He always wants to do something extra special at Christmas. By the way, have either of you seen Bill since school?"

"Why, yes, I was just talking to him," Mara said, her cheeks turning a beautiful pink hue.

"Come on, Mara," Janet urged, "You're keeping something from us!"

"Well, you see," Mara said simply, "Bill just asked me to go to the school prom with him tomorrow night, and I'm still a little bit excited!"

"Good for you, Mara," Janet said sincerely. "That's really good news!"

As Janet watched Mara's radiant face, she wondered how she or Bill or anyone else could ever have objected to inviting Mara Garber to church. And Janet knew now that Bill had been pondering this same strange problem for many days! [9]

SOLO: "A Noble Life" (tune: "Serenity" C. M.).
> A noble life, a simple faith,
> An open heart and hand—
> These are the lovely litanies
> Which all men understand.
>
> These are the firm-knit bonds of grace,
> Though hidden to the view,
> Which bind in sacred brotherhood
> All men the whole world through.
>   —A. S. ISAACS

CLOSING PRAYER:
We thank thee, our Father, for the bonds of Christian love and fellowship which link together all nations of the world. We are grateful for the contributions which the peoples of all races are making to the composite life of mankind. Help us to be more appreciative of the abilities of those whose background is different from our own. May we discover ways of strengthening the ties that unite us with the people of other nations. May we help and encourage those in our own country who have recently come from other lands. Above all, may we, by our deeds and by our words, show them the way of light and love which has been provided for all mankind by Jesus Christ. AMEN.

30. Choosing the High Road

SUGGESTIONS TO THE LEADER:
This program deals with the physical, emotional, and mental aspects of life, and stresses the importance of Christian growth and development in these important areas of life. Prepare enough copies of the check list so that each young person may have one. Be sure to have sufficient pencils available.

PRELUDE: "I'm Pressing on the Upward Way"

CALL TO WORSHIP:
Not that I have already obtained this or am already perfect; but I press on to make it my own, because Christ Jesus has made me his own. Brethren, I do not consider that I have made it my own; but one thing I do, forgetting what lies behind and straining forward to what lies ahead, I press on toward the goal for the prize of the upward call of God in Christ Jesus.[1]

PRAYER:
Help us, O God, to hear thy upward call within our minds and souls. May we earnestly desire to choose the high road in every area of life. Help us to walk with thee in all of life's experiences, so that we may press onward and upward each day. AMEN.

HYMN: "I'm Pressing on the Upward Way" or "Walk in the Light"

POEM:

> To every man there openeth
> A Way, and Ways, and a Way.
> And the High Soul climbs the High Way,
> And the Low Soul gropes the Low,

And in between, on the misty flats,
The rest drift to and fro.
But to every man there openeth
A High Way, and a Low.
And every man decideth
The way his soul shall go.[2]

—JOHN OXENHAM

LEADER:[3]

Every young person, as he stands at the threshold of life, is confronted with the challenge of choosing the high road. Life is a journey. There are many decisions that we must make along the way. We must constantly be deciding which road we will take. This is not always easy to do. There are many roads branching out in various directions, and it is easy to get off on a side road that leads us away from the high road of Christian growth and development.

A Christian young person has the responsibility of choosing the high road in every area of his life—physical, mental, emotional, and spiritual. All aspects of life are vitally important if we desire to follow the high road of Christian discipleship. (Distribute pencils and copies of the following check list.)

CHECK LIST:

PERTINENT PROBLEMS OF YOUTH

(Read thoughtfully the following statements, and check each one either "true," "false," or "uncertain.")

	True	False	Uncertain
1. The physical body has very little relationship to one's mental and spiritual life.	___	___	___
2. A Christian has a moral responsibility to observe the laws of good health.	___	___	___
3. Since many scientific tests indicate that smoking is harmful to the body, it is			

224

wrong for Christian young people to
smoke. _____ _____ _____

4. It is wrong for a Christian young person to drink alcoholic beverages—even
in small amounts. _____ _____ _____

5. Drinking alcoholic beverages is a personal matter which affects only the
individual who drinks. _____ _____ _____

6. Losing one's temper is a personal problem which has little relationship to
living the Christian life. _____ _____ _____

7. Faith and prayer can help a young person control such emotions as anger,
hatred, and jealousy. _____ _____ _____

8. Every aspect of life—physical, mental,
emotional, and spiritual—should be
dedicated to God and used for his
honor and glory. _____ _____ _____

A DISCUSSION OF THE CHECK LISTS:

Take time to discuss the check lists, encouraging each young person
to share his ideas and give his reasons for checking his list as he did.
Be sure to keep in mind during the discussion the theme of this meeting: "Choosing the High Road"—in every area of life.

A LIFE SITUATION:

Dave and Frank had been pals for many years. They were active
members of the same church, had graduated from high school
together, and were both enrolled as freshmen in the university in their
home town.

"Are you going to the youth fellowship party at the church tonight?"
Dave asked one Friday afternoon.

"No," Frank replied, "I'm going to a fraternity open house."

"What!" Dave exclaimed. "I thought we'd decided we didn't have the time or money to join a fraternity!"

"I've changed my mind," Frank explained. "I've decided I want a little more fun and excitement than I had during high school. Besides, all the 'big shots' on the campus belong to a fraternity."

"I'm not so sure about that," Dave said. "What about all the youth fellowship activities we've planned for this fall?"

"I'll go to most of them," Frank said, "but I won't be able to go tonight."

It was exactly four weeks before Frank showed up for a youth fellowship meeting.

"Where have you been keeping yourself?" Dave asked.

"I've been pretty busy with social activities," Frank said. "I told you I'm looking for fun and excitement."

"Have you found what you're looking for?" Dave asked rather abruptly.

"Why, yes, I guess so," Frank answered. "By the way, this group has really changed! I don't know half the gang here tonight."

"Come around a little more often and get acquainted," Dave advised.

It was several months before Frank made his appearance at another youth meeting. He stopped attending the college church-school class entirely. Only occasionally was he present for a church worship service.

At first Dave was provoked at Frank's behavior. By spring he was genuinely concerned. He knew that Frank had started smoking and was quite sure that he drank his share of cocktails at many of the social affairs that he attended. Frank never attended church any more, and at school he avoided Dave as much as possible.

Dave finally cornered Frank one day after school. "We've been missing you at church, Frank," he said. "Why don't you start coming to our youth activities again?"

"The last time I was there," Frank said, "everyone seemed different. I didn't know what was going on, and I felt very much out of place."

"I don't think we've changed that much, Frank," Dave said. "You just need to come a few times and get acquainted again."

"It would be pretty hard to come back," Frank said with a trace of wistfulness in his voice.

226

"Why would it, Frank?" Dave asked, feeling, for the first time, real sympathy for his friend.

"I don't know," Frank replied slowly. "Maybe I'm the one who has changed. Maybe that's the reason."

"Have you found fun and excitement?" Dave asked, remembering Frank's goal when he entered the university.

"I thought so," Frank answered, "especially at first. Now it's just one hectic round of activities. But," he added with the same trace of wistfulness, "once you get started in this kind of life, it's mighty hard to stop."

SHARING SESSION:

1. Is it possible to attend school activities and social events and still maintain one's interest in and loyalty to the church?

2. What was wrong with Frank's goal when he entered the university?

3. Can a young person become a part of a social-minded crowd without being influenced by it?

4. Why did Frank begin smoking and drinking?

5. Why did he feel out of place at youth fellowship meetings?

6. Should Dave and the other youth fellowship members have done more to keep Frank from drifting away from the church? What should they have done?

7. Do you think Frank will resume his activities in the church and again become a part of the youth group? Why is it difficult for him to do so?

SEARCHING THE SCRIPTURES:

1. What the Bible says about the physical aspect of life:

"Do you not know that your body is a temple of the Holy Spirit within you, which you have from God? You are not your own; you were bought with a price. So glorify God in your body." (I Cor. 6:19-20.)

This scripture passage emphasizes the importance of our physical bodies. It indicates that our bodies were entrusted to us for the purpose of bringing honor and glory to God. We should take the best possible care of our bodies and do nothing that would weaken, harm, or dishonor them.

"I appeal to you therefore, brethren, by the mercies of God, to present your bodies as a living sacrifice, holy and acceptable to God, which is your spiritual worship." (Rom. 12:1.)

This verse of scripture is a challenge to present our bodies to God as a *living* sacrifice. Are we aware of the amazing capabilities of our physical bodies? Are we grateful for the ability to breathe, to take nourishment, to use our brains, to speak, to work with our hands, to see and hear, to use all the varied and intricate muscles of our bodies? Or, do we take these marvelous blessings for granted? Do you suppose that the hundreds of polio patients in our country are aware of the priceless privilege of good health? Does this thought help us to realize the importance of appreciating and caring for our bodies?

2. What the Bible says about the emotional aspect of life:

"Let love be genuine; hate what is evil, hold fast to what is good; love one another with brotherly affection; outdo one another in showing honor. Never flag in zeal, be aglow with the Spirit, serve the Lord. Rejoice in your hope, be patient in tribulation, be constant in prayer." (Rom. 12:9-12.)

Many different emotions are mentioned in this scripture passage, such as, love, hatred, affection, zeal, enthusiasm, joy, patience, and persistence. The emotions are a vital and wonderful part of life. When emotions are directed along constructive channels, they provide the incentive for the most worth-while relationships and experiences of life.

"But the fruit of the Spirit is love, joy, peace, patience, kindness, goodness, faithfulness, gentleness, self-control; . . . And those who belong to Christ Jesus have crucified the flesh with its passions and desires." (Gal. 5:22-24.)

This helpful list of Christian virtues gives us guidance as we choose the high road of Christian growth in the realm of our emotions. Notice that self-control is listed in this passage as one of the characteristics of the Spirit-filled life. We must discipline our lives so that our emotions will be utilized in helpful, constructive ways. Our emotions are given to us by God; and when properly guided by God's Spirit, they are an important part of Christian discipleship and Christian growth.

228

3. What the Bible says about the mental aspect of life:

"Happy is the man who finds wisdom, and the man who gets understanding, for the gain from it is better than gain from silver and its profit better than gold. She is more precious than jewels, and nothing you desire can compare with her." (Prov. 3:13-15.)

This scripture passage from the Old Testament describes in beautiful language the value and significance of wisdom. Wisdom and understanding are of greater importance than knowledge. A wise person makes use of the knowledge he possesses and applies it helpfully and constructively in his daily living.

Jesus then said to the Jews who had believed in him, "If you continue in my word, you are my disciples, and you will know the truth, and the truth will make you free." (John 8:31-32.)

Jesus is the truth about God and about all the important issues of life. He wants us to know the truth as it is found in him and to experience the genuine freedom that comes with a possession of the truth. Real freedom and democracy are based on the truth of Christ as it is revealed in God's Word.

"I will pray with the spirit and I will pray with the mind also; I will sing with the spirit and I will sing with the mind also. Brethren, do not be children in your thinking; be babies in evil, but in thinking be mature." (I Cor. 14:14, 20.)

In these interesting verses the apostle Paul shows the importance of both emotion and intellect. Both should be utilized when we pray, when we sing, and in all the other experiences of life. One should not be emphasized to the exclusion of the other. Both mind and emotion should be dedicated to God and directed along paths that are righteous and worthy.

LEADER:

We have discovered from the Bible the importance of choosing the high road in every area of life. Every nook and corner of our lives should be dedicated to Jesus Christ. We should enter the inner throne room of our souls and, asking self to leave, we should invite our Lord to take his place upon the throne.

POEM:

Take Thou our minds, dear Lord, we humbly pray;
Give us the mind of Christ each passing day;
Teach us to know the truth that sets us free;
Grant us in all our thoughts to honor Thee.

Take Thou our hearts, O Christ, they are thine own;
Come Thou within our souls and claim Thy throne;
Help us to shed abroad Thy deathless love;
Use us to make the earth like heaven above.

Take Thou our wills, dear Lord. Hold Thou full sway;
Have in our inmost souls Thy perfect way;
Guard each sacred hour from selfish ease;
Guide our ordered lives as Thou dost please.

Take Thou ourselves, O Lord, heart, mind, and will;
Through our surrendered lives Thy plans fulfill.
We yield ourselves to Thee—time, talents, all;
We hear, and henceforth heed, Thy sovereign call.

—ANONYMOUS

HYMN (to be sung softly as a prayer): "Have Thine Own Way, Lord!"
or "Take My Life, and Let It Be"

CLOSING PRAYER:

Take complete possession of our lives, O Christ. Forgive us for the sins we have committed when we have tried to direct our own lives. Be our Master and Guide in every area of life and in every thought and experience. Help us to walk each day along the high road of Christian growth and discipleship. AMEN.

31. Flying the Beam

PRELUDE: "All the Way My Saviour Leads Me"

CALL TO WORSHIP:

> The fairest things are those that silent come;
>   You may not hear the first approach of morn,
> And though you listen as the golden sum
>   Of hours fade into dusk, no sound is born.
> When the stars dance on high no bugles blow;
>   The footsteps of the flowers fall silently,
> As softly come the blossoms of the snow;
>   And clouds float by in pale tranquility.
> No voices herald moonlight on a lake;
>   The silvery dew is still; these gifts are given
> As quietly as Christ, who for our sake
>   Was sent to us, the greatest gift of heaven.
> Tenderly now, as in the yesterday,
>   He leads earth-weary children in His way.[1]
>   —ELIZABETH SCOLLARD

HYMN: "Saviour, Like a Shepherd Lead Us" or "He Leadeth Me:
O Blessed Thought"

PRAYER:

We are grateful, O Christ, that you are our Saviour and Guide and
that you are able to lead us through every temptation and pitfall of
life. Help us to realize our need for growth and guidance and to go
forward, under your leadership, to a more complete understanding of
the meaning of Christian discipleship. AMEN.

231

SCRIPTURE:

But grace was given to each of us according to the measure of Christ's gift. And his gifts were that some should be apostles, some prophets, some evangelists, some pastors and teachers, for the equipment of the saints, for the work of ministry, for building up the body of Christ, until we all attain to the unity of the faith and of the knowledge of the Son of God, to mature manhood, to the measure of the stature of the fullness of Christ.[2]

LEADER: [3]

The Christian life is not a destination. It is a journey, a quest, a continual process of growth. We never "fully arrive" in the Christian life. No matter how far we travel along the Christian pathway, there are always vast vistas of experience and growth ahead of us to beckon us upward and onward.

The apostle Paul described the challenge of Christian growth by declaring that we should use the gifts which God has given us "until we all attain . . . to mature manhood, to the measure of the stature of the fullness of Christ."

POEM:

> Take us on the Quest of Beauty,
>   Poet Seer of Galilee,
> Making all our dreams creative,
>   Through their fellowship with Thee.
>
> Take us on the Quest of Knowledge,
>   Clearest Thinker man has known!
> Make our minds sincere and patient,
>   Satisfied by Truth alone.
>
> Take us on the Quest of Service,
>   Kingly Servant of man's needs,
> Let us work with Thee for others,
>   Anywhere Thy purpose leads.
>
> All along our Quest's far pathway,

232

Christ our Leader and our guide,
Make us conscious of Thy presence,
Walking always at our side.[4]
—Eleanor B. Stock

LEADER:

Airminded youth in today's world will be challenged to think of the Christian life as an airplane journey. An airplane makes its best progress when it stays "on the beam." A beam is a radio signal transmitted for the guidance of pilots. Therefore, pilots speak of "flying the beam." This means that a pilot is keeping his plane on the exact course indicated by the radio beam.

God has provided a "radio beam" for the Christian life. Christ is the Light of the world. He is our radio beacon or beam. By looking to him and keeping our minds fixed upon him, we can stay on the right course and keep going forward in the Christian life.

There are several specific aids which will help us stay "on the beam" in the realm of Christian growth and discipleship.

TALK I:

FLYING THE BEAM BY PRAYER

Prayer will help us stay "on the beam" in Christian discipleship. It will help us go forward "to mature manhood, to the measure of the stature of the fulness of Christ."

Jesus is our supreme example in the matter of prayer. He lived a life of prayer and communion with the Father. The Gospel of Mark tells us what Jesus did before a busy day of teaching and preaching in various towns of Galilee. He arose a great while before day, went out to a lonely place, and there he prayed.

In Matthew we read about a great throng which surrounded Jesus one day. He taught them, healed the sick, and fed more than five thousand of them. After this strenuous day of activity Jesus felt the need for quiet meditation and prayer. He dismissed the crowds and went into the hills by himself to pray.

Before choosing the twelve disciples, Jesus prayed—not for a few minutes, but throughout the night. On another occasion Jesus sent forth seventy of his disciples to preach the gospel. When the seventy disciples returned after a successful preaching mission, Jesus offered a prayer of thanksgiving.

Jesus also prayed at the tomb of Lazarus. He offered a prayer of gratitude, thanking God for raising Lazarus from the dead. This prayer of gratitude was offered *before* there was any evidence that Lazarus would be brought forth from the grave.

Jesus prayed in the Garden of Gethsemane. He prayed in agony that night, because he knew that the Cross lay immediately before him. He came from his prayer with a calm power that awed the mob which had come to arrest him.

If Jesus spent much time in prayer, surely we, too, need the strength and peace and guidance that come from prayer. We are in constant need of prayer if we are to stay "on the beam" in our Christian discipleship.

HYMN: "Sweet Hour of Prayer" or "Prayer Is the Soul's Sincere Desire"

TALK II:

FLYING THE BEAM BY BIBLE-READING

Growth in the spiritual realm comes through study, just as growth comes through study in other areas of life. As Christians, our textbook is the Bible. It is our chart and compass to guide us through life.

We should saturate our minds with the Word of God. Then we will be able to draw upon its storehouse of truths when we are faced with sudden temptations or when we must make on-the-spot decisions. The psalmist had this important use of the Scriptures in mind when he wrote, "I have laid up thy word in my heart, that I might not sin against thee." The psalmist emphasized another important purpose of God's Word: "Thy word is a lamp to my feet and a light to my path."

The apostle Paul wrote a letter of encouragement to a young man named Timothy. In this letter he listed a number of ways in which the Bible could be of guidance to Timothy and to every young person: "All scripture is inspired by God and profitable for teaching, for reproof, for correction, and for training in righteousness, that the man of God may be complete, equipped for every good work."

The Bible is a divine tool which God has placed at the disposal of each one of us. We must study and use this tool if we are to discover rich truths, just as a miner must use his tools if he is to discover rich veins of ore. The Bible may be compared, not only to a miner's tool, but also to the mine itself, for it contains teachings that are more valuable than precious jewels.

> Thy Word is like a deep, deep mine;
> And jewels rich and rare
> Are hidden in its mighty depths
> For every searcher there.[5]
> —EDWIN HODDER

The Bible is a book of power. Whenever it is read earnestly and followed faithfully, it transforms lives and communities. If we give it a chance, the Bible will be a source of guidance and inspiration to us in our daily decisions and experiences. It will be a mighty beacon light that will help us grow and glow as Christian disciples.

HYMN: "Thy Word Is like a Garden, Lord" or "Sing Them Over Again to Me"

TALK III:

FLYING THE BEAM BY SERVICE

The inspiration we receive from prayer and Bible-reading must be translated into action in our daily lives. The Bible frequently exhorts us to love God and our fellow men. This is emphasized in God's Word as the most important of all the commandments. We must demonstrate our love by deeds of loving service.

Through our church and its program of missionary activities, we will discover numerous avenues of Christian service. There are shut-ins to visit, missionaries to encourage and help, letters to write, classes to teach, programs to prepare. All types of talents can be utilized for the advancement of Christ's kingdom—musical talents, artistic talents, literary talents, manual skills, secretarial abilities, and all the rest!

Jesus' life was a constant demonstration of the importance of service.

He was interested in ministering to all the needs of mankind—physical, mental, social, and spiritual. Many of his teachings deal with the importance of unselfish service. On one occasion Jesus described the day of judgment as a time when the righteous will be commended for the service they have rendered to their fellow men. Jesus referred to himself as the King or Judge:

"Then the King will say to those at his right hand, 'Come, O blessed of my Father, inherit the kingdom prepared for you from the foundation of the world; for I was hungry and you gave me food, I was thirsty and you gave me drink, I was a stranger and you welcomed me, I was naked and you clothed me, I was sick and you visited me, I was in prison and you came to me.' Then the righteous will answer him, 'Lord, when did we see thee hungry and feed thee, or thirsty and give thee drink? And when did we see thee a stranger and welcome thee, or naked and clothe thee? And when did we see thee sick or in prison and visit thee?' And the King will answer them, 'Truly, I say to you, as you did it to one of the least of these my brethren, you did it to me.'" [6]

All the acts of service that we perform for the advancement of Christ's kingdom will strengthen our own faith and enable us to go forward in the Christian life. Deeds of love and kindness that we do for others in the name of Christ will help us stay "on the beam" in Christian discipleship.

HYMN: "O Master, Let Me Walk with Thee" or "We Thank Thee, Lord, Thy Paths of Service Lead"

TALK IV:

FLYING THE BEAM BY FAITH

It is our faith in Christ as our personal Saviour and Lord which is the ultimate test of whether or not we "fly the beam." Faith in Christ gives meaning to prayer and Bible-reading; it gives motivation and purpose to our acts of service.

Faith is real. It is dynamic. It can be experienced. It influences our thinking about sin and suffering, about life and death, about God and man. Faith influences our attitudes, our actions, our motives. Faith sets up the goals and purposes toward which we strive, and it determines the eagerness with which we work toward those goals.

Faith is more than a creed. It is more than an intellectual belief in God's existence. Faith is a conviction, a certainty, a loyalty. Faith is dedicating one's life to the will and purposes of God. True faith is the complete surrender of one's life to Jesus Christ and wholehearted loyalty to his cause.

How does faith in Christ enable us to stay "on the beam" in our daily activities and experiences? John, the beloved disciple, gives us the answer in these challenging words: "This is the victory that overcomes the world—*even our faith.*" Faith is the victory that overcomes the world and every problem the world can offer. Faith is the victory that overcomes every temptation, every disappointment, every worry, every heartache. Even defeat can be turned—through faith in Christ— into a spiritual victory. *What happens to us isn't nearly as important as the attitude we take toward the thing that happens.* Through a vital faith in Jesus Christ, we can take the constructive, victorious attitude that will enable us to discover spiritual triumph in the midst of disaster.

In a city in the Middle Western part of our country lives a humble Christian mother. She is slight of build and rather nervous and high strung. Through the years she has been devoted to her church and to her two sons. When both of her sons were sent overseas during World War II, many friends of the family said: "If anything happens to either of those boys, their mother will go to pieces."

Well, it did happen. The youngest son, a handsome lad twenty-one years of age, lost his life in a plane crash over the Pacific. The mother did not go to pieces. Her friends failed to realize the power of faith. Faith is practical. It can do wonderful things. This mother met her tragedy wtih poise and calm assurance. She did not waste time on self-pity. She continued her work in the church, teaching a class of boys who belonged to other mothers. Her son had been married before he went overseas, and the mother did all she could to help the young widow and the baby boy whom the young father had never seen. Two years later the daughter-in-law came to talk to this mother about a young man in whom she had become interested. The mother responded with the height of Christian unselfishness. She invited her daughter-in-law and the young man to her home for a delicious meal and an evening of fellowship. When they revealed to her that they were interested in marriage, she said to them, "I am thankful that my grandson will have such a fine father."

It takes a great faith in God and in the ultimate triumph of right to manifest a spirit like the spirit of this Christian mother. Faith is real. It can do marvelous things in the lives of humble people. Its measure is limitless. Faith can find a way to victory through every circumstance and experience.

A personal experience of faith in Christ is necessary for us to enter the Christian life. A growing, dynamic faith is necessary for growth in Christian discipleship. We must know Jesus Christ as Saviour, Master, and daily Companion if we would have a faith that is adequate for all the trials and testings of life.

LEADER:

Each one of us should dare to "fly the beam" as Christian disciples. We should dare to go forward in the Christian life. We should make prayer, Bible-reading, service, and faith more vital and meaningful in our daily experiences.

PERIOD OF SILENT PRAYER (as pianist plays softly "My Faith Looks Up to Thee")

HYMN (may be sung softly by the entire group or by a soloist): "My Faith Looks Up to Thee"

CLOSING PRAYER:

Forgive us, O Christ, for our failure to measure up to thy standards in our daily thoughts, words, and deeds. Increase our faith in thee and our dependence upon thy leadership. We earnestly pray that we may go forward with thee into new paths of Christian faith, dedication, and discipleship. AMEN.

32. Dedicating Our All to Christ
(A Candlelight Consecration Service)

SUGGESTIONS TO THE LEADER:
A medium-sized table and the following white candles will be needed for this service: 1 eighteen-inch candle, 4 twelve-inch candles, and sufficient small candles for the audience. The eighteen-inch candle with 2 twelve-inch candles on each side, should be arranged in candle-holders on the table. The tall center candle should be lighted before the service begins. The other candles may be lighted from the center candle at the appropriate times during the service. Each candlelighter will stand behind the candle that he is responsible for lighting. The leader may stand behind the tall center candle.

PRELUDE: "Follow the Gleam"

CALL TO WORSHIP:

> Lord, in the strength of grace,
>   With a glad heart and free,
> Myself, my residue of days,
>   I consecrate to Thee.
>
> Thy ransomed servant, I
>   Restore to Thee Thy own;
> And from this moment, live or die
>   To serve my God alone.
>   —CHARLES WESLEY

THE LORD'S PRAYER (in unison)

HYMN: "Now in the Days of Youth" or "Living for Jesus a Life That Is True"

POEM:

> O Sun of life, O wondrous shining Light,
> How pale our candles, flickering in the night!
> And yet we boast the splendor of their rays!
> Oh, make us humble, Lightener of our days.
>
> O Source of truth, O Wisdom past compare,
> Speak unto us, that we Thy truth may share.
> May some small portion of Thy heavenly lore
> Leaven our minds. Instruct us evermore.
>
> O Heart of God, O great unselfish Love,
> That came to earth, a Father's care to prove,
> We have but Thee; there is no other way
> To truth, to life, to God's eternal day.[1]
>
> —THOMAS CURTIS CLARK

LEADER:

Who shall separate us from the love of Christ? Shall tribulation, or distress, or persecution, or famine, or nakedness, or peril, or sword? No, in all these things we are more than conquerors through him who loved us. For I am sure that neither death, nor life, nor angels, nor principalities, nor things present, nor things to come, nor powers, nor height, nor death, nor anything else in all creation, will be able to separate us from the love of God in Christ Jesus our Lord.[2]

RESPONSE (by a soloist or by the entire group) (tune: "St. Catherine"):

> Jesus, Thy boundless love to me
> No thought can reach, no tongue declare;
> O knit my thankful heart to Thee,
> And reign without a rival there!
> Thine wholly, Thine alone, I am;
> Be Thou alone my constant Flame.

LEADER:

Beloved, let us love one another; for love is of God, and he who loves is born of God and knows God. He who does not love does not know God; for God is love. In this the love of God was made manifest among us, that God sent his only Son into the world, so that we might live through him.[3]

RESPONSE:

O grant that nothing in my soul
May dwell, but Thy pure love alone;
O may Thy love possess me whole,
My joy, my treasure, and my crown.
Strange fires far from my soul remove;
My every act, word, thought, be love.

LEADER:

Whoever confesses that Jesus is the Son of God, God abides in him, and he in God. So we know and believe the love God has for us. God is love, and he who abides in love abides in God, and God abides in him. There is no fear in love, but perfect love casts out fear. For fear has to do with punishment, and he who fears is not perfected in love. We love, because he first loved us.[4]

RESPONSE:

O love, how cheering is Thy ray!
All pain before Thy presence flies;
Care, anguish, sorrow, melt away,
Where-e'er Thy healing beams arise.
O Jesus, nothing may I see,
Nothing desire, or seek, but Thee![5]
—PAUL GERHARDT

LEADER:

In a concentration camp in Mandalay, Burma, is one of the most unusual churches in the world. In this concentration camp are a number of army officers from the Karen tribe of northern Burma. These officers have been in prison since 1950, when serious tension

241

developed between the Karens and the Burmese. Because these Karen officers are Christians, they have organized a church and are carrying on, in the concentration camp, an active ministry for Christ. More than six years of imprisonment and separation from their families have not dimmed their allegiance to Christ.

An American minister from Olympia, Washington, had the privilege of speaking at one of the worship services of this church within the concentration camp. After the service he met two deacons of the church, a church-school teacher, and the choir director—all of them prisoners far from their homes and families. One of the deacons told the American pastor: "There is a strong likelihood that several of us will lose our lives before any of us will be released. Whatever happens, we will not lose our faith in God."

These Karen Christians, under very difficult circumstances, are demonstrating their loyalty and devotion to Jesus Christ. The light of Christ illumines their hearts and minds even in the darkness of a concentration camp.

SOLO: "The Light of the World Is Jesus"

LEADER:

This tall lighted candle represents the Lord Jesus, who said: "I am the light of the world; he who follows me will not walk in darkness, but will have the light of life." As Christian youth, we desire to experience in greater measure the meaning of Christian discipleship. We desire to radiate the light of Christ and to dedicate our lives more wholeheartedly to him.

FIRST CANDLELIGHTER:

We should dedicate our bodies to Christ and ask him to use them to advance his kingdom upon the earth. Most of us have strong, healthy bodies. We could accomplish a tremendous amount of work for Christ, if we would dedicate our energy and strength to him and to his church.

The apostle Paul declared: "I appeal to you therefore, brethren, by the mercies of God, to present your bodies as a living sacrifice, holy and acceptable to God, which is your spiritual worship." Paul also reminded us: "Do you not know that your body is a temple of the Holy Spirit within you, which you have from God? You are not your own; you were bought with a price. So glorify God in your body."

This candle represents our physical strength, which we desire to dedicate to Christ. (Light first candle to right of center candle.)

SECOND CANDLELIGHTER:

Our minds are a marvelous gift from God and should be used for the glory of God and the building of his kingdom throughout the world. Do we ever stop to think of the multitude of fascinating pursuits which the mind enables us to do? Because of our minds we are able to think, to reason, to remember, to plan, and to create. In short, the mind is the focal point of all our human activity. Without our minds we would not have the full use of our bodies, our physical senses, our feelings, our attitudes, or any of the faculties which distinguish man from the beast of the field.

We should ask God to cleanse and purify our minds. We should develop our minds by studying the Bible and other stimulating books. We should give creative thought and effort to the work that we do to promote the kingdom of Christ. This candle symbolizes our minds, which we desire to dedicate to Christ. (Lights first candle to left of center candle.)

THIRD CANDLELIGHTER:

Time is a gift from God which is so vast that we cannot comprehend its immensity. It is difficult for us to think in terms of the long ages that are past or to project our thoughts into the eternities of the future. On the other hand, time, as it applies to our own lives, is so fleeting that we have difficulty in making wise use of it. We cannot bring back a single minute that is past. We cannot stop the ceaseless flow of time for one moment or borrow time from the future. We have only the moment that is the present to fill with beauty and worth-while living.

Too many of us let moments and even hours slip away without translating this precious gift of time into constructive thoughts and unselfish deeds. We should ask God to help us use our time in ways that will advance his kingdom in our own community and throughout the world. This candle is a symbol of our time, which we desire to dedicate to Christ. (Lights second candle to right of center candle.)

FOURTH CANDLELIGHTER:

In addition to the faculties of body and mind which are common to mankind, God has given each one of us special talents and abilities which we should use for God's glory. We should think of these individual talents as blessings which have been entrusted to us to use for the happiness and betterment of mankind. One of the glorious things about God's plan for mankind is the tremendous potential of each individual. Each one of us has a unique combination of capabilities which makes us unlike any person who has lived in the past and any person who will live in the future. For this reason, each individual can make a contribution to mankind which no one else can make.

As Christians, we should dedicate to God's use the talents and abilities which have been given to us. This includes our ability to work and earn money. A sacrificial portion of our money should be given to the church, which is God's agency upon the earth for proclaiming his message of salvation to mankind. This candle represents our talents and possessions, which we desire to dedicate to Christ. (Lights second candle to left of center candle.)

LEADER:

No man is common. Each one of us has unique and uncommon capabilities which we can use to bring blessings to others and glory to God. We may not yet have discovered the special contribution we should make to the kingdom of God. With the help of Christ, we will be able to find our place in God's plan.

As we light our individual candles from the tall white candle representing Christ, let us rededicate our lives to our Master and Lord. May we earnestly resolve to dedicate to him our strength, our minds, our time, our talents, our all. (The young people may light their individual candles from the center candle and form a circle around the room. While the young people light their candles and form the circle, the pianist may play softly "Are Ye Able, Said the Master.")

SOLO (as the young people hold their lighted candles): "Are Ye Able, Said the Master"

CLOSING PRAYER:

May we dedicate our lives to thee, O Christ, in a spirit of gratitude and love. We are grateful that you have shown us the way to make our lives purposeful and worth while. Help us to discover that the way of discipleship is the way of sacrificial service in our everyday contacts. May we demonstrate our dedication to thee by the light of love and kindness that we radiate to those about us. May our light shine more brightly because we have had a new experience of thy glory and thy radiance. AMEN.

RESPONSE (by the soloist or by the entire group):
"Lord, we are able."
Our spirits are Thine.
Remold them, make us,
Like Thee, divine.
Thy guiding radiance
Above us shall be
A beacon to God,
To love and loyalty.
—EARL MARLATT

(The leader may suggest that the young people leave quietly as the pianist continues to play the consecration hymn. The candles should be put out as the young people leave the room.)

Notes

PROGRAM 1. THE BIBLE THROUGH THE AGES
1. Pss. 19:7-9; 119:9-11, 105.
2. Rom. 15:4; II Tim. 3:16-17; I Pet. 1:24-25.
3. "God's Word." From *Masterpieces of Religious Verse*, Harper & Bros., 1948. Used by permission.

PROGRAM 2. HOW THE BIBLE HELPS US TODAY
1. Ps. 119:15-16, 18.
2. Matt. 7:21, 24.
3. Ps. 119:33-34.
4. Used by permission of Louis P. O'Connell, owner.

PROGRAM 3. WHAT GOD IS LIKE
1. Used by permission of John Haynes Holmes.
2. Isa. 64:8; Matt. 6:9-10; 7:11; I Cor. 8:5-6.
3. Ps. 90:1-2; John 4:23-24
4. Isa. 6:3; 57:15; I Pet. 1:14-16.
5. Pss. 40:10; 92:1-2; Lam. 3:22-23; I Cor. 1:9; 10:13.
6. Rom. 5:8; 8:38-39; I John 4:16; John 3:16.
7. I Tim. 1:17.

PROGRAM 4. HOW GOD MAKES HIMSELF KNOWN TO US
1. Pss. 19:1; 104:24; 95:1 2.
2. "Day Is Dying in the West."

PROGRAM 5. THE REALITY OF JESUS
1. "What Is Prayer?"

PROGRAM 6. WHAT JESUS MEANS TO US
1. "O Christ, the Way."
2. "The Way, the Truth, the Life."
3. Eph. 3:20-21.

PROGRAM 7. UNDERSTANDING THE HOLY SPIRIT
1. Used by permission of Allan Knight Chalmers.
2. Gen. 1:1-2.
3. Ps. 51:10-11; Isa. 61:1; Joel 2:28; Mic. 3:8; Zech. 4:6.
4. Matt. 3:16-17; 28:18-19.
5. John 14:16-17; 15:26; 16:7; Luke 24:49.
6. Acts 2:1-4.
7. John 3:5-6.
8. John 14:26; Rom. 14:17; 15:13; Gal. 5:22-23.
9. "Holy Spirit, Dwell with Me."

PROGRAM 8. HOW THE HOLY SPIRIT HELPS US TODAY
1. Used by permission of Mrs. Henry Hallam Tweedy.
2. John 3:5.
3. John 3:6.
4. John 14:16.
5. John 14:17.
6. John 14:26.
7. John 16:7-8.
8. John 16:13.
9. Acts 1:8.
10. Rom. 14:17.
11. This is the true story of the post-high youth group of the First Baptist Church, Lincoln, Nebraska.

PROGRAM 9. THE MEANING OF LIFE
1. "The Winds of Fate." Used by permission of Rand McNally & Co.
2. Luke 12:15-21; Jas. 4:13-16.
3. Gen. 1:27; 2:7 (K.J.V.); Matt. 4:3-4; John 3:5-7; II Cor. 4:6, 7, 16.
4. Matt. 6:19-21.
5. "The Way, the Truth, and the Life."

PROGRAM 10. FINDING THE ANSWER TO SIN
1. "The Master's Touch."
3. Jude 1:24-25.

PROGRAM 11. DISCOVERING THE WAY OF SALVATION
1. "Thy Will Be Done." Used by permission.
2. St. Augustine.

PROGRAM 12. LET CHRIST COME IN
1. "Every Youth." Used by permission of Mary S. Edgar.
2. John 6:35, 51; 3:16-18; Rev. 3:20.
3. "My Prayer." Copyright © Hope Publishing Co.
4. This story is a condensation of a sermon by Dr. Samuel M. Lindsay and is used by permission.

PROGRAM 13. HOW CHRIST CHANGES LIVES
1. Rom. 12:1-2; Phil. 4:8.
2. "Consecration."
3. The remainder of this program was originally published under the title "By Their Fruits" in the summer, 1955, issue of *High Call,* and is reprinted here by permission of the publisher, the American Baptist Publication Society.
4. Copyright © Hope Publishing Co.

PROGRAM 14. THE MISSION OF THE CHURCH
1. From *Hymns for Junior Worship.* Copyright, 1940, by The Presbyterian Board of Christian Education. Used by permission.
2. I Cor. 3:11.
3. Eph. 4:4-6.

4. Matt. 11:28-29.
5. Eph. 5:25-27.

PROGRAM 15. THE HOPE OF IMMORTALITY

1. "Our Christ." Copyright 1921 by Harry Webb Farrington. Used by permission of The Hymn Society of America.
2. "The Soul Eternal."
3. I John 4:7-9.
4. Rom. 8:35, 37-39.
5. John 11:25; 14:1-3, 19.
6. Matt. 28:1-7.
7. Acts 2:32, 36; 4:33.
8. This story originally appeared under the title "He Conquered Death," pupil's book of the junior-high course *Strong Son of God*, published in 1956 by the American Baptist Publication Society, and is reprinted here by permission of the publisher.

PROGRAM 16. THE FINAL TRIUMPH OF CHRIST'S KINGDOM

1. Phil. 2:9-11.
2. "An Affirmation." From *Masterpieces of Religious Verse*, Harper & Bros., 1948. Used by permission.
3. Mark 1:14-15; Luke 17:20-21.
4. Matt. 6:28-33.
5. Matt. 13:24-32.
6. I Tim. 1:17 (A.S.V.).

PROGRAM 17. PRAYER MAKES A DIFFERENCE

1. This program was originally published under the title "Men Who Live by Prayer" in the winter, 1951, issue of *High Call*, and is reprinted here by permission of the publisher, the American Baptist Publication Society.
2. Ps. 95:1-6.
3. The statements by Dr. Laubach are taken from two of his books—*Letters by a Modern Mystic* (New York: Student Volunteer Movement) and *Prayer, the Mightiest Force in the World* (Westwood, New Jersey: Fleming H. Revell Co.)—and are used by permission.
4. This impersonation is based on an actual interview which I had with Dr. Jones at Green Lake, Wisconsin, in July, 1951. The statements on prayer are Dr. Jones' own words, as he gave them during the interview.

PROGRAM 18. DISCOVERING THE MEANING OF PRAYER

1. From "The Vision Splendid." Used by permission of Erica Oxenham.
2. The remainder of this program was originally published under the title "Prayer— What and Why" in the winter, 1951, issue of *High Call*, and is reprinted here by permission of the publisher, the American Baptist Publication Society.
3. Luke 18:9-14.
4. Matt. 6:5-8.
5. Matt. 5:6; 7:7-11.
6. Matt. 14:23; Mark 1:35; Luke 6:12-13; Matt. 26:36-41.
7. "What Is Prayer?"

PROGRAM 19. EXPERIENCING THE REALITY OF PRAYER
1. Matt. 7:7-8.
2. From *The Hymnal for Youth*. Copyright, 1927, 1955, by The Presbyterian Board of Christian Education. Used by permission.
3. Luke 11:1-4.
4. The remainder of this program is adapted from a program entitled "My Personal Prayer Plan" and was originally published in the winter, 1951, issue of *High Call*. It is used by permission of the publisher, the American Baptist Publication Society.

PROGRAM 20. THE IMPORTANCE OF SHARING OUR FAITH
1. This program was originally published under the title "Why Be Evangelists?" in the fall, 1951, issue of *High Call*, and is reprinted here by permission of the publisher, the American Baptist Publication Society.
2. Matt. 28:18-20.
3. Heb. 13:20-21.

PROGRAM 21. REACHING OTHERS FOR CHRIST
1. Used by permission of John Haynes Holmes.
2. Matt. 9:35-38.
3. "Send Me."
4. The remainder of this program was originally published under the title "What's the Route?" in the fall, 1951, issue of *High Call*, and is reprinted here by permission of the publisher, the American Baptist Publication Society.
5. II Thess. 2:16-17.

PROGRAM 22. DISCOVERING OUR LIFEWORK
1. "Work," from *Music and Other Poems* by Henry van Dyke, copyright 1904 by Charles Scribner's Sons, 1932 by Henry van Dyke. Reprinted by permission of the Publisher.

PROGRAM 23. USING OUR LIVES FOR CHRIST
1. "The Faith of Christ's Freemen." Used by permission of Mrs. Thomas Curtis Clark.
2. Matt. 5:10-12.
4. Matt. 10:37-39.
5. "A Prayer."
6. The factual material in this story is from Mrs. Howard Taylor's *Borden of Yale* (China Inland Mission).
7. "Builders." Used by permission of Purd E. Deitz.

PROGRAM 24. THE MEANING OF CHRISTIAN FRIENDSHIP
1. "Hymn of At-One-Ment." Used by permission of John Haynes Holmes.
2. John 15:14-15.
3. John 13:34-35.
4. Matt. 18:21-22; 6:14-15.
5. Matt. 7:1-5.
6. Rom. 12:9-10, 14-15, 21.
7. I Cor. 6:19-20; Phil. 4:8.
8. John 15:10-11.

9. This skit was originally published in the summer, 1951, issue of *High Call,* and is reprinted here by permission of the publisher, the American Baptist Publication Society.
10. Num. 6:24-26.

PROGRAM 25. PREPARING FOR CHRISTIAN MARRIAGE
1. Col. 3:12-14.

PROGRAM 26. THERE'S MY IDEAL
1. "Dreams and Deeds."
2. The remainder of this program is adapted from a program which was originally published in the summer, 1952, issue of *High Call,* and is used by permission of the publisher, the American Baptist Publication Society.

PROGRAM 27. RIGHT ATTITUDES TOWARD MONEY
1. From *Masterpieces of Religious Verse,* Harper & Bros., 1948. Used by permission.
2. Matt. 19:16-22.
3. Used by permission of Etta W. Schlichter.

PROGRAM 28. THE MEANING OF CHRISTIAN STEWARDSHIP
1. Used by permission of Little, Brown & Co.
2. John 20:21; Matt. 28:19-20.
3. I Cor. 4:1-2.
4. Matt. 9:35-38.
5. John 15:1-11.
6. II Cor. 9:6-8.

PROGRAM 29. APPRECIATING PEOPLE OF OTHER RACES
1. Reprinted by permission of Virgil Markham.
2. "A Prayer for Brotherhood" from *A Book of Prayers for Use in an Indian College.* Used by permission of the Society for Promoting Christian Knowledge, London, England.
3. "O God of Light" from *Hymns for Worship.* Used by permission of the publisher, Association Press.
4. Eph. 4:4-6.
5. Eph. 2:13-14.
6. Eph. 2:17-20.
7. Gal. 3:25-28.
8. "No East or West." Used by permission of Erica Oxenham.
9. This story originally appeared in 1953 in a booklet for senior-high campers, and is reprinted here by permission of the publisher, the American Baptist Publication Society.

PROGRAM 30. CHOOSING THE HIGH ROAD
1. Phil. 3:12-14.
2. "The Ways." From *"Gentlemen—The King!"* by John Oxenham. The Pilgrim Press. Used by permission.
3. The remainder of this program is adapted from a program published in the fall, 1954, issue of *High Call,* and is used by permission of the publisher, the American Baptist Publication Society.

PROGRAM 31. FLYING THE BEAM
1. "He Leads."
2. Eph. 4:7, 11-13.
3. The remainder of this program is adapted from a program published in the fall, 1954, issue of *High Call,* and is used by permission of the publisher, the American Baptist Publication Society.
4. "The Prayer of the Quest." Used by permission of Eleanor B. Stock.
5. "Thy Word Is Like a Garden, Lord."

PROGRAM 32. DEDICATING OUR ALL TO CHRIST
1. "O Sun of Life." Used by permission of Mrs. Thomas Curtis Clark.
2. Rom. 8:35, 37-39.
3. I John 4:7-9.
4. I John 4:15-16, 18-19.
5. Translated by John Wesley.

Sources for Hymns

CODE: The letter refers to the hymnal, and the number to the page on which the hymn is found in the hymnal.

A . . . The New Hymnal for American Youth
B . . . The Broadman Hymnal (Southern Baptist)
C . . . Cokesbury Worship Hymnal (Methodist)
E . . . The Hymnal, 1940 (Episcopal)
F . . . Baptist Hymnal (Southern Baptist)
H . . . The Hymnal (Presbyterian U.S.A.)
L . . . The Lutheran Hymnal
M . . . The Methodist Hymnal
P . . . Pilgrim Hymnal (Congregational, now United Church of Christ)
S . . . Common Service Book (Lutheran)
W . . . Christian Worship (American Baptist and Disciples)
Y . . . The Hymnal for Youth (Presbyterian)

A Charge to Keep I Have
B—157; C—74; F—358; M—287; P—500; S—376; W—373

All Hail the Power of Jesus' Name
A—135; B—1; C—14; E—355; F—132; H—192; L—339; M—164; P—142; S—131; W—252; Y—122

Am I a Soldier of the Cross?
B—176; E—550; F—405; L—445; M—284; S—378

A Noble Life, A Simple Faith
W—512

"Are Ye Able," Said the Master
A—205; B—396; C—186; F—351; M—268; W—360

Blessed Assurance, Jesus Is Mine
B—120; C—64; F—269; M—238; P—489; W—412

Blest Be the Tie That Binds
A—312; B—239; C—87; E—495; F—366; H—343; L—464; M—416; P—37; W—476; Y—141

Break Thou the Bread of Life
A—71; B—192; C—88; F—178; H—216; M—387; P—412; W—461; Y—133

Breathe on Me, Breath of God
A—61; E—375; F—164; H—213; M—180; P—201; Y—130

Christ for the World We Sing
B—267; E—537; F—458; H—378; M—481; P—369; S—218; W—538; Y—250

Come, Thou Almighty King
A—38; B—4; C—9; E—271; F—12; H—52; L—239; M—2; P—10; S—164; W—122; Y—33

Come to the Saviour Now
F—226; H—220; M—190; W—278

Crown Him with Many Crowns
A—136; B—18; E—352; F—152; H—190; L—341; M—170; S—134; W—250; Y—120

Dear Lord and Father of Mankind
A—152; B—401; C—79; E—435; F—335; H—302; M—342; P—224; W—411; Y—150

Draw Thou My Soul, O Christ
A—149; F—314; M—297; P—232; W—299; Y—164

Faith of Our Fathers
A—256; B—201; C—86; E—393; F—252; H—267; M—256; P—220; W—348; Y—224

253

Father Almighty, Bless Us with Thy
Blessing
P—235; W—344

Fling Out the Banner
A—304; B—152; C—230; E—259; F
446; H—384; M—502; P—371; W—
540; Y—246

Give of Your Best to the Master
B—366; C—187; F—353; Y—176

God of Grace and God of Glory
C—235; E—524; F—465; M—279; W
—378; Y—236

God Who Touchest Earth with Beauty
A—223; F—45; W—315; Y—178

Gracious Spirit, Dwell with Me
H—214; P—186; W—270

Great Is Thy Faithfulness
F—47; W—165

Guide Me, O Thou Great Jehovah
B—181; C—44; E—434; F—55; H—
104; L—54; M—301; S—261; W—393

He Leadeth Me! O Blessed Thought!
B—422; C—35; E—426; F—58; H—
106; M—242; P—501; W—405; Y—54

Happy the Home When God Is There
C—97; F—374; M—428

Hark, the Voice of Jesus Calling
B—407; F—440; L—496; M—288; P
—504

Have Thine Own Way, Lord!
B—254; C—72; F—355; W—324; Y—
162

Holy Spirit, Hear Us
L—229; M—438; S—550

Holy Spirit, Truth Divine
A—60; C—20; E—377; H—208; M—
173; P—496; W—274; Y—128

How Firm a Foundation
A—74; B—199; C—48; E—564; F—
262; H—283; L—427; M—315; P—
211; S—344; W—406; Y—210

How Gentle God's Commands
H—279; M—69; P—205; W—399

How Lovely Is Thy Dwelling-place
M—383

I Know That My Redeemer Lives
B—413; F—127; L—200; M—329; S
—136; W—245; Y—184

I Love Thy Kingdom, Lord

A—311; B—196; C—8; E—388; F—
382; H—337; L—462; M—379; P—
404; S—199; W—428; Y—140

I Love to Tell the Story
B—371; C—65; F—141; H—443; M—
249; P—485; W—532; Y—193

I'm Pressing on the Upward Way
B—269; C—127; F—319

In Christ There Is No East or West
A—299; C—166; E—263; F—443; H
—341; M—507; P—389; W—480; Y
—243

I Need Thee Every Hour
A—150; B—193; C—54; E—438; F—
334; H—332; M—232; P—491; W—
341; Y—155

Into My Heart
B—321; C—190

I Serve a Risen Saviour
C—241; F—279

I've Found a Friend
B—28; C—93; F—261; M—241; P—
481; W—290; Y—190

I Would Be True
A—177; B—368; C—184; F—315; P
—469; W—361; Y—180

Jesus Calls Us
A—144; B—159; C—49; E—566; F—
360; H—223; L—270; M—233; P—
152; W—281; Y—198

Jesus, Saviour, Pilot me
A—160; B—158; C—71; F—337; H—
286; L—649; M—269; P—284; S—
270; W—409; Y—157

Jesus Shall Reign Where'er the Sun
A—305; B—150; C—13; E—542; F—
116; H—377; L—511; M—479; P—
373; S—219; W—527; Y—248

Jesus, Thou Joy of Loving Hearts
E—485; F—136; H—354; M—345; P
—415; S—354; W—419; Y—147

Jesus, Thy Boundless Love to Me
F—288; H—314; L—349; M—222; P
—278; S—355; W—380

Joyful, Joyful, We Adore Thee
A—43; E—281; F—44; H—5; M—12;
W—95; Y—6

Lead On, O King Eternal
A—199; B—236; C—21; E—554; F—

417; **H**—371; **M**—278; **P**—251; **W**—363; **Y**—226

Lift Up Our Hearts, O King of Kings
A—295; **H**—405; **M**—472

Light of the World, We Hail Thee
A—9; **F**—454; **H**—422; **M**—114; **P**—49; **W**—208; **Y**—281

Living for Jesus
B—373; **C**—173; **F**—352; **W**—304

Lord, for Tomorrow and Its Needs
A—317; **B**—259; **C**—102; **F**—339; **M**—314; **W**—327

Lord of All Being, Throned Afar
E—291; **H**—87; **M**—62; **P**—192; **W**—151; **Y**—56

Lord, Speak to Me, That I May Speak
A—251; **C**—167; **E**—574; **F**—340; **H** 399; **M**—460; **P**—339; **S**—212; **W**—470; **Y**—196

Love Divine, All Loves Excelling
A—67; **B**—19; **C**—22; **E**—479; **F**—2; **H**—308; **L**—351; **M**—372; **P**—270; **S**—276; **W**—379; **Y**—153

Master Speak! Thy Servant Heareth
M—221

More Love to Thee, O Christ
B—218; **C**—17; **E**—461; **F**—292; **H**—315; **M**—364; **P**—146; **W**—390; **Y**—191

My Faith Looks Up to Thee
A—155; **B**—209; **C**—122; **E**—449; **F**—257; **H**—285; **L**—394; **M**—213; **P**—498; **S**—360; **W**—355; **Y**—211

My God, I Thank Thee
A—51; **H**—73; **M**—9; **P**—11; **W**—109; **Y**—11

My Life, My Love, I Give to Thee
B—168; **C**—104; **F**—359; **W**—293

Now in the Days of Youth
A—146; **P**—477; **W**—300; **Y**—169

O God, Our Help in Ages Past
A—28; **B**—435; **C**—196; **E**—289; **F**—286; **H**—77; **L**—123; **M**—533; **P**—177; **S**—505; **W**—585; **Y**—40

O Happy Home, Where Thou Art Loved the Dearest
A—313; **F**—373; **L**—626; **M**—427; **W**—601; **Y**—262

O Jesus, I Have Promised

A—196; **B**—187; **C**—52; **E**—570; **F**—386; **H**—268; **M**—226; **P**—196; **W**—308; **Y**—174

O Jesus, Thou Art Standing
A—148; **B**—242; **C**—132; **E**—407; **F**—346; **H**—228; **M**—197; **P**—246; **S**—322; **W**—279; **Y**—201

O Master, Let Me Walk with Thee
A—197; **B**—202; **C**—50; **E**—572; **F**—426; **H**—364; **M**—259; **P**—291; **W**—306; **Y**—166

Open My Eyes, That I May See
B—351; **C**—89; **F**—312; **Y**—189

O Word of God Incarnate
A—68; **B**—75; **E**—402; **F**—183; **H**—215; **L**—294; **M**—386; **P**—421; **S**—169; **W**—434; **Y**—132

O Worship the King
A—36; **B**—2; **C**—7; **E**—288; **F**—20; **H**—2; **L**—17; **M**—4; **P**—5; **S**—294; **W**—94; **Y**—36

O Zion, Haste
A—306; **B**—151; **C**—16; **E**—261; **F**—451; **H**—382; **M**—475; **P**—372; **S**—224; **W**—529; **Y**—240

Praise God, from Whom All Blessings Flow
A—334; **B**—481; **C**—5; **E**—139; **F**—514; **L**—644; **M**—616; **P**—518; **W**—611; **Y**—2

Praise the Lord! Ye Heavens, Adore Him
A—30; **F**—9; **H**—10; **M**—11; **P**—7; **S**—300; **W**—110; **Y**—8

Prayer Is the Soul's Sincere Desire
B—264; **C**—73; **E**—419; **F**—336; **L**—454; **M**—303; **P**—227; **W**—335; **Y**—161

Rejoice, Ye Pure in Heart
A—27; **B**—285; **C**—24; **E**—579; **F**—17; **H**—297; **M**—358; **P**—476; **W**—418; **Y**—124

Rise Up, O Men of God!
A—254; **B**—186; **C**—147; **E**—535; **F**—445; **H**—401; **M**—267; **P**—313; **W**—374; **Y**—258

Saviour, Like a Shepherd Lead Us
B—13; **C**—69; **E**—247; **F**—344; **H**—458; **M**—337; **P**—492; **S**—565; **W**—401

Saviour, Thy Dying Love
B—149; C—33; F—400; H—396; L—
403; M—219; P—486; W—387; Y—
195

Sing Them Over Again to Me
B—233; C—96; F—181; P—482; W—
442

Soldiers of Christ, Arise
E—552; F—416; H—269; L—450; M
—282; P—258; S—384; Y—220

Spirit of God, Descend Upon My Heart
A—62; F—166; H—204; M—179; P—
223; W—272; Y—127

Spirit of Life, in This New Dawn
A—63; M—178

Spirit of the Living God
B—329; F—523

Stand Up, Stand Up for Jesus
A—201; B—31; C—224; E—562; F—
415; H—265; L—451; M—283; P—
507; W—371; Y—225

Sweet Hour of Prayer
B—263; C—12; F—327; M—302; P—
230; W—337

Take My Life, and Let It Be
A—198; B—174; C—53; E—408; F—
357; H—242; L—400; M—225; P—
195; S—382; W—296; Y—175

Take Time to Be Holy
B—291; C—57; F—367; M—251; P—
484; W—346

Tell Me the Old, Old Story
B—370; F—222; W—438

The Church's One Foundation
A—308; B—406; C—81; E—396; F—
380; H—333; L—473; M—381; P—
391; S—198; W—423; Y—138

The King of Love My Shepherd Is
A—50; E—345; F—280; H—99; L—
431; M—353; P—287; S—345; W—
169; Y—57

The Light of the World Is Jesus
B—330; F—88

There's a Wideness in God's Mercy
A—55; B—182; C—18; E—304; F—
48; H—93; M—76; P—180; S—256;

W—172; Y—50

This Is My Father's World
A—39; C—106; F—59; H—70; M—
72; P—464; W—171; Y—43

Thou My Everlasting Portion
B—223; C—189; F—354; M—235;
W—413

Thy Word Is Like a Garden, Lord
A—70; F—182; H—219

'Tis the Blessed Hour of Prayer
B—156; F—329; W—332

To the Knights in the Days of Old
A—230; C—182; Y—232

Walk in the Light
C—98; F—370; M—378; P—214; W
—479

We Gather Together
C—41; E—315; F—492; M—20; P—
29; W—117

We Give Thee but Thine Own
A—339; B—492; E—481; F—402; H
—394; L—441; M—456; P—333; S—
387; W—422

We Thank Thee, Lord, Thy Paths of
Service Lead
A—249; H—367; M—458; P—340;
W—495; Y—203

We've a Story to Tell to the Nations
A—302; B—379; C—158; F—455; M
—501; P—374; W—530; Y—238

We Would Be Building
W—489; Y—204

What a Friend We Have in Jesus
B—160; C—124; E—422; F—328; H
—257; L—457; M—240; P—478; W—
331; Y—158

Where Cross the Crowded Ways of Life
A—265; B—405; C—195; E—498; F
—464; H—410; M—465; P—140; S—
235; W—519; Y—253

Who Is on the Lord's Side?
A—202; B—63; F—413; H—272; P—
487; W—367; Y—222

Ye Servants of God, Your Master Proclaim
F—147; H—198; M—169; P—144; W
—258; Y—125